DATE DUE

	201-6503		Printed in USA

FIFTY YEARS
OF
GLYNDEBOURNE

FIFTY YEARS
OF
GLYNDEBOURNE

An Illustrated History

John Julius Norwich

JONATHAN CAPE
THIRTY-TWO BEDFORD SQUARE LONDON

The Glyndebourne pugs
drawing by Lila de Nobili

Title page drawing of Glyndebourne
by L. S. Lowry, 1959

First published 1985
Text copyright © John Julius Norwich 1985
Jonathan Cape Ltd, 32 Bedford Square, London WC1B 3EL

British Library Cataloguing in Publication Data

Norwich, John Julius
Fifty years of Glyndebourne: an illustrated
history.
1. Glyndebourne Festival Opera—History
782.1′07′942257   ML38.G63

ISBN 0–224–02310–1

Printed in Great Britain by Balding + Mansell
of Wisbech, Cambridgeshire

CONTENTS

1   Glyndebourne, *c.* 1895

INTRODUCTION

THIS BOOK IS PRIMARILY a picture book: a pictorial record of Glyndebourne, covering the first half-century of its history. Within its pages you will find, however, not only the sort of thing that you would expect to find in a similar book about any other opera company—set and costume designs and rehearsal photographs—but also pictures showing all the things that make Glyndebourne so different from everywhere else. Here, in fact, is every aspect of Glyndebourne life, public and private, musical and domestic, front of house and backstage, historical, comical and pastoral. Taken together, they form a composite portrait of what is surely the most improbable, illogical and utterly marvellous phenomenon to have appeared on the English cultural scene in the present century, providing at the same time a nostalgic reminder to most of us of the enchanted evenings we have spent thanks to the vision and determination of the late John Christie and, we hope, an enticement for all those unfortunates to whom Glyndebourne is still only a beautiful name.

But pictures, however evocative they may be, need words to go with them; and that is why I was asked some time ago to write a short history of Glyndebourne to accompany the present collection. As a fan of well over thirty years' standing I accepted with delight, and the last four months—punctuated as they have been by several daytime visits to Sussex, to immerse myself in old programmes and press-cutting books and to talk with many of those who have made the company what it is today—have been a joy indeed. For Glyndebourne is, in a very real sense, a family. The life that goes on within it is a family life, the house in which that life is led is a family house, and all those who come to work there in whatever capacity find themselves drawn into the family world, bound together not only by the prodigious challenge of putting on, night after night, one superb opera after another during a season that seems to lengthen year by year, but also by the glorious isolation from the world outside and—by no means least—the spell-binding beauty of the Downs which has inspired the whole enterprise since its inception. For a few short days I too felt part of that family; and I am eternally grateful to George and Mary Christie, Brian and Victoria Dickie, Helen O'Neill, Geoffrey Gilbertson and their colleagues for the warmth of their welcome and for all the help that they gave me.

This is not to say, though, that everything has been plain sailing. On the contrary, the job proved—like most jobs, I suppose—a good deal harder than I had expected. For anyone sitting down to write a history of Glyndebourne, three main problems soon become apparent. The first and greatest of these lies in the fact that the thing has already been done, and superlatively well at that. Mr Spike Hughes's *Glyndebourne* was first published in 1965 and tells the story in detail up to that time; its second edition contains a supplement that carries it on, somewhat more briefly, as far as 1979. In one way, of course, this has made my own task infinitely lighter: whereas Mr Hughes had to do all his own research—and with 83 productions of 54 operas performed over 46 years, this proved a formidable labour in itself—when my turn came so much of the material had already been superbly marshalled. On the other hand—and this is where the problem comes in—if one is given identical ingredients, it is not very easy to bake a radically different cake, though one can of course add a little more sugar here, an extra pinch of salt there: there is after all only one Glyndebourne story. I have tried to tell it in my own way, but I would like to acknowledge my debt to Mr Hughes's pioneering work.

The second problem is that the history of any opera company all too easily reduces itself to a list of the works performed and of the artists who performed them. So relentless an itemisation quickly becomes unreadable; even if a few critical comments were added, the bleak recital of 95 potted press notices of 60 different operas (for the totals have increased considerably even since Mr Hughes's second edition) would still be paralysingly dull. In an attempt to avoid this danger, I have devoted a third of my essay to what has always seemed to me the most astonishing part of the Glyndebourne miracle—the fact that the thing should have happened at all—and no less than half of it to the pre-war years during which it was acquiring its shape and style. The operatic history itself I have split up into decades, doing my best to find an overall pattern for each and discussing new productions not in any strict chronological order but wherever this pattern seemed to accommodate them most conveniently. If this appears confusing to readers with tidier minds than I have, I can only apologise, defending myself on the grounds that this somewhat haphazard treatment struck me as being more interesting and, frankly, more fun. If they get too confused, they can always resort to the chronological list of operas, conductors, producers, designers, choreographers and casts at the back of the book.

The third problem comes as a direct result of Glyndebourne's remarkable standards of excellence—standards which it has somehow contrived to sustain, with only a very few barely perceptible troughs, for half a century. Now a continuous torrent of praise can be—indeed, almost invariably is—music to the ears of the recipient, but all too quickly tends to grate on those of other people. If, therefore, I seem to have been occasionally sparing with my superlatives, this is more likely to be out of consideration for the reader than a sign of any

2　The Glyndebourne audience as seen by Henri Cartier-Bresson

personal lack of enthusiasm. By the same token, on the rare occasions when Glyndebourne has delivered up a dud, I have not hesitated to record the fact. To err is, after all, human; and the most human opera house in the world must surely be allowed its share of error.

And so, I trust, shall I be. My own first visit to Glyndebourne—a visit attended by certain embarrassing *contretemps* which have been recorded elsewhere★—took place as late as 1950. Since then I have spent much of my life out of England, and though nowadays I go to Glyndebourne as often as I can (or can afford), I am unable to boast anything like the attendance record that I should like. All too frequently, therefore, I have been obliged to quote critical opinions at second hand—though consoling myself with the reflection that the opinion of a professional music critic is bound to be a good deal more trustworthy than my own. I have been biased too, mentioning perhaps rather too often some of my favourite artists at the expense of others who may be every bit as brilliant but whom I have never personally seen on stage. Finally, I have been inconsistent. Why, you may ask, do I refer to *The Marriage of Figaro* and *The Magic Flute* in English throughout, while sticking to the original *Così fan tutte* and *Die Entführung aus dem Serail*? Simply because the first two are familiar names and to write *Le nozze di Figaro* or *Die Zauberflöte* would seem pretentious. On the other hand *Così fan tutte* is well-nigh untranslatable in English (certainly nobody ever tries to translate it) and *The Abduction from the Seraglio* (or perhaps *the Harem*) sounds clumsy and unfamiliar enough to justify my sticking to *Die Entführung*. Consistency has always seemed to me a most unworthy altar on which to sacrifice euphony or common sense.

But enough of this. As I write these words, the 1984 Glyndebourne season is just finishing and the Touring Company is already preparing to take the road in the autumn. Before they are printed, rehearsals will have begun for 1985; and by the time they are published, that season will in turn be upon us. What delights, discoveries or disappointments it may bring we cannot tell. Some things, however, are certain—that there will be much marvellous music, exquisitely played; that every artist and musician will give of his or her best; that the house will be full for every performance; that despite George Christie's continuing efforts, one or two Glyndebourne bats will find their way into the last acts; that the gardens will be at their most radiant, and not one jot the less so for the quantity of fair white cloths spread over the lawns; that many a bottle of champagne will be cooled in the lake; that a large number of people will be made very happy indeed, and will go on their several ways rejoicing; and that the great and liberal spirit of John Christie will beam down, benignly, over us all.

Cavaillon, August 1984   JOHN JULIUS NORWICH

★ *Glyndebourne, A Celebration*, edited by John Higgins, Jonathan Cape, 1984.

PART ONE

THE BEGINNINGS

IT HAD RAINED A little during the night, but the morning had dawned bright and clear, a perfect morning of late spring. In the gardens around the house, the herbaceous borders and flowering shrubs were ablaze with colour; beyond the almost invisible ha-ha, the Southdown sheep were safely grazing, the black and white Friesians mindlessly flicking their tails as they champed the damp grass. A gentle, pastoral calm reigned over all.

Or so, at least, it seemed. Elsewhere, however, the peace was something less than perfect. In the theatre, the carpenters and stage-hands were still hammering away at refractory pieces of scenery, shouting instructions to each other as the electricians wrestled with last-minute adjustments to the lighting; from the Dining Hall there came the constant clatter of crockery and cutlery, the squeaking and scraping of tables and chairs as they were dragged into position across the floor; from the drive, an almost continuous crunching of gravel and pealing of door-bells as the delivery vans drew up to unload ever more consignments of food and wine, posters and programmes, and gargantuan bunches of flowers. In the Organ Room—an oasis of relative calm amid the jangling telephones and rattling typewriters—the few remaining rough edges in the production were being patiently, painstakingly smoothed away. Meanwhile, as an integral part of all this activity, a bald and somewhat Pickwickian figure in leather shorts, embroidered braces and gym-shoes, holding under one arm a distinctly disgruntled pug, hastened from group to group—advising, admonishing, encouraging, cajoling, personally demonstrating how each and every job should be done and, not infrequently, doing it himself.

So passed the morning. The early afternoon was quieter, all those who could afford the time for a short siesta having seized the opportunity to take one. By four o'clock, however, the first motors were beginning to arrive, the first small groups stepping a little tentatively into the garden, most of the men—though there were exceptions—wearing white tie and tails, the women nearly all in long, chiffony dresses, the high heels of their gold-and-silver-strapped evening shoes causing unspeakable damage to the hitherto immaculate lawn. An hour later, after the arrival of the special train—it had left Victoria at 3.10 p.m. and

4   John Christie as infant (*c.* 1884), schoolboy (1895), keen motorist, and Army officer

cost ten shillings and sixpence for a first-class return—their numbers had swelled to some two hundred, comprising nearly all the music critics of the principal newspapers, most of the better-known figures of English musical life and a representative smattering of what was then known as 'society'. This last group included the Austrian Ambassador, Baron Frankenstein, who, with Prince and Princess Bismarck—the latter, it was noted with surprise, in a short day dress★—had been warmly greeted by the Pickwickian figure, now more appropriately clad, with whom he was happily quaffing Piesporter.

Suddenly, a trumpeter appeared on the terrace and blew the famous call from the last act of *Fidelio*. To those accustomed to more discreet announcements—as well as those who chanced to find themselves rather too near the trumpeter—the summons seemed somewhat peremptory; its insistence, however, was at least partly deliberate. Those privileged to be present that afternoon, it seemed to say, were not there simply to enjoy themselves. Just as they had been expected to dress suitably for the occasion, so they were now required to show proper respect for what they were about to receive. The message was not lost on them. Obediently, the little groups on the lawn drained their glasses and filed curiously into the small—and to many, surprisingly austere—oak-panelled theatre that adjoined the house. When all had taken their places, the lights dimmed and a tall, heavily-built man with thinning grey hair strode into the orchestra pit. The audience rose for the National Anthem, then subsided once more. Silence. The lights dimmed further. The tall man raised his baton.

Tiddle-iddle-um. Tiddle-iddle-iddle-iddle-iddle-iddle-um. It was the Overture to *The Marriage of Figaro.* The time was 5.45 p.m.; the day was Monday 28 May 1934. The Glyndebourne era had begun.

Although a little imagination may have been used to fill out the bare facts as recorded in the press and elsewhere, the above description of the first Glyndebourne opening is as accurate as the passage of half a century and the fallibility of human memory will allow. It is not, however, the beginning of the story. And as Glyndebourne was—and is—to a remarkable extent the creation of a single man, that story must start with him.

John Christie was born—before the doctor arrived, as he used proudly to relate—on 14 December 1882, of a well-to-do family of Swiss descent, the name having been anglicised from its earlier form Christin. On his mother's side, however, he could boast a far more ancient lineage, going back to well before the Norman Conquest. She was Lady Rosamond Wallop, third daughter of the fifth Earl of Portsmouth, and came of a family of which her nephew, the ninth Earl, was later to write: 'Of the known forebears in my English heritage there were a hundred and forty-nine direct (not collateral) ancestors who were Knights of the Garter, eleven who were canonised saints, and sixty-nine who were executed by their rulers, probably rightly.' At the age of thirteen the boy was sent to Eton, and four years later to the Royal Military

5 Lady Diana Cooper with Mr Maurice Baring, opening night, 28 May 1934

6 John Christie in May, 1934

★ Honesty compels the author to record that his mother, though not in the same party, had kept the Princess company in this respect.

Academy at Woolwich; but a bad riding accident soon put paid to all thoughts of a military career, and after taking a science degree at Cambridge he returned to Eton as an assistant master. There he was to spend the next sixteen years, apart from a period on active service during the First World War. How a man of nearly thirty-two, with a crushed foot on one leg and a damaged knee on the other and who had been virtually blinded in one eye by a rackets ball, contrived to get himself accepted into the King's Royal Rifle Corps remains something of a mystery: but John Christie did so, going on to acquire a reputation not only for conspicuous courage but—more surprisingly—for keeping his men cheerful under heavy fire by a method which one would have expected to produce the precisely contrary effect—reading them selections from *The Faerie Queene*. He also received yet another wound—though not serious enough, as he wrote to his mother, for him to 'get up any enthusiasm' about it. Finally, in 1916, he was invalided out of the Army with a Military Cross—having personally removed his name from the list of recommendations for the D.S.O.—and returned to schoolmastering.

Eton masters have always had reputations for mild eccentricity, and John Christie certainly kept up the standard. On his qualities as a teacher, opinions differ; but there is no doubt that he was immensely popular among the boys, driving them about in his huge and deafeningly noisy motor-car and frequently, on cold winter mornings, holding Early School★ in the comfort of his own house rather than the purgatory of an unheated classroom. (His pupils enjoyed it even more when, around 7.45 a.m., his butler, Childs, would appear to announce that 'Captain Christie has unfortunately overslept, but will be with you shortly, gentlemen.') It is unlikely that the Eton authorities altogether approved of such unorthodox practices; on the other hand, not many masters were prepared to buy costly items of scientific apparatus at their own expense for the benefit of the College, even if such apparatus did occasionally introduce its own hazards: as the Senior Science Master was later to remember, John Christie's purchases included 'an enormous induction coil . . . He earthed one end of this on the water pipes, which resulted in people all over Eton getting sparks out of their taps while he was working it'. Nor was it only in the scientific field that the Christie touch tended to manifest itself: as a member of the Officers' Training Corps soon after his return from the front, he is still remembered for one particular Field Day on which, having previously sent a boy (Wogan Philipps, the present Lord Milford) to reconnoitre the enemy's position disguised as an organ-grinder, he achieved an overwhelming victory by landing troops in their rear from a launch on the Thames.

John Christie left Eton for good in 1922, at the age of forty. Much as he had loved it, for some years already it had occupied only a part of his life—and a part which, he now realised, was growing steadily less important to him with every year that passed. Had he stayed any longer he would have been offered a boys' house, the additional responsibilities of which would have taken up

7 Three generations, 1895: William Langham Christie (1830–1913), Augustus Langham Christie (1857–1930), John Christie (1882–1962)

★ The first class of the day, which was held at 7.30 a.m. and continued for fifty minutes before breakfast. This barbaric practice was maintained at Eton until well after the end of the Second World War.

considerably more of his time and, moreover, would have put him under a strong moral obligation to remain at Eton for at least another fifteen years. It was clearly better that he should make the break now rather than later, and that he should henceforth devote his formidable energies to the large Sussex estate that had been effectively his since the death of his grandfather in 1913.

The history of that estate can be traced back to the twelfth century and perhaps even earlier, when it was the property of the Archbishops of Canterbury. Since then Glyndebourne has been owned by many different families; all of these, however, have been in some way interrelated, so that it has nearly always passed from one family to the next by inheritance rather than by purchase.★ The identities of the individual families need not concern us here (though it is pleasant to recall that between 1804 and 1824 the estate was owned by the prophetically-named Canon Francis Tutté); suffice it to say that in 1861 it passed to John Christie's grandfather, William. In those days it consisted of some 1500 acres; the house itself had an early fifteenth-century core of Sussex clunch, but had been effectively rebuilt in Elizabethan times. Neither house nor estate, it seems, was big enough to satisfy William Christie: in the years that followed he was to increase his land holding to over ten thousand acres and, less happily, to commission Ewan Christian to transform the house itself—giving it pyramid-capped towers and battlements and covering the old flint walls with garishly-diapered brickwork. He even added an Eton fives court, which his grandson subsequently demolished (together with much else) on the understandable grounds that as it had a rough brick floor it was impossible to play on.

John Christie never pretended that he thought his grandfather's architectural taste was other than execrable, and as soon as the war was over he began a characteristically ambitious programme of modernisation and improvement—including the building of the Organ Room, which has since become in a very real sense the focal point of the house. He was not himself particularly gifted as a musician—brief flirtations with the piano and 'cello had brought little pleasure to him and even less to his friends—but since his Cambridge days he had cherished a passion for Wagner, having attended the Bayreuth Festival as early as 1904 in company with the distinguished organist Dr Charles Hanford Lloyd, at that time Precentor of Eton. Lloyd had later become a life-long friend and seems to have been largely responsible for John Christie's continuing musical education; and it was in an effort to persuade him to pass his years of retirement in the nearby village of Ringmer that Christie offered to install at Glyndebourne an organ for him to play on. Alas, Lloyd died in 1919; but by this time work on the organ had already begun. It was to continue for no less than four years, a source of fascination but also of endless frustration to its owner, who spent altogether some £16,000 on it—and in 1923 actually bought the firm of Hill, Norman and Beard, the organ-builders responsible for the job—before being finally forced to admit that the instrument, despite (or perhaps because of) its numberless modifications, would never be the success for which he had hoped.

★ There is evidence to suggest that a certain Herbert Hay may just possibly have paid money for it in 1616; even so, the purchase would have been more technical than real, the vendor being his own uncle.

8 *Figaro* rehearsal in the Organ Room, 1939. Audrey Mildmay, Risë Stevens and Jani Strasser

9 Above, John Christie as Beckmesser, 1928

Once installed, however, the organ had to be played; and before long music in one form or another had become a constant feature of Glyndebourne life. The performers in those days were generally amateurs, reinforced when necessary with the occasional professional singer or instrumentalist; but little by little the programmes grew more ambitious, reaching a sort of climax on Sunday 3 June 1928 with the performance of a complete scene from an opera. This scene was not, as one might have expected, Mozartian but was taken from John Christie's beloved Wagner—the first scene of Act III of *Die Meistersinger*, set in Hans Sachs's house. Christie himself took the part of Beckmesser; that of Walther he entrusted to Steuart Wilson—later, as Sir Steuart, to be Head of Music at the BBC and later still, Musical Adviser to the Arts Council, one of his particular bugbears—and the roles of Sachs and Eva to Thornley and Dolly Gibson, the parents of the present Chairman of the National Trust. Only seven months later, on 5 and 6 January 1929, came a performance of the first act of *Die Entführung aus dem Serail*; on this occasion John Christie appeared not on the stage but among the nineteen-piece orchestra, playing the cymbals.

It was Christmas 1930 before opera was heard again at Glyndebourne, and even then it was not a new production but a repeat. John Christie had hoped for another performance of the *Meistersinger* act, but the Gibsons were unavailable and could not easily be replaced. The *Entführung* piece, on the other hand, was a good deal simpler to recast, and Dolly Gibson suggested for the role of Blonde a young friend of hers who had recently joined the Carl Rosa Company, Audrey Mildmay. Miss Mildmay was accordingly invited and was happy to accept, for a fee of five guineas plus free board and lodging at

10 Right, Audrey Mildmay
11 Far right, Audrey and John Christie in 1934

Glyndebourne for the week of rehearsals. As a financial reward it was scarcely princely and the performance as a whole seems to have been little less than a disaster, several of the audience being rendered so helpless with laughter that they were obliged to go and recover in the passage outside; but Miss Mildmay sang enchantingly, and that production—if it can so be called—proved to be the most fateful of her life.

For John Christie, it was love at first sight—even, perhaps, *first* love at first sight, since although he was nearly forty-nine he seems until that time to have taken little interest in women. It may or may not be true that, showing his guest round the house during that first Christmas week, he arrived at one particular bedroom and said in a matter-of-fact tone, 'This is where we shall sleep when we're married'; what is indisputable is that from that moment on he devoted virtually every waking hour to the wooing and winning of Audrey Mildmay. She for her part at first found it difficult to believe that this agreeable but eccentric bachelor eighteen years her senior was serious in his attentions; but she was not allowed to doubt him for long. His first present to her, a suitcase, came before she had left Glyndebourne (he also gave her double the agreed fee) and the weeks that followed produced an overwhelming succession of letters, invitations to dinner and the theatre, chocolates from Charbonnel, pheasants from Fortnum's and a continuous avalanche of flowers. Nor, when in early February the Carl Rosa went on tour, did the flow diminish. Hired cars now appeared outside the hotels and lodging-houses to mark John Christie's undying solicitude; it was only when, at Sheffield and in the presence of several of the cast of *The Bohemian Girl*, Audrey took delivery of an enormous box which was found to contain both a fur coat and fox stole, that she wrote to her admirer to protest. Eventually they agreed on a compromise: she kept the stole, the coat went back to the shop.

12   Portrait of Childs by Kenneth Green

There has long been a Glyndebourne legend according to which, later that spring with the tour completed, John and Audrey went three times in a fortnight to Covent Garden to hear *Der Rosenkavalier*; on the last occasion, so the story goes, he presented her at precisely the appropriate moment, with her own silver rose. If it never happened, one can only say that it certainly should have. But by now she had given up the struggle; and on 4 June 1931, at Queen Camel in Somerset, John Christie and Audrey Mildmay were declared man and wife. Childs, the butler, was best man. Later, at the reception, the new Mrs Christie asked him how he had ever allowed his employer to get married. Childs's reply was simple: 'I had to get my own back on him, didn't I, Madam?'

The Christie honeymoon was not, it must be admitted, all that it might have been. Audrey was quite seriously ill with simultaneous tonsillitis, colitis and anaemia, and by the time they returned to England they had both had their appendices out—John's operation having been not strictly necessary but insisted upon by him in order, as he put it, to keep his wife company. They managed, none the less, to hear the first three parts of *The Ring*, *Die Meistersinger*, *Schwanda the Bagpiper*, *Fidelio* and *Idomeneo* in Munich alone, before going on to hear more operas in Dresden and Berlin; they also spent long hours discussing the dream that had first brought them together and to which they were both to devote the greater part of their future lives—the dream of opera at Glyndebourne.

But no more than that. There was as yet no thought of any regular festival, performed exclusively by professionals of the highest quality to a paying public. Even John Christie's soaring ambition had not then envisaged anything remotely comparable to the sort of performance that we nowadays associate with his name. His idea at that time was certainly to extend and elaborate what he had done before: instead of the Organ Room he now proposed to use a small, purpose-built theatre that would allow him proper scenery, space for an orchestra and accommodation for perhaps 150 people. But he was still thinking in terms of amateur performances with occasional professional stiffening, to audiences of friends, tenants, and workers on the estate.

Home again and restored to his usual rude health, he at once began preparations for his new theatre, the announcement on 21 September that the recently-constituted National Government had abandoned the Gold Standard—a decision which seemed to him to invite galloping inflation—spurring him on faster than ever. Plans were drawn up, the kitchen garden was cleared and levelled, and all was made ready for the Ringmer Building Works—John Christie's own firm, one of several that he had founded soon after the war—to begin serious operations at the first signs of spring.

Already well before Christmas, however, everything was changed. The story is told of how one evening at dinner, while the Christies were discussing the project with their house guest, the stage designer Hamish Wilson, Audrey suddenly looked straight at her husband and said: 'If you're going to spend all that money, John, for God's sake do the thing properly.' That moment was, for the future of Glyndebourne, the most decisive one of all. Whether John Christie had been turning more ambitious schemes over in his mind already for some time and simply needed a word of encouragement from his wife before he adopted them, or whether her words took him completely by surprise, we shall never know; instinctively, however, he seems to have realised that she was right. Thenceforth, he dismissed all ideas of amateur productions and performances from his mind; for him, 'doing the thing properly' meant providing the best opera that could humanly be achieved—the best, in all probability, that had ever been seen or heard in this country. Glyndebourne, in short, was to be England's answer to Salzburg, even to Bayreuth—and not one jot inferior to either of them.

But this in turn meant building a bigger and better theatre. John Christie's continuing fears for the future of the pound—it had already slumped alarmingly—convinced him that there was no time to be lost. He immediately called in his old architect friend Edmond ('Bear') Warre—who had been responsible for the new Organ Room ten years earlier—and at the suggestion of the music critic Ernest Newman devoured every book and periodical concerned with modern German theatre design that he could lay his hands on. The first foundation trenches were filled in again and a new and more commodious site prepared, at right angles to the previous one. By January 1932, the building work had already begun.

13 Construction of the Organ Room; the drive in the foreground is now the main entrance to the Opera House

14 The house, Organ Room and Opera House, spring 1934

15 The auditorium and stage with *Figaro* Act IV set, 1934

THE OPERA HOUSE, GLYNDEBOURNE.   Reeves, Lewes

The new theatre was to have a seating capacity of 311—more than double that of its projected predecessor—and, as was obviously necessary in view of its more ambitious purpose, was to be far more lavishly provided with technical equipment and backstage facilities. It is difficult now to say who was principally responsible for the design: the initial drawings were certainly Warre's, but Hamish Wilson was regularly on hand with professional advice and John Christie seems, at least in the later stages, to have taken over most of the job himself. He had, of course, no architectural qualifications; but he was not the man to worry about trifles of that sort. After all, as he pointed out, in the sixteenth and seventeenth centuries many an English country gentleman was his own architect, and a very good one too. In any case Mr Sharp, Managing Director of the Ringmer Building Works, was present to give help when needed, and his own scientific training doubtless stood him in good stead. Although readily admitting that his theatre was designed and built 'in haste rather than in knowledge', he himself considered it a triumphant success. He wrote to his mother: 'I am pleased with the general appearance and lay-out . . . It may be advertised with me as architect! It would be funny if as a result I were asked to architect something else!'

So far as is known, he received no such invitation.★ None the less, although it could never perhaps be described as great architecture, the Glyndebourne theatre was a remarkable achievement for an amateur. It blended, as well as any building of its size and bulk could hope to blend, with the rest of the house and—on the whole—it worked. From the outset, John Christie was determined that its technical equipment and fixtures should be the very best available. Having first applied himself to a serious study of stage lighting, he scoured Europe for the material he wanted, eventually ordering a new and immensely sophisticated dimmer and lighting board from Siemens. At the time of its installation at Glyndebourne it was by far the most advanced lighting unit anywhere in the country, and it was to serve the theatre most effectively for the next thirty years, being eventually replaced only in the 1960s. John Christie was inordinately proud of it, as well he might be. All the auditorium lights, on the other hand, he designed himself, having them manufactured by another of his own local industries, the Glyndebourne Motor Works. He also bought, at second hand, an ingenious if sinister-looking device which, by puffing vast quantities of steam through various lengths of tubing, was said to be able to produce spectacular cloud effects on demand. Scenery hoists, cycloramas, acoustical apparatus, heating and air-conditioning plants— he became an expert on them all. Gadgets and stage mechanisms were to fascinate him throughout his life; but he took an almost obsessive interest in the structural work as well. Throughout 1932 and 1933, except during his absences abroad, he spent every day at Glyndebourne supervising the building operations down to the minutest detail—swarming up ladders, perching vertiginously on girders and scaffolding and frequently, stripped down to his shirtsleeves, working alongside his men.

★ Though his advice was sought during the planning of the Chichester Festival Theatre in the late 1950s.

But opera houses are no good without operas, and both the Christies were by now actively engaged in preparations for their opening season. Although John had some years before enjoyed a brief period as lessee of the theatre (which he always referred to as 'the Opera House') at Tunbridge Wells, he had no real experience of operatic management; and for this he was well aware that the qualities which he possessed in plenty—enthusiasm, determination and courage—were not enough. He needed experts; and in the summer of 1932 he set out to find them. Meanwhile for Audrey—who, it had always been understood, would be taking many of the leading roles—there was equally important work to be done. It was now well over a year since she had sung in public, and at the end of their summer holiday—spent in Germany and Austria and devoted, as in the previous year, to the hearing of the maximum number of operas in the minimum time—she stayed on in Vienna to work with one of the leading teachers of singing, a young Hungarian named Janos (Jani) Strasser. Her studies with him, during which she concentrated principally on *Lieder* and on the two Mozartian *soubrette* roles of Susanna and Zerlina, were an outstanding success—so much so that when her husband arrived to take her home for Christmas he immediately proposed that the Strassers should accompany them back to Glyndebourne. In later years, Strasser would recall how this extraordinary Englishman—dressed, as he remembered, more for the grouse moors than for the staid streets of Vienna—had appeared genuinely surprised when he and his wife declined to cancel all engagements and travel to England at a few hours' notice; but it was agreed that they should follow a little later, on a date to be subsequently arranged. When at the beginning of February 1933 they had still heard nothing, they assumed that the project had fallen through; then, one evening, their telephone rang. Where were they? Why had they not come? What had happened?

The Strassers delayed no longer. A fortnight later they arrived in Sussex. There they were to remain for the next five months, and Jani's association with Glyndebourne was to continue until his retirement as Head of Music Staff and Preparation nearly thirty-eight years later.

A beautiful miniature opera-house, which is intended to be the permanent home of international opera in England, has been built by Captain John Christie and his wife, who is well known as Miss Audrey Mildmay, the Carl Rosa Opera singer, at their home, Glyndebourne, between Glynde and Ringmer, in the heart of the Sussex Downs.

The work on it and the plans for its future have been kept secret. But it is nearly complete, and today I was allowed to inspect it.

It is a gem of modern theatre-planning, in one of the loveliest settings any theatre could have. It has a deep stage, with 'up to the minute' equipment, and an orchestra pit which will hold 60 players ... Every detail has been worked out mathematically to ensure perfect acoustics and a perfect view of the stage from every part.

It is proposed to produce many of the most famous operas—Wagner and Mozart particularly—and even to present the complete Wagner 'Ring'. The first performance is to be held early next summer, probably 'Don Giovanni' or 'Die Walküre'.

Captain Christie told me today details of his plans. 'The opera house is

OPERA IN THE
EART OF SUSSEX

TURE FOR A NEW
LE THEATRE

ORD" IN
NING IN

OPERA AMONG NIGHTINGALES

Covent Garden Crowd in a Garden

Strange things happened on the Sussex Downs last night.

A mother was suing her son for breach of promise.

A pageboy was hiding in a countess's wardrobe.

A mistress was changing clothes with her maid to the confusion of both their husbands.

t this was not a matter for the Sussex abulary. It was simply the playing for rst time in these surroundings of the "Figaro" at the opening of Mr. John 's garden opera house which adjoins sion at Glyndebourne, near Lewes. ust be the smallest and most efficient the world. Every modern electrical vice is here. and the acoustics are per- Only 320 people can squeeze inside, and hey must pay two guineas or thirty shillings or a seat, or twenty guineas for the box.

EVERY SEAT TAKEN

unique in many ways,' he said. 'The lighting is the first of its kind in England, and has only been tried twice in Europe. It is the invention of an Italian who sold his rights to Germany.

There will be two classes of performances—festival performances and instructional performances. For the first class any seat will cost £1, and for the second one the charge will be 7s. 6d.'

Home-Made Scenery

'We have asked Sir Thomas Beecham and his orchestra to come down here but that is not settled yet. We shall secure the services of two first-class singers from this country and from the Continent. My wife will take part.

'A wide range of opera is proposed. In addition to "The Ring" we shall produce "Parsifal" probably at Easter. English composers will be given every chance.

'All the scenery will be designed and made here. Some of the sets are already complete.'

Captain Christie has staged scenes from opera at Glyndebourne in the past—but only for the benefit of friends. He has one of the finest organs in the country.

So, a trifle unfortunately, wrote the Special Correspondent of the *Evening News* in its issue of 29 June 1933. It was the first item about John Christie's plans ever to appear in the British press. Reading it today, one cannot but feel astonishment that, only eleven months before the opening of the first Glyndebourne season, no firm plans had been made for anything. No singer—except of course Audrey herself—had yet been engaged; Sir Thomas Beecham had been invited to conduct, but had not replied. The only thing that seemed to be at least partly ready was the scenery, but that—as we now realise—must have been for the wrong operas. Of those works specifically mentioned by Christie in the course of the interview, only one—*Don Giovanni*—has ever to this day been performed at Glyndebourne, and that was not produced there until 1936, the last of the five best-known Mozart operas to be added to the repertoire.

Another surprising fact about the *Evening News* story is that it sank like a stone. Apart from a reprinting more or less verbatim two days later in another Northcliffe paper, the *Dundee Evening Telegraph*—in few of whose readers, one imagines, could it have aroused the slightest interest—a full three weeks now passed before another mention of John Christie's plans appeared in the national press; and even the lengthy article by one H. E. Wortham in the *Daily Telegraph* of 20 July added little to the public knowledge of what was afoot. There was, it was learnt, still no word from Sir Thomas; if he did not accept, Mr Christie might engage the orchestra from the Vienna Opera. As to the works to be performed in the opening season, *Die Meistersinger* was now added to the list of possibles. For the rest, 'even the festooned curtain rises and falls by a gadget Mr Christie has invented and made himself, so that it can be raised and lowered at any requisite speed by one man.' Mr Wortham also reported that 'an altogether delightful open-air beer garden is one of the theatre's adjuncts—and Mr Christie hints at the possibility of free beer.'

Despite even this agreeable prospect, the British public remained unimpressed. It was also, frankly, incredulous. The general reaction, even in the musical world, has been admirably summed up by Spike Hughes: 'The fact that the central figure of all this was referred to as 'Captain'—a title more often encountered among race-horse trainers than impresarios—made the whole project sound even more unlikely and cockeyed. We were used to bearded baronets concocting and even taking part as conductors in ingenious operatic schemes, but to find an officer and a gentleman not only embarking on an operatic escapade but actually building his own opera house to do it with was carrying eccentricity too far.'

A contributory cause of the prevailing apathy may well have been the continuing emphasis on Wagner. Except during the First World War, this composer had always been popular with the English opera-going public, but his work was regularly performed during the international seasons at Covent Garden and that, people felt, was probably enough. Moreover it was not immediately easy to see how the Glyndebourne pit, which by John Christie's own reckoning would accommodate only sixty orchestral players—a figure which itself was to prove a wild over-estimate—could possibly cope with the vast instrumental demands made by *Die Meistersinger* or *The Ring*. For patrons, too, the practical problems threatened to be considerable. Wagner operas could easily last five hours or more. Even at Covent Garden they began at tea-time; at Glyndebourne, if there were to be any question of the audiences' returning to London the same night, they would have to start directly after lunch, and that in turn would involve people leaving home soon after breakfast—already, presumably, in full evening dress.

Finally, in the summer of 1933, there was the international political situation to be considered. Hitler had come to power on 30 January; less than a month later the Reichstag had gone up in flames. Persecution of the Jews had begun in earnest on 1 April, with a national boycott of Jewish businesses and professions; by July, trade unions and all political parties other than the Nazis themselves had been suppressed. As the seriousness of these developments slowly came to be realised in England, a new wave of anti-German feeling began to gather momentum; Wagner in particular lost much of his appeal. Gradually, as the summer progressed, Audrey and Hamish Wilson together managed to wean John Christie away from his favourite, persuading him instead to focus his attentions on Mozart—whose operas, they pointed out, were infinitely better suited to the intimacy of the Glyndebourne stage and who enjoyed the additional advantage of being an Austrian. Even then, however, Christie does not seem to have made up his mind at once: in a long article that he wrote for the November issue of the *Monthly Musical Record*, his readers found no reference at all to the operas proposed for the following summer, by now only six months away.

Then, on 29 January 1934, there appeared an item—the first it had carried on the subject—in *The Times*:

A SUSSEX OPERA HOUSE
Mr Christie's Plans at Glyndebourne

The opera house which Mr J. L. Christie is building on his estate at

e Sketch

**THE
OPERA
HOUSE
AT
LYNDEBOURNE**

IRST NIGHT IMPRESSIONS
• • •
**WO WHOLE PAGES OF
PHOTOGRAPHS**

Glyndebourne in Sussex is nearing completion, and arrangements are in progress for its opening on May 28.

Mr Christie proposes to give 12 performances of *Così fan tutte* and *Figaro*, conducted by Herr Fritz Busch, with the members of the Busch Quartet as orchestral leaders, and a company of the best singers available . . .

Suddenly, everything seemed to have fallen into place. There was a new certainty in the air. The names of the works to be performed, the number of performances, the identity of the conductor, even the opening date—all these were clearly and precisely stated. It was perhaps a pity, in retrospect, that the announcement should have gone on to report that 'at a second Mozart festival in September it is hoped to add *Don Giovanni* and *Die Entführung* and that Sir Thomas Beecham will conduct', and even that 'further plans include a Christmas festival of Humperdinck's *Hänsel und Gretel* and *Königskinder*'; but it was at least careful to point out that 'these later schemes will naturally depend somewhat on the success of the earlier'.

16 Fritz Busch

What had happened, that plans for the opening season should have crystallised so suddenly and to such admirable effect? The short answer to that question is that John Christie had just encountered the first—and perhaps the greatest—of the several astonishing strokes of luck that were to come to him in the course of his life with opera. He had found Fritz Busch. Busch had until recently been Director of the Opera House at Dresden, and was little known in England. (He had in fact conducted the concert in London, four years before, at which the thirteen-year-old Yehudi Menuhin had made his English *début*, but on that occasion had been inevitably upstaged by the soloist.) A far more famous name in this country at the time was that of his brother Adolf, with whom the young Menuhin had studied and who gave regular performances here, both as a solo violinist and as leader of the Busch String Quartet.

It was as a soloist that Adolf Busch had been playing at Eastbourne one November night in 1933, when a rapidly-descending fog made it impossible for him to return to London; he and his quartet's secretary-cum-general-factotum, Miss Frances Dakyns, were accordingly prevailed upon to accept the hospitality of Mrs Rosamund Stutchbury, who lived high on the Downs a few miles away. After dinner the conversation turned, not surprisingly in the circumstances, to the subject of Glyndebourne: Mrs Stutchbury mentioned that her old friend John Christie was proposing to put on *Don Giovanni* the following summer and had not yet found a conductor. Half-jokingly, Adolf Busch suggested that he should invite his brother Fritz—since, as Miss Dakyns later remembered him saying, 'if anyone can conduct Mozart operas *he* can'. The next morning, before they left for London, Mrs Stutchbury drove her guests over to Glyndebourne.

A story has somehow grown up to the effect that until this moment John Christie had never heard of Fritz Busch. It seems difficult to believe: the Christies had attended several operas in Dresden in the summer of 1931, John had presumably also been there often during his many visits to Germany before his marriage, and it is surely unthinkable, given his interest in opera production, that he should not have known at least the name of the

Generalmusikdirektor and heard him conduct, even if he had never met him personally. He had obviously not thought of him in this particular connection, however, until Mrs Stutchbury and her friends made their suggestion. At any rate, he needed little convincing. At his request, Frances Dakyns wrote somewhat breathlessly:

> Dear Fritz,
>   There is a Mr Christie who has built an opera house (stage about the size of the Residenztheater in Munich, but no revolving stage) in the country at his house in Sussex, Glyndebourne, near Lewes—he has lots of money and a pretty wife—a singer—Zerlina. He is a good businessman and thinks that *good* opera in England can be made to pay—he will pay all production costs and all building costs of the theatre—there is therefore no rent to pay—only fees, salaries and wages. He would like to open with a fortnight's Mozart festival at the end of June (the last two weeks) or three weeks—he spoke of *Don Giovanni* or *Entführung*. He has asked Sir Thomas Beecham whether he will conduct a few performances, but would very much like to have you, if possible . . .
>   If you could conduct and take things over it would be the beginning of opera in England.

Fritz Busch was at that time in Copenhagen. Although not himself a Jew he had left Germany for good the previous May, in disgust at the Nazis' treatment of his Jewish friends and colleagues and at their constant interference in German musical life. They had done their utmost to persuade him to stay, first by offers of prestigious appointments—such as that of conductor at the 1933 Bayreuth Festival after Toscanini's famous cancellation of his contract—and then, when these failed, by threats; but Busch had treated all their approaches with equal contempt. He was now dividing his time between Denmark and the Argentine, where he had already for some years been Director of the annual opera season at the Teatro Colón in Buenos Aires.

His first reply to John Christie's invitation was a regretful refusal. His commitments in South America left him no time for Glyndebourne, much as the idea of it tempted him. Then, providentially, there came a financial crisis at the Colón: the 1933–4 season had to be drastically reduced in length. Hastily, Busch wrote again to Miss Dakyns, telling her that he might now after all be able to participate in what he called 'the beautiful opera project'. Only a week or two later, before he had seen Glyndebourne—before, indeed, he had even met John Christie—he agreed to take charge of the first Mozart festival, to run for a fortnight at the end of May and the beginning of June, at which two operas, *The Marriage of Figaro* and *Così fan tutte*, would be performed. It was immaterial that—as he was later to confess—he did so only because he was quite sure that this first festival would also be the last; the important thing was that the opening season at least was now in the best possible hands. Towards the end of January, Busch and his wife had their first meeting with John Christie— in Amsterdam.

One learns with some consternation that at this meeting, so crucial for the future of Glyndebourne, Christie revived an old idea of his—that of accompanying the opera with a string quartet, using an organ to fill in the wind parts. Many a conductor faced with such a proposal would, figuratively speaking, have laid down his baton there and then; fortunately for us all, Busch did not react as might have been feared. He merely told Christie, politely but firmly, that such an idea was out of the question. As Audrey had pointed out just over two years before, if the thing was worth doing at all it was worth doing properly. Christie did not insist: he quietly deferred to his new Musical Director and never mentioned the subject again.

Now it was Busch's turn to spring a surprise. He told John Christie that he would need a first-class producer. Christie at first seemed taken aback: his Organ Room operas had never been 'produced' in any real sense of the word—people had just come on stage, sung their parts and gone off again—and he had assumed that the various necessary moves and groupings would simply develop, organically and of themselves, in the course of rehearsals. Once again, however, he made no objection; if a producer was required, then a producer would be obtained. There and then he gave Busch authority to engage one.

A week or two later in Vienna, Busch ran into Max Reinhardt, then at the height of his fame. If, as Busch saw it, this most distinguished of living theatrical producers would agree to work at Glyndebourne, the success of John Christie's first season seemed certain. Reinhardt himself showed every sign of interest; like Busch, he was attracted by what appeared to be ideal conditions—the best singers, limitless rehearsal time, an exquisite and peaceful setting, discriminating audiences—and a Maecenas to pick up the bills. He had, moreover, long dreamed of working with Busch on a Mozart opera. In principle, at any rate, he was ready to accept; all that was now necessary was that John Christie should make him an offer that he could not refuse.

John Christie did indeed make an offer; but Reinhardt refused it. His world-wide reputation, and the spectacular scale of many of his productions, enabled him to command enormous fees; and Christie, for all his wealth and generosity, could not hope to match the great international impresarios like C. B. Cochran who, apart from anything else, expected to pay expenses and salaries out of profits. In fact, although no one realised it at the time, Reinhardt's refusal was almost certainly a blessing in disguise. His name would no doubt have pulled in the audiences, but his genius was too big for Glyndebourne. He would have felt constricted on the tiny stage, and the operas might easily have been swamped by the production. Temperamentally, too, he could never have settled down: he was a star and deeply conscious of the fact, he lived like a king with his court around him, and wherever he went, he was accustomed to being Number One. John Christie and he could never have got on together. Had he accepted the offer that was made to him, Glyndebourne's first season might well have been its last—if indeed it had taken place at all.

So Fritz Busch had to start looking again; and this time his eye fell on a large, outstandingly handsome man of forty-seven whose name was Carl—though he had actually been baptised Charles—Ebert. By birth a Berliner, he had for the first twenty years of his professional life enjoyed a successful career as an actor; gradually, however, his interests had turned more and more towards production, and particularly the production of opera. In 1927 he had left the

17   Above, Carl Ebert and Fritz Busch

18   Right, Carl Ebert

stage for good to become *Generalintendant* of the Hessische Landestheater in Darmstadt; four years later, he had returned to Berlin to take over the Städtische (Charlottenburg) Oper. There Fritz Busch had been deeply impressed by his work—so deeply in fact that when he was asked to conduct *Die Entführung* at the 1932 Salzburg Festival he agreed only on condition that Ebert was engaged to produce it. The result had been a critical triumph and had been followed shortly afterwards by an equally memorable *Ballo in maschera* at the Charlottenburg, after which Ebert had tried to persuade his friend to join him permanently in Berlin; but Busch had no wish to leave Dresden. As things turned out, his decision to stay there mattered little, for within a few months both men had sought voluntary exile abroad.

It was thus on Busch's recommendation that John Christie wrote to Ebert. His first two letters remained unanswered, but a telegram at last had the desired effect and Ebert agreed to come. He was still frankly sceptical; although Busch's name had naturally been mentioned in the letters, he had had as yet no opportunity of hearing about the project directly from his friend. On the other hand, having so recently uprooted himself, he was without a permanent job—and, as he later admitted, it seemed a heaven-sent opportunity to visit England for the first time.

His initial impressions can hardly have been favourable. The February weather was appalling, the language incomprehensible and, worst of all, there were serious faults in the design of the theatre. John Christie showed him round, pointed out his beloved cloud machine and demonstrated the lighting system with justifiable pride, but seemed totally uninterested when Ebert pointed out that he had provided no means of flying the scenery and no storage dock; all that existed was a single tall door on one side, through which every set would have to be taken out as soon as it was struck and before the next could be brought in by the same way. Ebert did his best to impress upon him the seriousness of this defect, but Christie would not listen; by now he was interested only in hearing Ebert's opinions about the correct positioning of the bells in *Parsifal*. Finally it was agreed that his two distinguished guests would have a week to look around, discuss matters between themselves and decide what could and could not be done. Then all three would meet for a conference.

During that week Ebert, believing that his host had no inkling of the magnitude of the task before him, took it upon himself to prepare a rough budget. This included all those little things which he suspected—probably rightly—might have been forgotten: rehearsal time and overtime, travel expenses for the chorus, printing of programmes, fire precautions, cloak room tickets and countless other similar items, over and above the major outgoings on wages, salaries and professional fees. Did Mr Christie really understand what—and how much—he was letting himself in for? Mr Christie, looking a little surprised, replied that he did indeed understand. These considerations, he reminded his guest, were no one's business but his own. All he wanted from Professor Ebert was the answer to a single question: was he or was he not prepared to work at Glyndebourne?

Such was Ebert's first—but by no means his last—experience of what he always described as John Christie's 'marvellous stubbornness'. He said no more about the budget. As to the question he had been asked, the answer was yes—on one condition. In all artistic matters, the final decisions must rest with Busch and himself. The selection of singers, the works to be performed, the number of rehearsals required and all other similar questions would of course be fully discussed with Christie beforehand; but his two artistic directors must have the last word.

They had expected this to prove a stumbling block; but John Christie accepted without hesitation. The three men shook hands. Glyndebourne, at last, was in business.

There remained, however, a prodigious amount of work to be done. Three and a half months is not a very long time in which to prepare, cast, produce and rehearse two full-length operas to the highest standards, with international casts and on an untried and in some ways inadequate stage. The international telephone service, too, was still in its infancy; to track down a travelling foreign artist might easily take a week or more. The desperate need now was for a highly efficient and experienced executive who knew the ways of the operatic world and who could be entrusted with the task of building up the whole administrative organisation of the new company, the actual engagement of the chosen singers and the preparation of contracts. Mercifully, Busch and Ebert knew just the man; miraculously, he was available.

Rudolf Bing was a Viennese who had formerly been in charge of one of the most important Austrian theatrical and concert agencies, in which capacity he

19 Left, Fritz Busch, John Christie and Rudolf Bing, with Tuppy the pug, spring 1935 when the scenery tower was being built
20 Right, 1939: Carl Ebert, Hans Peter Busch (*standing*), Fritz Busch and Rudolf Bing

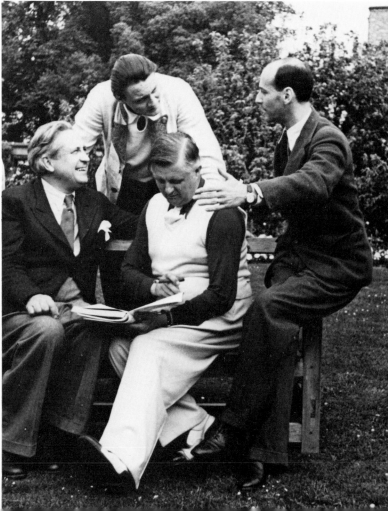

had been largely responsible for the management of the first festival to be organised by the International Society for Contemporary Music at Salzburg in 1923. Later he had taken over Artists' Management at Darmstadt under Ebert, and had worked with him again as his assistant when he moved to Charlottenburg. When the Nazis came to power in 1933, however, Bing—a Jew—had been obliged to leave hurriedly and return to his native city; but even there he was finding it difficult, in those troubled times, to pick up the threads of his old career. Fritz Busch knew of his problems all too well. When he wrote to Bing, encouraging him to accept John Christie's offer, he ended his letter with the words: 'Even for a small sum of money, it would be worth your while—particularly since, if it succeeds, it will mean work for you in the future.' It certainly did. Bing, who came to Glyndebourne for a hundred pounds—a sum which included his travelling expenses—was promoted the following year to be General Manager, a post he was to hold until 1949 when he left to take over the Metropolitan Opera in New York. For the time being, however, he had no official position on the Glyndebourne staff; a General Manager had already been engaged in the person of one Alfred Nightingale, chosen by John Christie partly for his name and partly for his presumed experience as former Manager of Covent Garden. Only later was it to emerge that Nightingale's responsibilities there had been largely confined to front-of-house organisation: as we shall see, his lack of expertise in the handling of artists and their contracts was before long to bring Glyndebourne to the verge of disaster. But during these first months, though Bing with his cosmopolitan background was immediately made responsible for the hiring and contracting of all continental artists (Nightingale speaking no foreign language) he had to be content to serve in a junior and somewhat nebulous capacity.

By the beginning of March, things began to move a good deal more quickly. One of the major problems at this time was the recruitment of an orchestra. John Christie's earlier announcement that the various string sections were to be led by members of the Busch String Quartet was now seen to have been over-optimistic, as were his plans to engage several other distinguished foreign instrumentalists. As might have been expected, the Musicians' Union put its foot down. The orchestra, it decreed, must be British to a man. Presumably because it had no corporate entity other than that conferred on it by Glyndebourne, this orchestra as finally constituted received no billing at all in the first season's programme: all that patrons were told was that its Leader was George Stratton and that, 'Every Member of the Orchestra and the Chorus has been personally selected'. (It would have been surprising had they not been.) Most of the thirty-three players eventually engaged were in fact drawn from the London Symphony Orchestra; they included, that first season, the celebrated oboist Evelyn Rothwell, later Lady Barbirolli.

The names of the principal singers were announced at the beginning of April. It is safe to say that apart from Audrey Mildmay and a handful of other British singers like Norman Allin, Roy Henderson and Heddle Nash, very few of the names listed rang any familiar bell to most people; but from the outset it was Glyndebourne casting policy that big names, for their own sake, would count for nothing. The only consideration would be for quality; the principal roles would be given not necessarily to the famous, but to those singers, known or unknown, best able to do them justice. Certainly the company as announced was nothing if not international: the seventeen leading singers in the two operas—eleven in *Figaro* and six in *Così fan tutte*—included two Germans, an Austrian, an American, an Italian, a Czech and a Finn.

Audrey herself was to sing Susanna. There were, inevitably, many people who suspected that this young Englishwoman, despite her success with the Carl Rosa, had been given the star part only because she was married to John Christie; this was a cross that she had to bear throughout the rest of her tragically short life, and owing to the sad brevity of her professional career— she never sang at Glyndebourne after 1940—there may be some who believe it even today. It may therefore be of interest to quote from the report written after her audition in March by Fritz Busch—and not, of course, intended for the eyes of her husband. She made, wrote Busch, a somewhat disappointing start, due partly to nervousness and partly to a certain weakness after her recent confinement. (The Christies' first child, their daughter Rosamond, had been born the previous October.) After that, however, she revealed 'a delightful voice, well-trained and full of artistry. Sang Susanna, Italian good, and she has a great sense of style. Even better at expressing lyrical emotion than gay good spirits. Strongly recommended. If properly used, her talent would have success in Dresden and Berlin. Request, on my recommendation, that she be given the part of Susanna. Undoubtedly a good actress, and a serious worker. After tea she sang with great taste half-a-dozen songs to what she called my "very expressive accompaniment".' He added that in the normal course he would have engaged her at once for Dresden.

Within a few days of Audrey's audition, another still more important one

21 Audrey Mildmay, Risë Stevens, Maria Markan rehearse in the Green Room with Jani Strasser

was given: this time, to the theatre itself. From the moment it was built John Christie never lost an opportunity to praise its acoustics to the skies, but until March 1934 it had never actually been tried out with a proper orchestral performance in a full auditorium. The decision was therefore taken to invite the Intimate Opera Company down to Glyndebourne with three one-act productions from their repertoire—Mozart's *Bastien and Bastienne*, Pergolesi's *La serva padrona* and *Love in a Coffee Cup*, an operatic adaptation of Bach's *Coffee Cantata*. The music was to be provided by the Boyd Neel String Orchestra, the audience were all individually invited and there were so many acceptances that the entire performance had to be given twice. As it turned out, the exercise proved to have been well worth while: the orchestra sounded distinctly muffled, and the floor of the pit was raised by a foot in consequence. It was also decided to darken the walls surrounding the proscenium arch, which were reflecting too much light from the players' desks.

22   Rudolf Bing with Wardrobe Mistress Juliette Magny discussing costume designs

Structural alterations to his theatre were always of immense interest to John Christie. Once these were completed, however, he seems to have felt himself underemployed. It is not easy for ordinary mortals to understand how anyone in his position, with his first season's opening by now only some two months away, would not have found the physical and nervous strain already almost unbearable; but his energies had always been double those of everyone around him and, with much of the day-to-day work now safely in the hands of Busch, Ebert and Bing—who had doubtless made it clear that they preferred as far as possible to be allowed to get on with it undisturbed—he was suddenly conscious of time lying rather heavily on his own. Gradually, as the opening night approached, the pace would build up and the tension rise again; but for the moment there was, as far as he personally was concerned, a lull. If, therefore, his assistance was no longer required for the opening season, he might as well start planning the next.

It had by now become clear to him that his statement to the press at the end of January—or at least that part of it which referred to Glyndebourne's future plans—had been premature. For financial reasons alone—quite apart from the need on the part of everybody for a bit of a holiday when the first season was over—the idea of a re-opening in September with two new productions was obviously out of the question, and that of the two Humperdinck operas at Christmas, to say the least, in doubt. But this did not mean that John Christie was running out of steam: for the summer of 1935 he now suggested the postponed *Hänsel und Gretel*, together with *Der Rosenkavalier* and—despite the pleadings of his wife and Hamish Wilson, by now an established member of the Glyndebourne staff—*Die Walküre* and *Siegfried*.

All this was duly reported with some amazement by Francis Toye, Music Critic of the *Morning Post*. He continued:

But this is not the limit of Mr Christie's ambitions, for he confided in me his desire to produce the *Meistersinger* with a chorus of 200! I will confess that this seems to me exaggerated, for, even presuming he could get 200 people on the stage—which I very much doubt—a chorus of that size would be excessive for a theatre seating at most 320 people ... Except in the matter of Mozart my personal operatic tastes scarcely coincide with Mr Christie's; for his enthusiasm seems to be exclusively confined to the Austro-German orbit.

I would have preferred to hear Verdi's *Falstaff* or Purcell's *Fairy Queen* rather than *Walküre* or *Rosenkavalier* in such typically English surroundings as those of Glyndebourne. I like them better, to begin with, and I think the choice would be more interesting and appropriate.

This, however, is an entirely personal matter. If Mr Christie's tastes are what they are, no one in the world has earned a better right to indulge them. Practical wisdom he can and will obtain with experience.

He already possesses things that cannot be taught: imagination, enthusiasm, unflagging energy, and unbounded optimism. Such qualities have enabled men to win unexpected triumphs over seemingly insuperable objects before. Should they win through once again at Glyndebourne it will be a cause of rejoicing to anyone who appreciates the inestimable value of idealism.

Had Mr Toye known it, John Christie had yet another project up his sleeve: that April, while applying to the Lewes magistrates for permission to sell intoxicating liquor during his festival, he requested an additional licence to enable him, on Good Friday and Easter Sunday 1935, to stage performances of *Parsifal*. The Chairman of the Bench replied regretting that it was not within his power to give authority for any theatrical performance on a Sunday, but assuring the applicant that there would be no objection to a performance on Good Friday. The liquor licence was, fortunately, granted at once.

John Christie was soon once again fully occupied. As April turned to May and the appointed time for the opening approached, press interest increased and there was hardly a day when he was not called upon to give an interview. Several of the interviewers seemed, it must be admitted, rather more interested in 'Captain Christie' (as he was nearly always called) than in his operatic undertakings; and with his unpredictable behaviour and his various eccentricities of manner and of dress—particularly the *lederhosen* and what one reporter referred to as 'the oldest pair of tennis shoes I have ever seen'—he was indeed the answer to the feature-writers' prayer. For their more serious colleagues, however, the principal problems were first to keep up with the relentless fusillade of facts and ideas to which they were subjected and then to try and get them into print with the minimum of distortion. Newspaper stenographers and sub-editors fifty years ago tended to be a good deal less sophisticated than their present-day successors, especially where foreign names and languages were concerned; and when the articles had to be telephoned through by way of the crackly Ringmer telephone exchange the results could be even more calamitous. Mr Spike Hughes has recorded that the unfortunate Willi Domgraf-Fassbänder, who had been booked to sing both the title role in *Figaro* and Guglielmo in *Così fan tutte*, was variously described as Dom Graf Fassbander, Domgraf-Fassbäinder, Domgraf-Fass-Bender, Fässbenderan and Fassba Ender. Only *The Times*, apparently, got it right first time. Meanwhile, continues Mr Hughes, 'the *Morning Post* writer found his story of a *Figaro* rehearsal printed with references to the singing of Willi Domgraffassbaender, the 'Count Jerraviva' of Roy Henderson, and a character with a name like a soft drink who was called Cherribina and sang a song which began "Voi eh sapeto".'

Between interviews, John Christie spent a good deal of time drafting, in his own inimitable style, a prospectus covering every aspect of his enterprise. It began with what might be called the Glyndebourne Manifesto:

At the ancient Tudor Manor House of Glyndebourne, situated in a beautiful wooded stretch of the Sussex Downs near Lewes, has been erected an Opera House fully equipped for the worthy presentation of Opera, and designed on the most modern lines for the comfortable accommodation of the audience.

Here, from time to time, beginning with an opening season of two weeks from Monday, 28th May, to Sunday, 10th June, during which Mozart's *Figaro* and *Così fan tutte* will be performed, will be given Festival seasons of Opera which, it is hoped, will ultimately make of Glyndebourne an artistic and musical centre to which visitors will come from all parts of the world as they do to Salzburg and Bayreuth.

Two main intentions lie behind the enterprise. The first is to stage in this country productions of opera which, from the point of view of their singers and orchestra, of the beauty of costume and décor and of the care and finish of the presentation, can rank with the best that the European Opera Houses can offer. The second is to inspire in artists and audience alike by the charm and beauty of the theatre's surroundings something of that spirit of Festival which characterises the famous musical and dramatic Festivals abroad.

The next section, maintaining the same direct, straight-from-the-shoulder approach, set out the prices. These were:

On first nights	Box (seat nine) 20 gns		Stalls	£2	0 0
Subsequently	Box (seat nine) 20 gns		Stalls	£2	0 0
			and	£1	10 0
Sunday Orchestral Concerts			Stalls		12 6

There had been much comment in the press about these prices. Two pounds in 1934 was an unheard-of amount to pay for a seat in any theatre; to Audrey herself, the idea of asking so much had seemed 'quite mad', while Francis Toye, writing for the relatively affluent readers of the *Morning Post*, had given it as his opinion that John Christie was asking for 'a sum which comparatively few would or could pay'. But Christie had defended his prices stoutly. 'English opera fails', he had announced to the *Manchester Guardian* at the end of March, 'because it is not good enough. Opera must be expensive. There is a fallacy in England that opera ought to be cheap. It is not cheap anywhere else in the world except in England, and here, because it is cheap, it is bad.' At Glyndebourne opera would be expensive, but it would be good.

The prospectus now turned its attention to other matters which might be expected to be of interest to patrons coming to Glyndebourne for the first time. The management, they were informed, had provided them not only with a spacious car park but also with 'an excellent landing ground for aeroplanes 100 yards from the Opera House'. (The first sky-borne arrivals did not in fact make their appearance for another twenty-eight years.) If, once safely at Glyndebourne, they felt in need of sustenance, they could be served with a full dinner during one of the intervals, provided only that twenty-four hours' notice was given. Alternatively, 'patrons may bring their own refreshments and consume

them in the Dining Hall, and in that case may, if they wish, be waited on by their own servants.' There was no mention, as yet, of picnics, but the prospectus did go on to provide a brief description of the gardens:

> The Opera House is surrounded with beautiful lawns and gardens which will be at the disposal of the public. Within a quarter-of-a-mile's stroll of the house is a chain of woodland pools following the course of a Downland stream, leading to coppices carpeted with wild flowers. The grounds are encircled by gracious hills and in whichever direction one looks the eye is met by views of unspoiled natural loveliness.

This lyrical flow ceased abruptly, however, and the prospectus came down to earth again with a chapter covering the Opera House, the Orchestra and the Stage. The first section (by an unfortunate error headed *The Stage*) gave detailed information about the building:

> The Opera House is a rectangular building designed in simple Tudor style, and built of materials already mellowed by time so that there is nothing to clash with the natural surroundings or the older architecture of the Manor House. All the seats are so arranged on one tier that a perfect view of the whole stage can be obtained from each one. The 300 stalls which form the capacity of the auditorium are specially designed with a view to comfort. Each seat is numbered and is allotted to a corresponding number in the roomy cloakrooms. There are also comfortable retiring rooms for ladies and gentlemen. At the back of the stalls is a box holding nine seats, approached by a separate entrance from an open terrace. While the seating throughout is roomy and comfortable, certain seats at the ends of the rows have been made specially wide for the benefit of patrons who wish for extra space, or for invalids. In a separate stage box are four seats which have been set aside for the free use of members of institutions for the Blind.

The section headed *The Orchestra* was a bit disappointing; it revealed virtually nothing about the individual players, merely emphasising that they would be completely out of sight in the pit and would not therefore distract the audience's attention from what was happening on stage. The rest was largely given over to Fritz Busch's *curriculum vitae*. Finally, under the heading *The Opera House*, came John Christie's essay on his beloved stage:

> It is no exaggeration to say that the technical equipment of the stage is second to none in this country. The dimensions permit the adequate mounting of elaborate and full-scale productions. Every modern device for the rapid and easy change of the heaviest scenery has been installed, as well as equipment for the production of any stage effect or illusion for which Grand Opera calls.
>
> Particular attention has been paid to the lighting installation, which is of the most complete and modern description, and contains many features still unknown in the theatres of this country. While the technical details of the improvements are highly interesting, it is enough to say here that the proper lighting of operatic productions, in which English opera-houses have hitherto lagged badly behind, will bring new and unsuspected beauties to the most veteran opera-lover.
>
> All the settings used in the operas have been made and painted in the Glyndebourne workshops. The setting of every opera is being viewed

26 and 27   Members of the audience enjoy the gardens and are intrigued to find bits of scenery stacked outside the stage door: 28 May 1934

35

afresh, and the designs show a healthy disregard of some of the old tawdry conventions, while not sacrificing visual beauty to exaggerated modernism.

With the prospectus safely out of the way and the press finally glutted with far more information than it needed or could possibly hope to digest, John Christie was now able to put the finishing touches to his theatre. No detail was too trivial for his notice. The ladies of the cast were particularly grateful to discover that he had carefully had the doors of their 'comfortable retiring room' made wide enough for them to enter when wearing their crinolines. (Those of the audience may have been very slightly taken aback to find their corresponding amenities labelled *Damen* and those of their escorts *Herren*, but it is doubtful whether such innocent whimsicalities caused any serious confusion or embarrassment.) At one moment he was seriously considering the building of kennels for the patrons' dogs and the provision of meals for them while their masters and mistresses were enjoying more sophisticated refreshment in the theatre; reluctantly, however, he was persuaded that relatively few people took their dogs with them to the opera, and that those few would almost certainly have made their own arrangements for them.

28 Above, Members of the chorus relax in the Green Room

Audrey, too, was working as she had perhaps never worked before. For any serious young singer, her first Susanna is a milestone in her career and a responsibility not lightly to be undertaken; but for her it was something more than that, for she knew that on her performance depended not just her own reputation but that of Glyndebourne itself. If she did well in so distinguished a company, she would become an international star overnight and would silence those who persisted in dismissing her as a second-league singer with a rich husband. If she failed, that opinion would gain ground and Glyndebourne's much-vaunted seriousness of purpose and emphasis on quality would be held up to ridicule as so much hot air.

29 Below, Constance Willis

But her professional anxieties were not all that Audrey had to cope with during those terrifying weeks. She was also the mistress of a large country house, and the capacities of that house were now being strained to the utmost. At a time when any other singer might have expected—and many would have *demanded*—peace and quiet, time for contemplation and reflection and an opportunity to study her role without interruption, she found herself a hard-pressed hostess, obliged to provide lodging for what must have seemed an ever-increasing number of her fellow-artists and board for a good many more. Worse still, she had to be able to move at a moment's notice from one role to the other—from that of a conscientious member of the company, obedient to every command from Busch or Ebert, to that of *châtelaine* of Glyndebourne, looking after a heterogeneous and polyglot collection of singers and musicians (and in many cases their husbands and wives as well), humouring their eccentricities, indulging their dietary fads and, above all, ensuring that they were comfortable and happy—since, apart from other considerations, any dissatisfaction or resentment that they might feel would almost certainly show in their performance.

Opera singers, as is well known, are not always the easiest people to handle, and the company at Glyndebourne that first summer was no exception. One of the difficulties was caused by the fact that all the principal artists had been hired (on Busch's authority) by Rudolf Bing before he left Vienna or knew anything about the conditions under which they would be working: many of them had accepted only because of the prospect of being associated with Busch and Ebert. Bing—as he later recorded in his autobiography—had been given to understand that the artists would live 'at the castle' and had made something of a selling-point of this when approaching them: 'later, when the wife of the baritone Willi Domgraf-Fassbänder found herself living at a hotel in Lewes (a very lovely hotel, by the way) she complained bitterly that the only reason she had encouraged her husband to accept this engagement was her understanding that she would live in a castle.' On 11 May we find John Christie writing to his mother: 'All is going well except that we have untold troubles with one of the German singers—or particularly with his wife—also with an Austrian singer, both of whom are superb artists.' A glance at the cast list—in which Christie always insisted on including the nationalities of the singers against their names—suggests that the other guilty party on this occasion must have been Luise Helletsgruber. Just what trouble she caused has now been long forgotten, which is probably just as well; but whatever it may have been, we can be reasonably sure that, like most of the other troubles of this kind, it was Audrey who bore the brunt of it.

In addition to which—to make things even harder for her—she may well have been feeling considerably below the top of her form. Some time around the beginning of May, Audrey discovered that, for the second time, she was pregnant.

However much they might have read about it in the newspapers, the first-night audience that arrived, by train or motor, at Glyndebourne on 28 May 1934 can have had only the haziest idea of what lay in store for them; and such expectations as they may have cherished probably varied a good deal, depending on the reasons for which they had come. Some felt themselves to be on a serious musical pilgrimage, word having gone round among the *cognoscenti* that this was to be the most perfectly staged and exquisitely performed Mozart opera ever heard in England—with the additional interest that it would be in Italian, a rare treat in those days when throughout Europe opera was almost invariably sung in the local vernacular.★ Some had made the journey to Sussex in order not to miss a much-publicised social occasion, to see and be seen. Some had come frankly for the sake of the jaunt—for the potential fun to be had from what many people still considered the most crackpot scheme they had ever heard of. Some were there simply because they knew and loved the Christies and were determined to give them all the support they could. But whatever their motivations or their expectations, it is hard to believe that anyone left disappointed.

The magic began the moment they walked into the garden. Even among the old *habitués* of today, the first sight of the Glyndebourne garden after a year's

30 Audrey Christie with George, 1935

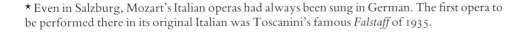

★ Even in Salzburg, Mozart's Italian operas had always been sung in German. The first opera to be performed there in its original Italian was Toscanini's famous *Falstaff* of 1935.

absence prompts a sudden intake of breath; and, by all accounts, it had never looked more beautiful than on that golden evening. There were, it need hardly be said, no picnics; to settle down for a *déjeuner*—or even a *dîner*—*sur l'herbe* in another man's garden presupposes a degree of familiarity with both man and garden that few of those present had yet acquired. To most, it was a time for exploration of all that this magical place had to offer, for a quiet unwinding from the noise and tensions of the road, for absorbing the peace and tranquillity of the Downs—and, of course, for preparation.

All but the most erudite of opera-goers feel the need of a little homework before the rising of the curtain, and the plot of *The Marriage of Figaro* is more intricate than most. (How many readers of these words, I wonder, could explain precisely off the cuff why it is so important to find that pin at the beginning of the Fourth Act?) At Glyndebourne, however, there was no excuse for anyone not being properly briefed. Patrons throughout that first season were surprised and delighted to be handed, on their arrival, a free programme of no less than twenty pages between gold covers containing, as well as the expected cast lists and synopses of the plots of both *Figaro* and *Così fan tutte*, two photographs (Glyndebourne from the south and the interior of the Opera House), two maps (the route from London to Glyndebourne and the approaches to house, theatre and car park), a short biography of Mozart and—most characteristic of all—two brief essays, the authorship of which could not be for a single moment in doubt. The first of these was entitled 'Acoustics' and ran as follows:

> This Festival Opera House has been built by the Ringmer Building Works, who have, in conjunction with their architectural and acoustic advisers, undertaken to build a building where the *acoustics* are satisfactory. They have succeeded in producing a building where *the acoustics are supremely good*. Every whisper on the stage can be heard all over the auditorium. There is no echo to any sound made on the stage. The singers have never found any building so good to sing in. *This work is of National Importance*. The results are not accidental. At first the results were good; then, as the work progressed further, very good; then when the chairs were installed, as bad as they could be; and now the acoustics have been corrected (at a cost of a few pounds), so that, at last, they are marvellously good. The result has not been accidental, but is the result of the application of Science, of elementary Physics, and chiefly of commonsense. The balance of sound even in the front row is almost perfect. This is accidental, but 'it never rains but it pours'.

The second piece was odder still, in that John Christie, not content with encouraging people to visit Glyndebourne, actually tried to persuade them to settle nearby:

WHERE TO LIVE

Why not come and live within reach of this Festival Opera House? The Opera House needs your support so that its Festivals can be extended, so that there can be more Festivals, so that there can be Concerts, so that there can be Shakespearean Festivals, so that there can be Lectures. If you come to this district you can help this scheme. You will have Downs, Sea-air, Woods and 'Kultur'. If you scatter yourselves over England you are too far away to

GLYNDEBOURNE
FESTIVAL OPERA HOUSE
LEWES   Lessees Manager   JOHN CHRISTIE, LTD, ALFRED NIGHTINGALE   SUSSEX

FOR TWO WEEKS
MONDAY, 28 MAY to SUNDAY, 10 JUNE

MOZART FESTIVAL IN ITALIAN

THE ORIGINAL TEXT
"FIGARO"
"COSI FAN TUTTE"
SUNDAY ORCHESTRAL CONCERTS

FIRST WEEK.			
Monday,	28th May	5.15 p.m.	"FIGARO"
Tuesday,	29th May	5.15 p.m.	"COSI FAN TUTTE"
Wednesday,	30th May	5.15 p.m.	"COSI FAN TUTTE"
Thursday,	31st May	5.15 p.m.	"FIGARO"
Friday,	1st June	7.0 p.m.	"COSI FAN TUTTE"
Saturday,	2nd June	5.15 p.m.	"FIGARO"
Sunday,	3rd June	3.30 p.m.	ORCHESTRAL CONCERT
SECOND WEEK.			
Monday,	4th June	5.15 p.m.	"FIGARO"
Tuesday,	5th June	5.15 p.m.	"COSI FAN TUTTE"
Wednesday,	6th June	5.15 p.m.	"FIGARO"
Thursday,	7th June	5.15 p.m.	"COSI FAN TUTTE"
Friday,	8th June	7.0 p.m.	"FIGARO"
Saturday,	9th June	5.15 p.m.	"COSI FAN TUTTE"
Sunday,	10th June	3.30 p.m.	ORCHESTRAL CONCERT

Opera Prices: Box (Seat Nine) 20 Gns. Stalls, £2 0s. 0d. & £1 10s.
Sunday Orchestral Concerts: Stalls, 12s. 6d.
Box Office Telephones: RINGMER 28 and NORTH 3003 (3 lines)
AND USUAL AGENTS

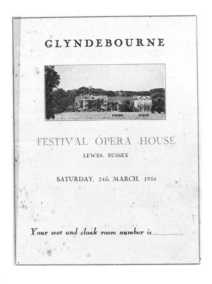

support this enterprise. If you are near at hand you can enjoy superb intellectual food which you cannot get elsewhere. Make this an artistic and creative centre. You will then enjoy this marvellous county all the more.

There is an excellent service of comfortable express trains to London and there are good roads for motoring. The county contains many famous schools for those who bring a family to the district.

No mass migration to East Sussex seems to have resulted from this appeal. In any event, if any patron did consider taking so momentous a step, he is a good deal more likely to have been swayed by the beauty of Glyndebourne itself than by the words of John Christie. Nor was anything more ever heard of a Shakespearean Festival, an idea which probably occurred to the writer on the spur of the moment and which he immediately afterwards forgot.★ So much the better. Glyndebourne was meant and made for opera, not the drama; nor, after the early days, did it ever stand in particular need of a body of local supporters. It was soon to prove well able to look after itself.

The first night was a triumph, as John Christie had known all along that it would be. The orchestra—who had loved Fritz Busch from the beginning of the very first rehearsal, when he had lifted his baton for the overture and then dropped it again, before a note had been played, with the words, 'Already, is too loud'—gave him everything they had; and the whole performance, reported *The Times*, 'was conspicuous for the sense of unity between sight and

★ Although there was a production of *The Taming of the Shrew* in Italian—*La bisbetica domata*—to celebrate the Shakespeare quatercentenary in 1964.

31 Left, Cartoon by Osbert Lancaster

32 Right, Audrey Mildmay as Susanna with John Brownlee as Count Almaviva

sound'. Audrey Mildmay captivated all eyes and ears with her freshness and charm and also—a rare quality indeed on that evening—the purity of her Italian. This language proved, on the other hand, a severe stumbling-block for the German-speaking singers, to whom it was almost completely unfamiliar; the rapid-fire recitatives of Luise Helletsgruber's Cherubino were, by all accounts, largely incomprehensible. Apart from this, however, she sang ravishingly, as did Aulikki Rautawaara as the Countess. Moreover—and this was rarer still, so much so as to be virtually unparalleled in those distant days— all three ladies looked as enchanting as they sounded. Of the men, Willi Domgraf-Fassbänder incurred some criticism for what many felt to be a rather over-boisterous Figaro; but his artistry and musicianship were never in doubt. Heddle Nash provided a superbly stylish Don Basilio, coming into his own particularly in the last act, when the inclusion of the usually omitted aria *In quegli anni* gave him a scene to himself. That same act brought another bonus, unrehearsed and unexpected: the entrance into Hamish Wilson's moonlit garden of a number of local bats, adding greatly to the artistic verisimilitude and even—if that were possible—to the general enjoyment. No wonder that, when the final curtain fell, the audience cheered and cheered; as the *Yorkshire Post* summed up a trifle primly, 'the only thing that outran the carefully applied scale of this performance was the quite undisciplined enthusiasm at the end'. The *News Chronicle* went further. 'The first performance', it wrote, 'was as near perfection as anybody has the right to hope for.' Best of all, however, was the *New Statesman*:

> ... All this—good theatre, adequate accommodation, beautiful site—could have been provided as a setting of the mediocre, the less than mediocre, or the downright bad. It is a tribute to the extraordinary qualities of Mr Christie

that in this theatre on its opening night, last Monday, he gave us the finest production of Mozart's *Figaro* that has ever, to my knowledge, been given in this country.

Certain critics, to be sure, noted with surprise Fritz Busch's practice of personally accompanying the recitatives on the piano rather than the harpsichord, and objected rather more strongly to his refusal to allow unwritten *appoggiaturas*; but these were conscious decisions, open to different opinions. The only serious defect about which everybody—including Busch—agreed was, ironically, the one thing of which John Christie had been proudest: the acoustics. There had been no opportunity to put to proper test the various alterations that had been made after the experimental performances two months before; and whereas the Boyd Neel players had sounded muffled, the very much larger orchestra required for *Figaro* gave quite the opposite impression. Particularly in the big concerted numbers with trumpets, percussion and full chorus, the opera suffered what was felicitously described in the *Sunday Times* as 'tonal elephantiasis' and the audience were almost blasted out of their seats. Fortunately both orchestra and singers were able to scale down their performances on subsequent evenings; but the dry Glyndebourne acoustics were to remain a problem for many years to come.

On the second evening, Tuesday 29 May, the curtain rose on *Così fan tutte*. The house was, to say the least, disappointing: John Christie was always to maintain that only seven people arrived on the special train and that the entire audience numbered just fifty-four. This may be a slight underestimate, but the theatre was certainly less than half full; nor were the later performances

35 *Così fan tutte*, 1934: Willi Domgraf-Fassbänder, Heddle Nash, Ina Souez, Luise Helletsgruber

markedly better attended. The first-night excitement was over; it should be remembered, too, that fifty years ago *Così fan tutte* was nowhere near so well known as it is today, and had furthermore a reputation for dullness as inexplicable as it was undeserved.

That reputation, however, did not survive the first night. The work proved an even greater *tour de force* than *Figaro* had been—the more so as it came, to most of those present, as a revelation. Of the six principals, three—Nash, Domgraf-Fassbänder and Helletsgruber—had also sung in *Figaro*; of the newcomers, the Czechoslovak Irene Eisinger sang Despina and Vincenzo Bettoni—Glyndebourne's first Italian—Don Alfonso; but the triumph of the evening was the Fiordiligi of Ina Souez, a young singer from Colorado who had married an Englishman and settled in this country. Richard Capell, Music Critic of the *Daily Telegraph*, voiced the opinion of virtually all his colleagues when he wrote the following morning: 'Readers may be asked to make a note of our opinion that such a *Così fan tutte* has not before been seen in our time. On this particular score, Salzburg is not placed.'

The first season ended with a deficit of £7,000, and John Christie was delighted. He had expected, he said, to lose a good deal more than that. He had never thought of his Opera House as a profit-making concern. The important thing was that he had proved his point: opera could be produced in England to as high a standard as was to be found in any of the great musical centres of Europe—possibly even higher. As to the disappointing audiences, he was not worried: the press notices had been uniformly enthusiastic, the general publicity had been excellent, those who had made the journey would tell their friends and the word would spread rapidly. He had no doubt that far more people would come next year.

As usual, his optimism was to prove justified. The first-year patrons, few on the ground as they may have been, had returned to their homes enraptured—not only by the music and the idyllic setting but by the whole atmosphere of Glyndebourne itself: by the feeling, which is every bit as strong today as it must have been fifty years ago, that one is not simply a paying patron but also a guest, welcomed into a charming and comfortable private house. In those days the Organ Room served as the principal foyer, while those who ordered dinner found the food to be delicious—English country house cooking at its best. (The *agneau de South Down rôti* came in for particular praise.) The wines, too, were excellent; chosen as they were by John Christie himself, one is hardly surprised to discover that they were exclusively German. The cheapest—a Schloss Reinhartshausener Cabinet of 1920—sold for just six shillings, while for a Deidesheimer Leinhöhle Riesling of 1921 you were set back two pounds—a very considerable price to pay for a bottle of wine in the 1930s, being the same as that of a seat for the opera itself.

The artists seem to have enjoyed themselves as much as the patrons. They cannot, admittedly, have much liked playing night after night to half-empty houses; on the other hand, they had been able to work under ideal conditions with a conductor and a producer of international stature; they had received universal critical acclaim, ending with a prestigious contract with His Master's

Voice, who recorded all the concerted ensembles of *Figaro* as soon as the season was over—most of the remainder, with a complete *Così fan tutte*, followed in 1935—and, last but not least, they too had fallen under the Glyndebourne spell. Whether they complained of having to share dressing-rooms—there were, that first year, only two to accommodate all the principals—we do not know; but they could hardly fail to have been touched to find, on the opening night, a half-bottle of champagne on each dressing-table with the compliments of Mrs Christie. At any rate, they were virtually all to return to Glyndebourne for the next season—the sole exception among the foreign contingent being Vincenzo Bettoni, who was to be replaced as Don Alfonso by the Australian John Brownlee.

The critics, too, in their retrospective summings-up of the first season, stressed once again the importance and magnitude of John Christie's achievement and paid Glyndebourne the additional compliment of accepting it as being henceforth part of the English musical scene. Countless suggestions were made for operas which might suitably be performed in subsequent years—suggestions among which the name of Wagner was noticeably absent—and for various other ways in which the Festival might be improved, the worst of which must surely have been that of A. H. Fox-Strangways of the *Observer* who proposed that in future it should be held in February. Already a few misgivings were expressed lest Glyndebourne should become a fashionable and social, rather than a strictly musical occasion; no one, however, suggested that its motives were anything but the highest, and all looked forward eagerly—and confidently—to 1935.

So too—as he cheerfully set off for a short fishing holiday in Norway—did John Christie.

PART TWO

THE 1930s

O N 1 JANUARY 1935, two announcements were made simultaneously from Glyndebourne. The first was to the effect that Mrs John Christie had the previous day given birth to a son, George; the second provided details of the programme which had been decided upon for the following summer's festival. In addition to *The Marriage of Figaro* and *Così fan tutte* there would be performances of Mozart's two German operas, *Die Entführung aus dem Serail* and *The Magic Flute*.

These two new operas, however, had not yet been cast, and the next two or three months were anything but easy. Whereas in 1934 Glyndebourne was an unknown quantity and the artists were prepared to give it and John Christie the benefit of the doubt, by 1935 it had acquired a reputation. Thus, as its fame increased, so did their demands. In those days the normal fee for a leading singer stood at around £25 per performance; but Spike Hughes has told us that, to give but two examples, a German tenor recommended for the secondary part of Pedrillo (in *Die Entführung*) asked £80 *and* was unwilling to arrive before the dress rehearsal, while 'a young soprano, just beginning her career in Germany and totally unknown in this country, asked more for appearing as Constanze and the Queen of the Night than Lotte Lehmann was paid at Covent Garden. (John Christie never thought the Queen of the Night justified much of a fee, since the part consisted of only "five minutes' singing and no acting".)' Such fees were obviously well beyond Glyndebourne's budget, and for the unfortunate Rudi Bing—now at last an established member of the staff, with the somewhat surprising title of 'Assistant Producer'—there was much hard bargaining to be done before all the contracts were safely signed.

Other problems were caused by that occupational disease of opera singers, professional pride. Early in January John Christie announced happily that his wife, now fully restored to health and vigour after her *accouchement*, would sing Pamina in *The Magic Flute*—news which would have been greeted with delight had it not been for the fact that Aulikki Rautawaara had already been engaged and her contract signed. Audrey, when she heard, was naturally ready to renounce the part; but the situation was now further complicated by Luise Helletsgruber who, having herself hoped to sing Pamina, agreed to accept the lesser role of First Lady only if Mrs Christie sang that of the heroine. Finally the combined efforts of Busch and Bing—and, one suspects, of Audrey herself, who was after all giving up far more than Miss Helletsgruber—persuaded her to reconsider: when the time came, she sang the First Lady to Miss Rautawaara's Pamina, and very beautifully too.

Poor Miss Helletsgruber: her voice—and, it must be said, her looks—seem to have been a good deal superior to her intelligence. The article she wrote in her local Viennese newspaper, the *Neue Freie Presse*, is still a treasured memory at Glyndebourne. Entitled 'As a Mozart Singer in England', it described Lewes as boasting no less than four first-class hotels and such a wealth of 'old-time' architecture as to have earned it the name of 'the English Nuremberg'. John Christie himself was 'one of England's most celebrated antique dealers' and was married to a singer called Audrey Middlemay. Neither Busch nor Ebert was mentioned at all.

But the most serious problem of all those that bedevilled the first months of 1935 was that of contracts. With the foreign singers there was no difficulty: Rudolf Bing was a thoroughly efficient professional with long experience of artists' management. The trouble came with the English singers and the orchestra. John Christie had no such experience and Alfred Nightingale, despite his Covent Garden background, very little more. Both seem to have assumed that any artist or musician invited to Glyndebourne, even orally the previous year, would consider himself or herself irrevocably committed and would turn down all other invitations for the period in question as a matter of course; it is certainly difficult to find any other explanation for the fact that, only six weeks before the opening of the new season, one-third of the orchestra were discovered to have been given no contracts at all and to have accordingly accepted other engagements.

This was bad enough, but worse was to come. In mid-April it emerged that, as a result of this same lackadaisical attitude, Ina Souez was also without a contract and had consequently agreed, during the precise weeks of the Glyndebourne season, to sing Micaela in Sir Thomas Beecham's *Carmen* at Covent Garden. For Fritz Busch, on holiday in Sorrento, this news came as the last straw. He cabled back a furious ultimatum. There were now only five weeks before the opening—no time to engage and adequately to rehearse another singer, even if one could be found. Either Souez sang, or he himself would resign. 'I *demand*', he wrote to Bing, ' ... that the five guilty ones [i.e. Christie, Bing, Nightingale, Souez and the head of Busch's Musical Staff, Hans Oppenheim] do *everything*, with, without or against Beecham, with the help of the King, or Parliament, or friend, or foe, no matter H O W: that I have Souez at the necessary rehearsals and the 4–5 performances of *Così* ... That is my last word.'

Exactly what was done remains a mystery. Relations with Beecham and Covent Garden, separately and together, were not such as to give any direct appeal in that quarter the faintest hope of success. Eventually, however, Souez herself appears to have taken the decision. She cancelled her London engagement and informed Busch, who was now in Rome, that she would after all be available for the *Così* performances. The news reached Glyndebourne on 5 May, and was greeted with jubilation. The fact that it had been announced just twenty-four hours previously that the part of Fiordiligi would be taken by a totally unknown singer named Falconieri was unfortunate, but could not be helped. Miss Falconieri was informed that her services would not after all be required and, just three weeks later, the second season opened.

This narrow escape from disaster taught Glyndebourne a valuable lesson: that high professionalism was every bit as important on the administrative side as it was on the artistic. At the end of that same season, Alfred Nightingale followed Miss Falconieri into oblivion and was replaced as General Manager by Bing. The name seemed somehow less appropriate, but from every other point of view the improvement was immediate and dramatic. John Christie's great triumvirate was now complete.

The new season opened on 27 May with *The Magic Flute*—the opening had been originally scheduled for the 29th, but was brought forward so as not to conflict with the Covent Garden gala for George V's Silver Jubilee. It was generally accounted a triumph, above all for Fritz Busch's inspired conception of the work as a whole; the only serious weakness was the Queen of the Night. As we have already seen, the casting of this part had presented problems from the outset, and it was only after the failure of several attempts to engage other, better, singers that Busch had in desperation agreed to the summoning of a Czech singer by the name of Míla Kocová. Now John Christie's remark about the Queen of the Night was perfectly true as far as it went: the role is, in terms of duration, extremely small. Unfortunately, however, it includes two of the most fiendishly difficult arias Mozart ever wrote, and if the singer concerned fails to carry them off with sufficient *bravura* she risks bringing the whole opera down about her ears. Madame Kocová did not quite do this; none the less, it was obvious by the first interval that she should never have left Prague. So painful indeed was her interpretation that she lasted only two or three evenings before being replaced by the Scottish singer Noel Eadie, who also took over all five of her performances as Constanze in *Die Entführung*.

Another, minor, irritation was the way in which Willi Domgraf-Fassbänder, as Papageno, was allowed to intersperse his German dialogue with heavily-accented jokes in English. They raised few laughs, only much unnecessary embarrassment all round. It was one of the rare lapses of taste that can be recorded against Carl Ebert—who, however, went a long way towards making amends by appearing personally in the role of *Der Sprecher* (not that of High Priest, as stated in the programme) and earning himself a small ovation. For the rest, though the men sang well the ultimate accolades went to the ladies: Rautawaara's Pamina and Helletsgruber's First Lady were both exquisite, and there was an enchanting Papagena by Irene Eisinger—who had inexplicably changed her nationality since her last appearance at Glyndebourne, having been described in 1934 as Czech, in 1935 as Austrian.

Die Entführung followed on 19 June. Once again Ebert made a personal appearance, this time in the speaking part of Pasha Selim; but once again the palm went to Miss Eisinger, for a bewitching Blonde. The other memorable success was that of the Norwegian Ivar Andrésen as Osmin, in which role his sense of comedy and immaculate timing came as a considerable surprise to

39   Above, *Die Zauberflöte*, 1937: Roy Henderson, Thorkild Norval, Winifred Radford, Jean Beckwith, Molly Mitchell

40   Left, John and Audrey Christie with Rosamond and George, August 1939

those who had previously seen him only as a majestic Sarastro in *The Magic Flute*; but no account of the production would be complete without a mention of the *tour de force* as the Dumb Slave (*der Stumme*) of Childs, the Glyndebourne butler. His past experience—gathered, he later explained, in an institution for the deaf and dumb in which he had once worked—stood him in good stead, and his performance is said to have been hilarious.

This second season was more than twice the length of the first. In 1934 there had been twelve performances in fourteen days; in 1935 twenty-five performances extended over a little more than a month. It was thus only to be expected that the deficit should have been proportionately greater; in fact it proved to be almost exactly £10,000—only 30 per cent more than in the previous year—a fact which gave much pleasure to John Christie, confirming—as he believed it did—his oft-stated opinion that Glyndebourne would in time make a profit. There were other figures, too, to give him encouragement: we do not know how many dinners were provided in the splendid new Dining Hall that he had built for his patrons, but the 966 bottles of German wine sold during the season represented an increase of more than 700 per cent on the nightly average. Momentum, it seemed, was gathering fast.

The high spot of 1936, where Glyndebourne was concerned, was the introduction of *Don Giovanni* into the repertoire, the other four productions continuing as before apart from certain changes in cast. To everyone's sorrow, Irene Eisinger had been signed up by C. B. Cochran for his review at the Adelphi, *Follow the Sun*; Willi Domgraf-Fassbänder, too, was unavailable; he had been seriously ill and was not yet sufficiently recovered to return to the stage—though he would be there again in 1937. The great Mariano Stabile took over Figaro, while Guglielmo in *Così fan tutte* was entrusted to Roy Henderson. Both, it was generally agreed, were improvements; and the two operas, additionally helped by Audrey Mildmay's still more enchanting Susanna in the one, and the by now predictably outstanding performances by Ina Souez and Luise Helletsgruber in the other, were the great successes of the year. *Die Entführung* also received enthusiastic notices, thanks largely to the Blonde of the young Irma Beilke from Dresden. She was every bit as good as Eisinger, the critics agreed, and what more need be said? Only the ideal Constanze still eluded Busch and Bing; the Swiss soprano Julia Moor, though perhaps an improvement on the luckless Madame Kocová, still fell short of Glyndebourne standards, just as she did, inevitably, in her single appearance as the Queen of the Night—after which poor, long-suffering Miss Eadie took over once again. Indeed it was *The Magic Flute* that provided the greatest disappointment of the season. The cast was not at its best, and the orchestra had unwisely been entrusted to Hans Oppenheim, who conducted so mechanically that Busch was obliged to relieve him at the third performance.

But all critical eyes and ears were fixed on the long-awaited *Don Giovanni*, with which the season began on 29 May; and for the third time running a Glyndebourne first night provided a performance that no one present would ever forget. As Donna Anna and Donna Elvira respectively, Ina Souez and Luise Helletsgruber once again fulfilled every expectation; so did Audrey

41 Audrey Mildmay as Zerlina and
John Brownlee as Don Giovanni

Mildmay as Zerlina. John Brownlee was a handsome, swashbuckling Don, even if he did seem to lack that essential touch of evil which Mozart threads so persistently through the music. In the role of Leporello, Salvatore Baccaloni almost ran away with the show—a rich, fruity Italian *buffo* with a face that made you laugh just to look at it, a voice 'reeking', in the words of one critic, 'of garlic and olive oil', and a natural comic talent such as Glyndebourne had never seen before. Roy Henderson was a fine and sensitive Masetto, and if the Hungarian Don Ottavio was a little disappointing, everyone agreed that it was a thankless part anyway. As always, Busch revealed more hidden beauties in that miraculous score than anyone knew were there. Such criticisms as there were, surprisingly, were levelled at Carl Ebert—especially for his introduction of a group of half-naked courtesans in the last Act. Today, accustomed as we are to the liberties taken by modern producers, I suspect that we might rather have enjoyed them; but in 1936 they struck people as vulgar and even offensive. Ebert, it seemed, had still not quite got the measure of an English—or at least a Glyndebourne—audience; but this was only a minor blemish in a production that set new standards for all subsequent productions of *Don Giovanni* in England. His Master's Voice, thank heaven, recorded it in full, and the BBC broadcast the first Act—the first time that any music from Glyndebourne was heard on the wireless.

The fame of the new opera house was now rapidly spreading. No longer did the artists find themselves performing to half-empty houses. Whether or not the sandwich-men whom John Christie rather improbably paid to walk up and down the pavement outside the Queen's Hall after concerts there were having the desired effect, we cannot tell; but most evenings found the house sold out

42   Ilse Bing (no relation of Rudolf) came from Germany at Ebert's invitation to photograph the productions. She believes these were the first photographs to be taken of opera during performances, rather than at specially staged photo-calls (see also nos 43 and 44). Here, *Don Giovanni*, 1937

43 and 44   Over page, *Le nozze di Figaro*, 1937

49

and when the curtain came down for the last time that summer—after thirty-two performances spread over thirty-eight days—the deficit was revealed as a mere £4,000. That year, too, the wine sales were even more comforting—an average of eighty bottles a night, bringing the total to some 2,500 in all. How much of this, one wonders, was due to John Christie's new Wine List? In 1936, for the first time, every wine offered had been given an appropriate Greek quotation, sometimes from famous writers like Homer and Sappho but more often from obscure writers of whom few Glyndebourne patrons can ever have heard. (One tag baffled even the compiler, who attributed it simply to 'Who?'.) None was translated; it therefore needed more than a little erudition to discover, for example, that the 1934 Forster Jesuitengarten smelt (in the words of Homer) 'of violets and roses and hyacinth'. John Christie greatly enjoyed translating these quotations for the benefit of the diners, normally giving the credit for their compilation to his old Eton friend C. M. Wells. (They were in fact supplied by Audrey's father, the Reverend Aubrey St John Mildmay, but Christie's detestation of his father-in-law had now grown to such proportions that he could not bring himself to admit it.) Anyway few of the patrons can have cared; they had a new talking-point at dinner, and one more had been added to the increasing number of quirkish eccentricities that made Glyndebourne—quite apart from the glorious music it provided—so utterly unlike everywhere else.

Of 1937 there is relatively little to say. For Glyndebourne it was a year of consolidation. Fritz Busch—he was strongly in favour of dropping *Die Entführung*—had still not recovered from the nightly massacre of its German dialogue by the quintessentially Italian Baccaloni, and there was an idea that it might be replaced (this was, after all, Coronation Year) by an English work, or at least something on an English theme. His first choice, Verdi's *Falstaff*, was rejected (surprisingly, since it was later to become a Glyndebourne favourite) as being too difficult and expensive to mount. Ralph Vaughan Williams's essay on a similar theme, *Sir John in Love*, was then suggested; but permission was refused by the composer himself, who had been outspokenly critical of Glyndebourne in the past and who also understandably felt that to include his modest work in a programme with four of the greatest operas ever written would do no good to its reputation—or indeed his own. Busch then proposed Gluck's *Orphée* (in its French version) which was vetoed by John Christie, and John Christie suggested *La Traviata* which was vetoed by Busch. Finally, in despair, they agreed to have no new productions at all and simply to repeat the 1936 programme, including *Die Entführung*.

It all seemed a bit of an anticlimax; and sadder still was the fact that in April Audrey Mildmay was suddenly taken ill and was obliged to cancel all her appearances for the coming season. Susanna was sung by Irene Eisinger—now happily returned from the West End and no worse for her experience—who manfully assumed in addition the roles of Despina, Blonde and, in some performances until the strain of so much work began to tell, Papagena; Zerlina was taken over by a comely young Czech soprano, Marita Farell, who also sang Cherubino. Three other notable first appearances on the Glyndebourne stage

were those of the Italian tenor Dino Borgioli as Don Ottavio, the English bass Norman Walker as the Commendatore and the Speaker in Act I of *The Magic Flute* (Ebert taking over in Act II), and the German Herbert Alsen, who performed with equal brilliance the widely differing roles of Osmin and Sarastro—in which latter role he was supported by a magnificent chorus of Priests including no less than ten unemployed Welshmen, mostly miners.

But if the programme was unadventurous, it was still more successful than in the previous year. This was in part due to the fact that the auditorium had been considerably enlarged during the winter and now seated 442—impressive testimony in itself to Glyndebourne's growing popularity. To cater for the increased numbers, two new Dining Halls had also been opened and named, in a pretty compliment to John Christie's maternal ancestors, Over and Middle Wallop. Another innovation was the provision of dressing rooms—not, as might be thought, for the artists (for whom they were still in short supply) but for those patrons whose lives were so disorganised that they were not able to change into evening clothes before their arrival.

All these improvements (and several others backstage) were a source of much pride to John Christie. He was prouder still, however, to announce at the close of the season—which ended with an additional performance of *Don Giovanni* to meet insistent popular demand—that it had resulted in 'a little profit', namely £2,723.6s. Admittedly the absence of any new productions had made possible a considerable saving, not only in scenery and costumes but also in expensive orchestral rehearsals; but the fact remained that John Christie, who had always maintained that first-class opera—even in deepest Sussex— could be made to pay, had now, after just four years, proved himself right.

The financial success of the 1937 festival, together with his firm (if still optimistic) belief that, if it maintained its existing standards, Glyndebourne could by now guarantee a full house on virtually every evening of the season, emboldened John Christie to embark on still more ambitious structural alterations. By the following summer his theatre could accommodate 451 seats in the stalls, another 64 in the balcony (not counting the Christies' own box), plus three public boxes with four seats in each. Foyers, entrances and cloak-rooms were also enlarged to cope with the increased numbers. Still more important from the point of view of the productions, the stage area had been expanded; it now measured 59 ft from the footlights to the centre of the cyclorama which had been installed the previous year. Finally, to Carl Ebert's immense relief, a proper fly-tower had been built above the stage, into which the scenery could be flown instead of being pushed laboriously through doors and stacked against walls.

Meanwhile, there was the 1938 programme to be considered. Clearly Glyndebourne must move forward; new productions could no longer be postponed. Equally clearly, it must extend its range away from Mozart. John Christie was still pressing for his beloved *Don Pasquale*, with Audrey singing Norina. Neither Busch nor Ebert was particularly keen on the idea, and both knew that by the terms of their initial agreement, so firmly insisted upon four years previously, they could justifiably maintain their opposition to it; they felt, however, that the time had come to be diplomatic. Glyndebourne was, after all, John Christie's creation, and it was he who was picking up the bills—which, incidentally, included a 50 per cent rise in salary for both of them. Moreover, he was allowing them to function with an artistic and financial freedom which no commercial opera house could have contemplated. And so they agreed—on two conditions. First, Audrey must go and study in Italy. Donizetti's *bel canto* style was a world away from Mozart, and she had much to learn before she could hope to meet Busch's exacting standards. Second, *Don Pasquale* could not be the only new offering for 1938; audiences must also be given something meatier and more substantial. It was Rudolf Bing who first suggested Verdi's *Macbeth*. Busch was not at first much taken with the idea, but it had considerable appeal for Carl Ebert, and he and Bing together finally won their colleague over.

Fifty years ago, the greatness of Verdi as a composer was by no means universally acknowledged in England, and much of his work was still unknown. One of the attractions of *Macbeth* was that despite having had its first performance as early as 1847—to say nothing of its obvious British associations—it had never once been professionally produced in this country. Its disadvantages were the well-known unadventurousness of English audiences (and particularly the Glyndebourne one) who might easily stay away in droves, and the problems of casting—which gave Fritz Busch, he later admitted, the biggest headache of his entire operatic career.

Those first months of 1938 were further complicated by the march of political events in Europe. Already nearly a month before Hitler's invasion of

47   *Macbeth* (designer Caspar Neher)

Austria, on 16 February, Arturo Toscanini announced that he had cancelled his engagement with the Salzburg Festival. Busch immediately tried to secure him for at least one opera at Glyndebourne, and negotiations were still in progress when, on 12 March, the *Anschluss* took place. On that day, Rudolf Bing actually found himself in Vienna. Returning hurriedly by the first available train, he was horrified when it stopped at the frontier and all Austrian passengers were informed that they were forbidden to leave the country. By a miracle, he had in his possession an official Austrian *Grenzempfehlung*—literally, a 'frontier recommendation'—which he had promised to deliver to an English Member of Parliament. Hiding his own Austrian passport, he managed to cross into Czechoslovakia under this borrowed identity; had he not succeeded he would almost certainly have been held by the Nazis throughout the war—which, as a Jew, he would have been unlikely to survive.

Perhaps fortunately, Toscanini decided to conduct no operas in 1938—Bing had never wanted him at Glyndebourne anyway—and the season opened on 21 May with *Macbeth*. The whole production had been thrown into jeopardy on the 11th when the Lady Macbeth, Iva Pacetti (who had been signed up, after countless frustrations, only a month before) suddenly fell ill and cancelled; it was saved by the last-minute engagement of Vera Schwarz, a striking blonde who after a week of unremitting rehearsals was by the first night almost too exhausted to sing—though her appearance and acting are said to have been magnificent. The Macbeth, however, a young Italian-American named Francesco Valentino who possessed what Busch described as 'the most beautiful baritone voice I have heard for years', scored a notable triumph—as did David Lloyd, a Welsh miner's son who sang Macduff to perfection. In the last Act, several of the English and Scottish soldiers may have looked oddly familiar to some members of the audience, particularly if they had dined in one or other of the Wallops. They had in fact been largely recruited from the restaurant staff, who had done a quick change after the dinner interval.

It must also have been refreshing to regular audiences to see, at last, a Glyndebourne production not to have been designed by Hamish Wilson. Wilson was, as we know, an old friend of the Christies and one who had played a vital role in the whole genesis of Glyndebourne; but his sets (usually complemented with costumes by his sister, Ann Litherland) were—as old photographs make all too plain—sadly amateurish. It is a matter of some surprise that Carl Ebert should have accepted them so passively year after year—particularly since by this time such designers as Rex Whistler, Cecil Beaton and Oliver Messel had all begun working in the theatre. Caspar Neher, who had collaborated with Busch and Ebert in their famous Charlottenburg *Ballo in maschera* of 1932, was not perhaps quite in the same league as these; but at least he was thoroughly professional and he made a change. The *Don Pasquale*, alas, was again entrusted to Wilson; after 1938, however, John Christie seems at last to have accepted that his friend was not of Glyndebourne calibre and his name mercifully disappears from the programme.

Don Pasquale was the last production of the season, following repeats of *Figaro*, *Don Giovanni* and *Così fan tutte*. (*Die Entführung* and *The Magic Flute* were dropped, and not revived until new productions were mounted in 1950

48   Cartoon sketched by Caspar Neher during *Macbeth* rehearsals: Ebert, Busch, Bing and John Christie

and 1956 respectively.) It, too, proved hugely successful; Ebert played the high comedy for all it was worth and the audience, as *The Times* reported, 'roared and shouted like any shilling gallery'. Audrey, fresh from her studies in Italy, sang ravishingly opposite the Ernesto of Dino Borgioli, forty-eight years old but still at the top of his form, while the two old stalwarts Baccaloni and Stabile together regularly brought the house down. Here again there were plenty of in-jokes for the *cognoscenti*, including memorable appearances by Mrs Ashton, the Glyndebourne cook, as Don Pasquale's (silent) housekeeper and by Tuppy, the reigning pug, who took a somewhat reluctant curtain call.

Macbeth had been an undoubted *succès d'estime*—Desmond Shawe-Taylor numbers it 'among the most memorable and formative experiences' of his operatic life—but, as Bing had feared, it did badly at the box office. Of its ten performances the last five showed a marked improvement, but by then the damage had been done and, as the production had been an expensive one, a loss was inevitable. It amounted to some £7,000, a fact which John Christie chose not to make public, preferring his favourite annual statistic of the amount of wine sold—4,000 bottles, a new record.

The decision to introduce no new productions in 1939 was, however, taken less on financial grounds than in the light of the rapidly deteriorating political situation. The last pre-war season was thus essentially the same as its predecessor, apart from certain changes of cast. The greatest blow in this respect was the unavailability of Aulikki Rautawaara who, having sung the Countess every year since the beginning, had become a Glyndebourne institution. Fritz Busch tried hard to persuade Audrey to take over the role. Her voice, he told her, had now matured sufficiently and he was sure she could make a success of it. (He, Ebert and Bing were also increasingly concerned at the political innocence which she shared with her husband and which had allowed her to accept an invitation to sing Susanna at Salzburg that summer; secretly, he hoped that if she started singing the Countess she might find Susanna no longer possible and so be obliged to cancel.)★ But Audrey refused. Her voice, she said, was not yet ready. The part eventually went to a certain Maria Markan, whose engagement had a particular appeal for John Christie— who collected singers' nationalities like other people collect stamps—since it enabled him to write '(Icelandic)' after her name on the programme. He was still more delighted when he discovered that Margherita Grandi, who was the new Lady Macbeth, had been born in Hobart; in appearance, character and antecedents she could hardly have been more Italian, but as long as she sang at Glyndebourne 'Tasmanian' she remained. These two were among the greatest successes of the season; the third was the young American soprano Risë Stevens, who sang Cherubino—in which role she was to return sixteen years later, in 1955—and Dorabella.

The season ended on Saturday 15 July. After the curtain calls, John Christie stepped forward to make his customary speech. These speeches had also become something of a tradition. They usually took the form of expressions of

49 Francesco Valentino as Macbeth and Margherita Grandi as Lady Macbeth

★ In the event she was prevented from appearing by the Foreign Office.

thanks to various people and departments, a brief announcement—almost always inaccurate—of the next year's programme, an extended passage in praise of some new front-of-house facility or backstage equipment, a few digs at Covent Garden and a remark or two about the dog. On this occasion, however, he advanced, unsmiling, to the footlights.

'Ladies and Gentlemen,' he said, 'I regret that I have some very serious news.'

There was silence. During the summer of 1939, serious news could be serious indeed.

'For the first time since 1908, Harrow has beaten Eton at Lords.'

It had been a good season musically, an improvement on 1938. It had made a small profit, and the BBC had broadcast two of the operas complete, with individual acts from the other three. On the following day, 16 July, John Christie announced a programme for 1940, which was to include a production of *Carmen* with Risë Stevens.

Alas, that programme was never realised. Six weeks later, Hitler invaded Poland. On 3 September, Britain and France declared war.

50   Risë Stevens rehearsing with Jani Strasser

51 Wartime evacuees from London enjoying the Glyndebourne gardens, 1940

PART THREE

THE 1950s

THE FACT THAT THERE is no section in this book headed 'The 1940s' is easily explained. In the years from 1940 to 1949 inclusive, only one opera—and that in a singularly undistinguished production—was mounted by the Glyndebourne company at Glyndebourne.

It was, of course, inevitable that the 1940 programme should have been cancelled: apart from anything else, the house itself had been converted into a vast nursery school for 260 children evacuated from London. Besides, Busch was in Stockholm (whence he went later to America) and Ebert in Ankara, where he had accepted an invitation from the Turkish Government to build up a Turkish National Theatre. Both being technically enemy aliens—though both had made their detestation of Hitler clear enough seven years before—they would have stood no chance of being allowed back into England, where in any case they would almost certainly have been interned. It was important, however, that Glyndebourne's name should not be forgotten; and partly at least to keep it before the public, Rudolf Bing organised in January 1940 a production by John Gielgud of John Gay's *The Beggar's Opera* starring Audrey Mildmay as Polly, Roy Henderson as Peachum and Michael Redgrave as Macheath. It opened in Brighton and went on to Cardiff, Liverpool, Manchester, Glasgow and Edinburgh before winding up at the Haymarket Theatre in London. But it was never performed at Glyndebourne and, despite its splendid cast, was only a moderate success. When it closed, Audrey took her two children to Canada, remaining there and in the United States for the next four years—and, in 1943, making what was to be her last appearance on any stage when she sang Susanna in Montreal under Sir Thomas Beecham. Bing, for his part, took a job for the duration of the war with Glyndebourne's old supporter, the John Lewis Partnership, in which he soon rose to be a manager at Peter Jones in Sloane Square.

With the end of the war in 1945 Glyndebourne entered the saddest period of its history. There was no shortage of ideas, but the whole enterprise seemed to have lost not only its momentum but its sense of direction as well. The opera house, to be sure, opened its doors again in July 1946 for the world première of Benjamin Britten's *The Rape of Lucretia*, but this was produced by a breakaway company from Sadler's Wells (soon to become famous as the English Opera

Group) and was thus not really a Glyndebourne creation. In 1947 the star of the previous year, the young Kathleen Ferrier, returned to sing Gluck's *Orpheus* in Italian; here at last was something that Glyndebourne could call its own. Carl Ebert, back from Turkey, directed; the conductor, in Fritz Busch's continuing absence, was his old colleague from the Charlottenburg days, Fritz Stiedry. It should have been a triumph, but somehow the spark was not there. Miss Ferrier was new to opera and her Italian, to say the least, shaky; Stiedry's conducting was oddly lacklustre; and the whole production seemed tired and devoid of style—particularly the ballet, which drew critical comment ranging from 'commonplace' to 'deplorable'. Audiences welcomed with relief the return of the English Opera Group with a revival of *The Rape of Lucretia* and the première of Britten's new comic chamber opera, *Albert Herring*; John Christie, on the other hand, remained openly unconvinced. He had never made any secret of his dislike of modern English opera. 'I suppose it's all right for some people,' he would mutter gloomily to patrons in the foyer, 'but it's not really *our* sort of thing, you know.'

On this melancholy note Glyndebourne closed for the season; and for the next two years, as far as opera was concerned, the theatre remained dark.★ The company, however, was by no means idle. In 1940, in Edinburgh with *The Beggar's Opera*, Audrey Christie had gazed up at the Castle and murmured to Rudolf Bing: 'What a place for a festival!', and as early as 1945 Bing—now back with Glyndebourne—had formally proposed to the Lord Provost that an annual Festival of Music and Drama should be held in the city, with Glyndebourne providing the organisation and expertise—though not, he was careful to add, the financial backing. The proposal was accepted, and in August 1947 Ebert, Bing and the new Assistant Manager Moran Caplat took the two pre-war productions of *Figaro* and *Macbeth* to the King's Theatre. The next year they returned to Scotland with the old *Don Giovanni* (under Rafael Kubelik, with recitatives accompanied on the harpsichord for the first time in any Glyndebourne production) and a new *Così fan tutte* designed by Rolf Gérard; and in 1949 there were seven more performances of the latter, together with a *Ballo in maschera* conducted by Vittorio Gui, with Margherita Grandi and Ljuba Welitsch alternating as Amelia. But none of these was seen in Sussex.

There were several reasons. What with post-war taxation and the difficulties of restoring his estates to their proper condition after five years of war, John Christie was for the first time feeling the pinch. For some years now he had been bombarding ministers and senior civil servants with letters, stressing the necessity of proper government financing for the arts; he had even suggested the amalgamation of Glyndebourne with Sadler's Wells, possibly with Covent Garden (whose freehold he had recently attempted to buy) thrown in; but all these schemes had come to nothing. Then, when opera had returned to Glyndebourne after the war, it had been with *The Rape of Lucretia* which he cordially disliked (he complained after the première that there was 'no music in it') and *Orpheus* which he had already vehemently opposed in 1937. Finally, he

52 Above left, Set design by John Piper for *Albert Herring*

53 Below far left, *Albert Herring*, 1947: Frederick Sharp, Peter Pears, Nancy Evans

54 Below left, Benjamin Britten and Frederick Ashton at *Albert Herring* rehearsal

★ There were a few concerts, with Sir Thomas Beecham conducting his own orchestra, the Royal Philharmonic.

was becoming worried about Audrey. She had not been her old self since her return to England, and her health was now slowly but steadily deteriorating.

Rudolf Bing, too, was depressed. He looked in vain, as he later admitted, for 'the happy atmosphere of pre-war days', and was increasingly doubtful of Glyndebourne's survival. He was not to stay for long, however: in May 1949 he was offered the post of General Manager of the Metropolitan Opera in New York, and there he was to remain for the rest of his professional life. He was a great loss to Glyndebourne, but in the circumstances prevailing at the time he can hardly be blamed for accepting an offer that must have seemed irresistible. In Edinburgh, his place was taken by his assistant, Ian Hunter; at Glynde-bourne, by the thirty-two-year-old Moran Caplat, who was to continue as General Administrator until his retirement in 1981.

Within months of his taking over, Caplat achieved a major triumph: he persuaded Fritz Busch to return to where he belonged. Busch's absence was not the least unhappy feature of those first depressing post-war years; had he been back at the helm, like Ebert, by 1946 or thereabouts Glyndebourne would, one suspects, have found its impetus and direction—and regained its old morale—a good deal sooner than it did. And what made the situation all the sadder was its cause: a quite unnecessary and, in retrospect, almost ridiculous quarrel nearly ten years before over the *Macbeth* production, which Busch had foolishly appropriated without acknowledgment. When, in America during the war, he had passed over Audrey—who desperately needed the money—and engaged another singer for Susanna, the bad feeling between him and the Christies had increased still further. So things continued until the summer of 1949, when Moran Caplat, who had never met Busch and had had no part in the quarrel, invited him to conduct in 1950. Busch agreed at once, and the hatchet was buried.

With the return of Fritz Busch the whole atmosphere changed. Much of the credit, certainly, must go to him; much too to Mr John Spedan Lewis of the John Lewis Partnership, who had been an enthusiastic supporter of Glynde-bourne since its beginning and who now offered to underwrite the 1950 season

55   Fritz Busch, John Christie and Carl Ebert

56   Right, *The Beggar's Opera*, 1940: Michael Redgrave and Audrey Mildmay

to the tune of £12,500. The season itself was to be modest enough—seven performances each of productions of *Die Entführung* and *Così* new to Sussex★; but the Busch-Ebert team was back, and that was what mattered. In January, when the details of the programme were announced, the statement to the press began: 'At last in 1950 Glyndebourne is restarting its own Festival at Glyndebourne.' It was the message that everyone had been waiting to hear.

The 1950s mark the first great decade in the history of Glyndebourne. The 1930s are naturally unforgettable to all those old enough and fortunate enough to have known them; but they provided only seven operas in six seasons, the first of which offered two productions only while two others consisted merely of repetitions from the existing repertoire. Though the standards of music and of stage direction were outstanding from the start, in matters of style the infant company was still finding its feet; the decor and costumes, in particular, seldom rose above the mediocre. None the less, it was developing fast; given a few more years of peace, it would almost certainly have realised its full potential. Alas, the war struck before it could do so, putting it into a state of suspended animation and casting it into a limbo from which it took ten years to emerge.

Then, in 1950, the long-delayed recovery began at last; and in the ten years that followed Glyndebourne finally attained the fullness of its flower. The artistic direction was back in the hands of the two men who had shaped it from its earliest beginnings—though one of them was to be taken from it all too soon—and the old traditions were resumed. Once more little groups of people in evening dress (though the dinner jacket had now largely supplanted the tail coat) could be seen standing rather self-consciously about in Victoria Station in the early afternoon, carrying small but expensive-looking hampers. Once more a wing-collared John Christie, pug under arm (its rear end usually facing forward) would be found bustling about in the foyer, greeting his guests, expatiating on new improvements, extolling the singers, explaining the plot or the wine list. And once more, on first nights, there was delivered to every dressing room a half-bottle of 'Mrs Christie's Champagne'.

The one thing that was sadly and sorely missed was Mrs Christie's active participation. She had returned from North America in 1945 with the firm resolve to give up singing for good. Throughout those years of exile her art had been her only source of income, there being no way of having money sent from England in war-time. Either you earned or you borrowed; and Audrey from the start had been determined to earn. By travelling constantly, performing in the occasional opera and singing in countless concerts the length and breadth of Canada and the United States, she had been able to support unaided her two children, a friend, the friend's daughter and a particularly useless governess; but the physical and emotional strain had been appalling—and not helped by the necessarily long absences from home—while for much of the time the family was living, quite literally, from hand to mouth. George Christie has a clear recollection of asking for a second helping one morning at breakfast, and of his mother's reply: 'Certainly not—we're down to eleven dollars.'

★ The latter, however, had been seen at Edinburgh in 1948 and 1949.

57   Above right, Make-up sketch by Oliver Messel for Richard Lewis as Idomeneo

58   Below right, Richard Lewis

59   Far right, *Ariadne* rehearsal, 1950: Sir Thomas Beecham, Oliver Messel, Carl Ebert with Peter Anders (Bacchus) and Hilde Zadek (Ariadne)

But once back at Glyndebourne, Audrey's health would in any case soon have obliged her to retire from active musical life. Her totally incapacitating migraines were becoming more and more frequent, and were now accompanied by such pain in the back of the neck and the upper spine as to cause her sometimes to scream aloud in agony. The root of the trouble was never properly diagnosed. (Her son thinks that it was probably not cancer.) Major spinal surgery proved unavailing, and before long her only relief was in increasingly heavy doses of drugs, which awoke in their turn a new dread of addiction. Her suffering during her last years must have cast a bleak and unhappy cloud over Glyndebourne's regeneration.

On the other hand, that regeneration brought her untold comfort. Once Busch was back where he belonged, it moved surprisingly quickly. Even in the field of stage design, things were looking up. The two Sussex productions for 1950 both had sets by Rolf Gérard. They were much criticised on grounds of vulgarity, but once again they possessed the great advantage of not being by Hamish Wilson. The real breakthrough that summer, however, was made not in Sussex but at Edinburgh, where a production of *Ariadne auf Naxos* was designed by the man who, more than anyone else, was to put his stamp on the Glyndebourne of the 1950s—Oliver Messel. (In the pit, incidentally, for that production was Sir Thomas Beecham, conducting a Glyndebourne opera for the only time in his career.) Sussex audiences were not to see this *Ariadne* for another three years, but Messel's *Idomeneo* came in 1951, and during the decade he was to design no less than seven more operas—every one an explosion of fantasy, humour and sumptuous colour that proved irresistible to audiences and critics alike. By 1956 no less than four of the six operas performed— *Idomeneo*, *Figaro*, *Die Entführung* and *The Magic Flute*—were designed by him, and the same was true of both 1957 (when the first two were replaced by

Ariadne and *Le Comte Ory*) and 1959 (when for the last two there were substituted *La Cenerentola* and Carl Ebert's farewell production as Artistic Director, *Der Rosenkavalier*). With a total of nine productions designed for Glyndebourne, Messel's record remains, in 1984, still unbeaten.★

There was another designer too, whose influence on the Glyndebourne style of the 1950s cannot possibly be ignored. Osbert Lancaster provided only three décors during that decade—though he was later to do two others, *La pietra del paragone* in 1964, and *The Rising of the Moon* in 1970—but they were, in their way, equally memorable. His vision of the world could hardly have been more different: while Oliver created one Italianate rococo extravaganza after another, Osbert replied with four-square, down-to-earth English sanity. Only the humour was common to both; but while Oliver's sprang organically from the luxuriance of his designs, with Osbert one never felt too far away from Drayneflete, or the world of the *Daily Express* Pocket Cartoon. *The Rake's Progress* of 1953 and *Falstaff* of 1955 were ideally suited to his style, and he made the most of them; his third, *L'italiana in Algeri* of 1957, was perhaps slightly less so, but he created some sparkling sets all the same and the comparative failure of the production—during the whole decade, the only full-length work produced at Glyndebourne that was never once revived—was no more due to him than it was to Vittorio Gui, Peter Ebert, Oralia Dominguez in the name part or indeed to Rossini himself. (The audience just sat on their hands, and that was that.) Apart from these two designers, Hugh Casson made his Glyndebourne *début* in 1953 with a memorable *Alceste* and the young Peter Rice did a splendid job the following year with Busoni's *Arlecchino*. John Piper was not entirely unfamiliar

65 *Arlecchino*, 1954 (designer Peter Rice): Geraint Evans, Douglas Craig, Fritz Ollendorf, Murray Dickie, Elaine Malbin

★ Though John Bury, with eight, is now running him close.

to Sussex opera-goers, having designed the *Rape of Lucretia* just after the war; but no one who saw it will ever forget his dark, brooding *Don Giovanni* of five years later. For all its brilliance and its humour, *Don Giovanni* remains a tragedy, the only one Mozart ever wrote; never, I think, have we been made more conscious of the fact.

It was during a performance of this *Don Giovanni* of 1951 that Fritz Busch was suddenly taken ill and could no longer continue after the first act. Fortunately the Assistant Conductor, John Pritchard, was tracked down to the beach at Eastbourne and, despite the fact that his car caught fire on the way, managed to get to Glyndebourne by the end of the dinner interval. Fortunately, too, Busch's indisposition was short-lived; but the incident can now be seen as a fateful premonition of what was to come. Less than two months after the end of the season, on 14 September, he died of a sudden heart attack in the Savoy Hotel. He was sixty-one. Readers of this book will not need to be told how shattering was the loss to Glyndebourne. Busch had found it in 1934 with its tiny theatre not yet completed, full of good intentions but without experience, shape or direction; he it was who moulded it, guided it and made it great. Not only was he one of the outstanding Mozart conductors of all time; he was also a man of modesty, charm and unfailing good humour, who settled happily and effortlessly into the unique and peculiarly English ambiance in which he found himself—something of which few—if any—other musicians of his calibre would have been capable.

The death of Fritz Busch was the first tragedy that befell the company during that decade; alas, it was not the last. Less than two years later there came another, more poignant still. On 31 May 1953, just two days before the young Queen's Coronation, Audrey Mildmay died at Glyndebourne after a long and painful illness, aged only fifty-two. Her influence, like that of Busch, had been immeasurable; without her, the Opera House would probably have remained little more than a rich man's toy. While taking constant care never to tread on her husband's dreams, she had always somehow managed to keep his feet firmly on the ground. 'For God's sake,' she had urged him twenty-two years before, 'do the thing properly'. Thanks to her, he had done it properly, and she for her part had not only given him help and encouragement and her own expert professional advice, but had gone on to create that special atmosphere that made Glyndebourne, for artists as well as patrons, unlike any other opera house in the world. She had been sadly missed during the 1952 season, when she had been away receiving treatment in a nursing home; in 1953 her loss seemed almost unbearable, leaving as it did a void that could never be filled.

Her dying wish had been that the Festival should open as planned, and her husband had promised her that it would—on 7 June, exactly a week after her death. She will have derived additional consolation from the knowledge that the future of Glyndebourne was being assured by the formation of a special trust—in which, however, the Christie family would continue to play a key role. Indeed, as a visible sign of the continuing importance of the family traditions, the 1953 programme included a new name among the credits: the 'Producer's Assistant' was none other than John and Audrey's son George Christie, now eighteen.

66–68 Designs by John Piper

66 Above left, *The Rape of Lucretia*

67 Below left, Costume designs for
The Rape of Lucretia

68 Above, *Don Giovanni*

John Christie never really recovered from his wife's death. Even Glyndebourne itself, though continuing to go musically from strength to strength, was never quite the same—above all for the artists, who could not forget that unique sureness of touch with which she had combined the role of a warm, welcoming and infinitely considerate hostess with that of a dedicated professional singer. For Fritz Busch, on the other hand, there emerged in the very first season after his death if not a substitute, at least an unofficial successor who was to put his own individual stamp on music at Glyndebourne for the next thirteen years. Vittorio Gui had been responsible for *Così fan tutte* and *Un ballo in maschera* in 1948 and 1949 at Edinburgh, but not until 1952 did he ever conduct in Sussex. In that year, however, he was in the pit for three out of the four productions, including the Messel-Ebert *Cenerentola* which inaugurated Glyndebourne's famous Rossini revival.★ *The Barber of Seville*—with the first of his great discoveries for Glyndebourne, the irresistible Graziella Sciutti—followed two years later, *Le Comte Ory* the year after that (although it had originally been produced at Edinburgh in 1954) and, as we have seen, the equally dazzling if less successful *L'italiana in Algeri* in 1957. The first Italian to be engaged as a principal conductor at Glyndebourne—though Alberto Erede, a member of Busch's staff, had taken over a few performances in 1938 and 1939—he brought a welcome breath of the South into the opera house. He did not, however, confine himself to the Italian *buffo* style at which he was supreme; there were also three operas by Mozart (*Figaro*, *Così fan tutte* and *The Magic Flute*), two by Verdi (*Macbeth* and *Falstaff*) and other productions as different as *Alceste* and *Fidelio*. In the 1960s, as we shall shortly see, he was to cast his net wider still.

69   *Le Comte Ory*, 1954: Ian Wallace and Fernanda Cadoni

The other conductor whose name appeared most frequently in the programmes of the 1950s was John Pritchard. We had first heard of him as a member of the Music Staff as early as 1947, when he was only twenty-six; four years later he was conducting some performances of four different productions; in 1952 he was given sole charge of *Idomeneo* and by the end of the decade he had ten operas to his credit, as against Gui's eleven. His first major success was the *Ariadne auf Naxos* of 1953—the one that Messel had designed and Beecham had conducted at Edinburgh in 1950—which was memorable above all for the *début* as Zerbinetta of the young American *coloratura* Mattiwilda Dobbs and for the flawless performances of two of Glyndebourne's best-loved singers, Sesto Bruscantini and Sena Jurinac, who took an afternoon off on 19 June to get married in Lewes and were both back on stage the same evening in *Così fan tutte*. This was the opera in which Miss Jurinac—'Bosnian', as John Christie gleefully recorded—had first appeared for Glyndebourne, in the 1949 Edinburgh production; in that year she had sung Dorabella, but in

---

★ This was the production at a performance of which John Christie was awarded, on the Glyndebourne stage, during the dinner interval, a high-ranking decoration by the German Ambassador. As he and the Ambassador emerged through the pass door into the Red Foyer they were greeted by Sock, the pug of the period. John Christie immediately removed the red silk collar of the decoration from his own neck and, with the Ambassador still standing next to him, hung it around the dog's, saying as he did so, 'You know, Sock, I think you deserve this as much as I do.'

1950 she switched to Fiordiligi, in which role she was to make her last appearance in Sussex in 1956. Between whiles she repeated it every season except 1955, when we heard her instead as Donna Anna and the Countess. In 1951 she made history by singing Ilia in the first-ever professional production in England of *Idomeneo*, written 170 years earlier; the title role was sung by Richard Lewis, while that of Electra was given to a virtually unknown Swedish singer named Birgit Nilsson. Lovely as Jurinac's Mozart singing was, however, for many of us her Composer, in the Prologue of *Ariadne*, was the most meltingly beautiful thing she ever did at Glyndebourne. As for her husband, he was equally superb both as Don Alfonso and Guglielmo in *Così fan tutte* as well as making a glorious Dandini, year after year, in *La Cenerentola*; but of the six roles he sang in Sussex between 1951 and 1959 his ultimate *tour de force* was probably his Figaro in *The Barber of Seville* in 1954, in which he was brilliantly supported not only by the delectable Miss Sciutti (was that the year in which her name was so unattractively mis-spelt 'Scuitti'?) but also by the ever-popular Ian Wallace as Dr Bartolo and, as Almaviva, by the Spaniard Juan Oncina—who played his own guitar accompaniment to the serenade.

And there were other things as well as *The Barber of Seville* to make 1954 a memorable year for Glyndebourne. With Busoni's *Arlecchino*—which was given as a curtain-raiser to *Ariadne*—we saw the first opera (apart from *The Rape of Lucretia*, which was not really a Glyndebourne creation) not to have been produced by Carl Ebert. He doubtless kept a paternal eye on proceedings, however, the new producer being his son Peter, who had first joined the

71 *Arlecchino*, 1954: Murray Dickie and Elaine Malbin

73

Glyndebourne staff as his assistant seven years before. In the next ten years Peter Ebert was to produce two more operas in Sussex and to revive five more of his father's productions—including, in 1955, a *Forza del destino* for Edinburgh (with Jurinac as Leonora) which, sad to record, was never brought to Glyndebourne. Another Edinburgh production was more fortunate: Stravinsky's *The Rake's Progress*, first seen there in 1953, came south in the following year. The first fully-staged production of the work in the British Isles, it failed to appeal to John Christie—who also objected to it on the grounds that 'he couldn't imagine hearing the overture played on a concert platform'. (It has no overture.) 'I'm told I may come round to it,' he added hopefully; but he never did. As things turned out, *The Rake's Progress* became quite a favourite with Glyndebourne audiences—the Lancaster sets may have had something to do with it—returning three times more during the 1950s and once more in 1963.★ On every occasion the part of Tom Rakewell was sung by Richard Lewis, another Glyndebourne regular whose thrilling tenor was heard in Mozart, Gluck, Strauss or Beethoven, in every year but one during the decade.

On the strictly musical front, 1954 was also to be remembered for the appearance in the pit of Georg Solti, conducting a *Don Giovanni* with the American James Pease in the title part and the predictably perfect Sena Jurinac as Donna Elvira. (Unfortunately this first appearance was also his last, at any rate up to the time of writing. Is it too much to hope that he will return again to Glyndebourne for at least one more opera before his retirement?) The same year saw the Company's first visit abroad—to the West Berlin Festival, where it gave two performances of *La Cenerentola*—and the formation of the Glyndebourne Arts Trust; at this point, therefore, it might be a good idea to discuss very briefly the financing of the opera house in the difficult post-war years.

Already at the beginning of the decade it had become clear that the whole financial basis of Glyndebourne would have to be rethought: it could no longer rely on box office income for the lion's share of its receipts and on John Christie's fabled generosity for the rest. The first step in this rethinking was the establishment of a Glyndebourne Festival Society, whose declared objective was the raising of £25,000 a year: individual members would receive, in return for their subscription of £26 11s., two free seats and a copy of the annual programme book, while Corporate Members were given four seats, but were asked for £105. Firms were also encouraged to take full-page advertisements in the book, for which they would pay £500; the originator of this idea, Mr Miki (later Sir Nicholas) Sekers of the West Cumberland Silk Mills, suggested a target of forty such advertisers, who would together thus bring in a total of £20,000 gross. Next, in 1954, came the formation of the Glyndebourne Arts Trust, which took over the lease of all the principal buildings and some hundred acres of the estate for sixty-six years less a day from John Christie at a peppercorn rent, and also assumed responsibility for the continuation of the opera—specifically agreeing that 'Mr Christie and his colleagues, who have brought the Festival to its present high level of distinction, shall continue to be responsible for its direction and administration'. The Trust was, in its turn, to

78   Ilva Ligabue, Fernanda Cadoni, Geraint Evans and Oralia Dominguez in *Falstaff*, 1957

★ To say nothing of the new production, designed by David Hockney, in 1975.

79   *The Rake's Progress*,
      1954: Richard Lewis,
      Marina de Gabarain and
      Chorus

80   The basket scene,
      Falstaff, 1957

81　Above, Teresa Berganza as
Cherubino, 1958

82　Below, *Il segreto di Susanna*, 1958
(designer Carl Toms): Mary Costa
and Michel Roux

work in co-operation with a new company to be known as Glyndebourne Productions Ltd, whose function was to prepare the artistic and financial programmes for each season and to submit an annual budget for approval by the Trust.

For the time being at least, Glyndebourne's future seemed assured; and, as if in very slightly premature recognition of his achievement, Her Majesty the Queen had, in her 1954 New Year List, elevated John Christie to the rank of Companion of Honour.

In 1955 Glyndebourne came of age, celebrating the fact with a new *Figaro* and *Don Giovanni* and with the introduction from Edinburgh of *Le Comte Ory*. The credits for the first and last included the names of Carl Ebert, Oliver Messel and Vittorio Gui; Carl Ebert, John Piper and John Pritchard were responsible for the second. The year also marked the end of the company's regular association with the Scottish Festival. Edinburgh was, in a very real sense, the child of Glyndebourne, and had been of considerable value to its parent in the early post-war years, enabling the company to re-launch itself without undue financial risk to John Christie at a time when he could ill afford it. By the 1950s, however, this value was rapidly diminishing as the seasons in Sussex were once again gathering momentum. The 1951 Edinburgh visit proved a flop, so much so that in the following year the Hamburg Opera was invited instead. In 1953, with *Idomeneo*, *Cenerentola* and the first *Rake's Progress*, all went well; so too did the 1954 season (*Le Comte Ory*, *Così fan tutte* and *Ariadne auf Naxos*), while in 1955 Glyndebourne distinguished itself even more brilliantly with the Jurinac *Forza del destino*—why did it never come to Sussex?—*The Barber of Seville* and a superb *Falstaff* with Fernando Corena, conducted, owing to the illness of Gui, by Carlo Maria Giulini. (This was the unforgettable occasion when Osbert Lancaster proposed introducing a grotesque Lady Godiva on a hobby-horse into the last Act in Windsor Forest, only to be reminded by John Christie that, as her direct descendant, he was not going to allow anyone to make a monkey out of her.) That 1955 season was a triumph; but after it the special relationship was no more. Only once since then has the Company visited Edinburgh—in 1960, when it returned like any other guest company, with a revival of *Falstaff* (sung now by Geraint Evans) and *I Puritani* with Joan Sutherland.

At home in Sussex, Glyndebourne marked the bicentenary of Mozart's birth in 1956 by performances of all six of his major operas, with new sets by Messel for *Die Entführung* and *The Magic Flute* and Mattiwilda Dobbs sailing effortlessly through the two great challenges of Mozart singing, the roles of Constanze and the Queen of the Night. Geraint Evans, already a favourite with Glyndebourne audiences, gave us his first Papageno and Joan Sutherland made her Sussex début as the Countess. Sadly, however—although we did not know it—this was the last season for Sena Jurinac. When it was over (after a total of forty-eight performances, a Glyndebourne record) the company took *Figaro*, *Don Giovanni* and *La Cenerentola* for a fortnight to Liverpool, its first appearance in an English provincial city. The visit was a tremendous success, being fully reported not only in the local but also in the national press—one of whose sub-editors headed the critical notice of *The Marriage of Figaro* with the

83 Joan Sutherland, Cora Canne-
Meijer and Monica Sinclair as the
Three Ladies (*Die Zauberflöte*), 1956
(designer Oliver Messel)

caption 'MOZART'S MELODIOUS BEDROOM FARCE'. One had somehow never thought of it quite like that before.

Less than two years after Liverpool, in May 1958, there came a still more prestigious visit—to Paris, for the international *Théâtre des Nations* season at the Sarah-Bernhardt, with four performances each of *Le Comte Ory* and *Falstaff*. The former, despite being one of the only three operas written by Rossini to a French libretto, was received with only moderate enthusiasm; the latter, however, was every bit as much of a triumph as it had been at Edinburgh. Evans's characterisation was maturing all the time; Graziella Sciutti and the young and still unknown Ilva Ligabue made an enchanting pair as Nannetta and Alice; while the delightful Mexican contralto Oralia Dominguez endeared herself to everybody as Mistress Quickly, inspiring Desmond Shawe-Taylor to describe her face as 'a producer's gift: ripe, round and shining, like a melon that has seen a joke'.

The Glyndebourne season that followed less than a fortnight later included both these operas, plus five revivals—though Miss Sciutti, singing Susanna for the only time in Sussex, and the still unfamiliar Teresa Berganza as Cherubino made *The Marriage of Figaro* sound like new. The only real innovation was Wolf-Ferrari's one-act *Il segreto di Susanna*, another curtain-raiser for *Ariadne*. There was, however, one more excitement in 1958: the announcement of George Christie's engagement to Mary Nicholson. It came on 4 June, the twenty-seventh anniversary of the marriage of his parents, and the wedding took place on 8 August. Shortly afterwards there followed another piece of news to interest all lovers of Glyndebourne, to the effect that George had assumed the responsibilities not only of marriage but also of the chairmanship of Glyndebourne Productions Ltd, on the retirement of his father—who would, however, retain a seat on the Board.

84 George and Mary Christie, 1960

The last year of the decade was both happy and sad. It was happy because Glyndebourne was celebrating its Silver Jubilee and was able to extend its programme longer than ever before, from the end of May to the middle of August, with a record-breaking total of sixty-eight performances during a summer when temperatures were those of the Côte d'Azur and it seemed that the sun would never cease to shine. It was sad because Carl Ebert, now seventy-two, had announced his retirement as Artistic Director at the end of the season. He was not quite the last of the old guard—there remained Jani Strasser, the Chief Technician Jack Gough and Moran Caplat's Personal Assistant Janet Moores, as well as John Christie himself—but his artistic contribution had been unequalled. Only Fritz Busch had done more to mould Glyndebourne; but Busch was there only eight seasons, while 'the Professor' had served for twenty, producing during that time no less than thirty different operas, nearly all of which were repeated several times in successive years, often with different casts. His productions did not always escape criticism: occasionally his work was accused of being fussy and over-full of unnecessary business. He was, however, generally regarded in the profession as being the greatest operatic director of his time, and was certainly the first in England to see opera as the drama it should be, rather than a concert with costumes and scenery. When we consider how lamentably low were the standards of opera production in England before his arrival—John Christie himself, it will be remembered, had in the early days questioned the need for any producer at all—we can be in no real doubt of the immense influence he had on the younger generation of producers around him.

For Ebert's last production as Artistic Director he selected *Der Rosenkavalier*—an ambitious choice indeed for so small a theatre. The size of the Glyndebourne pit meant that the orchestra could be nowhere near up to the strength intended by the composer; the music was therefore played according to an orchestral arrangement that had been agreed between Fritz Busch and Richard Strauss himself between the wars. The cast was unbeatable—it included Régine Crespin, Elisabeth Söderström, Anneliese Rothenberger and Oscar Czerwenka—and the production itself made a worthy climax to Ebert's career. (Though it was not, as we shall see, to be his last opera for Glyndebourne.) At the end of the opening performance there occurred a richly comic scene. A short ceremony had been arranged on stage, in the course of which John Christie was to present his retiring Artistic Director with a silver rose-bowl. Christie made one of his most characteristic speeches, which lasted twenty-five minutes and in which he told the audience exactly what he thought about Covent Garden, the Arts Council and several other organisations whose representatives were his guests for the evening; he failed, however, to make any mention of Carl Ebert or the rose-bowl, and when he finished, having completely forgotten his original purpose, he started to walk off the stage with the bowl still in his hands. It was only thanks to Moran Caplat, who pursued him with a whispered reminder, that the presentation was finally made.

The other new opera for Jubilee Year was *Fidelio*—the first production, incidentally, to make use of Glyndebourne's new rehearsal stage. (Incredibly enough, until 1959 all full rehearsals, if they could not be held on the stage itself,

85–86 *Der Rosenkavalier*, 1959
(designer Oliver Messel): Elisabeth
Söderström, Régine Crespin,
Anneliese Rothenberger

took place in the Mildmay Restaurant, John Christie having always opposed the construction of proper rehearsal facilities on the grounds that it would involve the felling of an old ilex of which he was particularly fond.) *Fidelio* was the opera that Fritz Busch had always longed to do at Glyndebourne, but that Carl Ebert had always turned down as unsuitable. Perhaps he still held the same view; at any rate he did not produce it himself, entrusting it instead to Günther Rennert, who thus made his most distinguished *début* for a company of which, at the end of the season, he and Vittorio Gui were to be appointed 'Artistic Counsellors'. With Gré Brouwenstijn and Richard Lewis in the leading roles it could hardly fail: the audience cheered it to the echo.

Less successful, on the other hand, was the Jubilee *Figaro*. Shortly before its opening Geraint Evans burnt himself severely in a domestic accident and was able to sing only the last four performances; Teresa Berganza miscalculated the date of her baby's arrival and was obliged to withdraw altogether,★ her place being taken by Josephine Veasey, who was also due to give birth before the end of the year; and the conducting by Peter Maag—also a last-minute substitute— was described by one critic as 'bewilderingly eccentric', his harpsichord continuo as sounding like a 'parrot scraping its beak along the bars of its cage'. All in all, it was a sad disappointment; but with *Figaro* and *Der Rosenkavalier*

★ Though she had managed—quite memorably—two glorious performances of *La Cenerentola* earlier in the season.

87   Left, *Fidelio*, 1959 (designer Ita Maximowna), Act I, Scene I: Mihály Székely, Kim Borg, Esie Monson, Duncan Robertson, Gré Brouwenstijn

88   Below, Maximowna with Günther Rennert and Assistant Producer Anthony Besch

89   Right, The Prisoners' chorus

Glyndebourne could at least congratulate itself on two notable successes. And what other opera house has ever managed to engage *two* pregnant Cherubinos in a single season?

Perhaps, however, a greater reason for satisfaction than any of these was the expansion of Glyndebourne audiences over the decade, thanks to the BBC. Broadcasts in the pre-war years had been, to say the least, tentative; in 1946, however, the introduction of the Third Programme extended the possibilities a hundredfold. At last the music of Glyndebourne was available to all who wished to hear it: thus, in 1954 alone, no less than fifteen performances (including those from Edinburgh) were broadcast within four months. Television, too, had moved in. Already in 1951 there had been a live transmission of Fritz Busch's final performance of *Così fan tutte*, and similar broadcasts followed every year through the 1950s. By the end of the decade, Glyndebourne had become a household word: as Lionel Salter, then Head of Music Productions at BBC Television, pointed out in 1957, 'the number of people who watched the Glyndebourne relay of Rossini's *Le Comte Ory* would be equivalent to full houses at Glyndebourne every single night throughout the year, Sundays included, for fifteen years'. How thrilled John Christie must have been with that!

90   Cover by Osbert Lancaster for the 1960 Programme Book. Behind John Christie (with
     pug), Vittorio Gui can be seen in animated conversation with Moran Caplat. On the far right,
     Jack Gough and Head Gardener Mr Harvey survey the scene.

PART FOUR

THE 1960s

GLYNDEBOURNE ENTERED THE 1960s conscious that this was the beginning not just of a new decade but of a new chapter in its history. In the absence of Carl Ebert, its future was almost impossible to imagine. The influence of 'the Professor' had been everywhere—not just in the operas that he personally had produced, not even restricted to the field of production: the genial, paternal figure with his shock of white hair had long been an institution, with the Glyndebourne staff and the patrons alike, second only to John Christie himself.

Both the very special position that Ebert had enjoyed, and Glyndebourne's recognition that he was ultimately irreplaceable were evident to all careful readers of the 1960 programme book. The post of Artistic Director, which he had filled with such distinction and for so long, was seen to have been abolished; instead we found listed two 'Artistic Counsellors'—Vittorio Gui, who was given as a secondary title 'Head of Music', and Günther Rennert, now described as 'Head of Production'. It seemed to many people an odd arrangement, and a curiously tentative one; were the two of them not authorised to take over the complete direction, but only to give expert advice? If so, whom were they to advise, and where did the ultimate responsibility lie? These questions were never satisfactorily answered, and the mystery became still more opaque in 1963 when an additional post of 'Music Counsellor' was instituted for John Pritchard; what, one wondered, had Gui been counselling about? In the following year Gui's name no longer appeared at the head of the programme, since he refused to be in any way associated with what he considered a tasteless travesty of Rossini's *La pietra del paragone*, concocted by his colleague Rennert and a German collaborator and included in the 1964 repertoire; he finally agreed to conduct six performances of *The Magic Flute*, and he was to return, as a guest conductor, in 1965 for *Figaro* and some performances of a new production of Cimarosa's *Il matrimonio segreto*, but he was by now eighty and at the end of that season Glyndebourne regretfully bade him farewell.

The company indeed owed him much. In eighteen years, Gui had been responsible—if we include the 1948 *Ballo in maschera* at Edinburgh, which never came to Sussex—for no less than sixteen operas, by seven different

91 Above, Costume design by Desmond Heeley for *I Puritani*

92 Below, Joan Sutherland in *I Puritani*, 1960

composers; and although he will probably be remembered above all for his incomparable performances of Rossini, none of us who heard it will easily forget the glorious *I Puritani* with which the decade opened—Joan Sutherland singing with an effortless brilliance that took everybody's breath away—nor the *Pelléas et Mélisande* that followed two years later. This, surely, was one of the greatest achievements in the whole history of Glyndebourne. Gui—who had known Debussy well—brought out, time and time again, hidden beauties in the score whose existence many of us had not even suspected. Denise Duval was a superb Mélisande—she was warmly congratulated after the first performance by Dame Maggie Teyte herself, who had been chosen by the composer to succeed Mary Garden in the same part when the work was first produced at the Opéra-Comique—Kerstin Meyer an exquisite Geneviève and Michel Roux a magnificent Golaud; Beni Montresor's designs seemed exactly right, and the production was in the hands of none other than Carl Ebert himself, who had emerged from retirement for his final contribution to Glyndebourne. It proved also to be his finest.

The other great excitement of the 1962 season was *L'incoronazione di Poppea*, first performed 320 years before and now receiving its first professional production in Britain. The score had been arranged specially for Glyndebourne by Raymond Leppard, and may have shocked an occasional purist; for most of us, however, it was an unadulterated joy—dramatic, inventive and laced with irresistible flashes of humour when the occasion demanded. It was the first of four seventeenth-century operas that Mr Leppard has given us at Glyndebourne so far, and we can only implore him not to stop.

Despite these two successive *tours de force*, 1962 was the saddest year Glyndebourne had known; for on 4 July, just an hour or so before the curtain went up on *Così fan tutte*, John Christie died. He had never properly recovered from an operation for cataract some weeks before. It had been unsuccessful and had left him almost completely blind. For the first time, though he had appeared in the foyer as usual—unrecognised by many of his old friends owing to the patriarchal white beard he had grown after he could no longer shave himself—he had not taken his seat in the Glyndebourne Box on the opening night. His death was not announced until the end of the performance, and it was only on the following evening that the audience was able to honour his memory by standing in silence for two minutes before the beginning of *Figaro*. After that, the season went on as planned, and as he would have wished.

To say that John Christie was deeply missed would be an understatement. In a very real sense, he *was* Glyndebourne; the place seemed empty and incomplete without him. But for several years already—even before he handed over the chairmanship to his son—he had increasingly left the direction of the company to Moran Caplat, who was by now firmly in control. On the purely artistic side, Glyndebourne suffered even more seriously from the loss, effectively within the same three years, of both Carl Ebert and Vittorio Gui. From this double blow it took a long time to recover; and for the rest of the 1960s it showed, again and again, the want of firm artistic direction at the top. John Pritchard, who inherited Gui's position in 1964, worked hard to weld the

93 John Christie, photographed by
Anthony Armstrong-Jones for
Vogue, 1958

company together; but his time was limited and he had heavy commitments elsewhere, as did his colleague Günther Rennert.

George Christie was conscious of the decline, but for some years powerless to stop it. His position was a difficult one. He had lived in the world of opera since his birth—and indeed before it, having been embryonically present at the very first night of Glyndebourne in 1934—but although Chairman of the company he held no administrative position and was all too conscious of his youth and inexperience. After five years with the Gulbenkian Foundation, he resigned in 1962 to devote himself to Glyndebourne; but even then he very sensibly kept himself in the background until he was sure of his abilities. Only towards the end of the decade did he begin to make his presence firmly felt; in view of the results, one can only regret that he did not do so earlier.

To Richard Lewis — Admetus —
Glyndebourne — 1958 — Hugh Casson

Poppaea — Preliminary Study.

Perhaps it was inevitable that, in the absence of the two artistic giants, the quality of many of the productions during those years should have suffered. It must be admitted, moreover, that not all the failures could be justifiably blamed on Glyndebourne, except possibly in so far as the works concerned were unwisely chosen in the first place. Such a one was Hans Werner Henze's *Elegy for Young Lovers*, which was given its world première in English (the original language, since the libretto was by W. H. Auden and Chester Kallman) in 1961. Powerfully produced by Günther Rennert, exquisitely designed by Lila de Nobili and with Elisabeth Söderström and Kerstin Meyer in the cast, it deserved something more than the tame reception it received; but then Glyndebourne audiences have never been outstandingly *avant-garde* and their reaction was not entirely to be wondered at. It was, perhaps predictably, shared by John Christie himself. Spike Hughes tells of how one evening Christie met Auden and Kallman in the garden and, not having the faintest idea who they were, greeted them amicably and got into conversation. In the course of it, one of them mentioned that they had written the libretto of *Elegy for Young Lovers*. John Christie's face clouded. 'Oh dear,' he murmured, 'You shouldn't have, really you shouldn't', and walked sadly back into the house.

But if standards during the 1960s were more variable than they had been in the previous decade, the best was still as good as ever it had been. Among the new productions, 1961 brought an utterly magical *Elisir d'amore*, produced by Franco Zeffirelli and designed by him in the style of old Italian theatrical prints; its revival in the following year was even better, bringing in as it did Sesto

98   Left, *Elegy for Young Lovers*, 1961 (designer Lila de Nobili): André Turp, Dorothy Dorow, Carlos Alexander, Elisabeth Söderström
99   Right, Elisabeth Söderström as the Countess in *Capriccio*

100 *Dido and Aeneas*, 1966 (designer Lorenzo Ghiglia): Thomas Hemsley and Janet Baker in the title roles

Bruscantini and Mirella Freni to join Luigi Alva as the three principals. Then in 1963 came the first fully-staged presentation in England of Richard Strauss's last opera *Capriccio*, produced by Günther Rennert and with Elisabeth Söderström singing her first Countess. But perhaps the most outstanding of all was the *Dido and Aeneas* of 1966, with Janet Baker—who had herself spent two seasons in the Glyndebourne Chorus during the 1950s—and Thomas Hemsley in the title roles. Lorenzo Ghiglia gave it a glowing baroque set, with painted gauzes against which the bronze and gold costumes stood out majestically; the production was by Franco Enriquez, Gui's stepson, on whom—more even than on Günther Rennert—the mantle of Carl Ebert seemed to have fallen. Beginning with *I Puritani* in 1960, he produced seven more operas during the next ten years, including Donizetti's *Anna Bolena* which, with *Il matrimonio segreto*, was the principal new offering for 1965. This work, which had originally been conceived as a vehicle for Giuditta Pasta and had caused something of a sensation when revived by Callas at the Scala eight years before, relies heavily on the singer in the title role; on this occasion that singer was the Turkish soprano Leyla Gencer. She was the first Turk to sing at Glyndebourne—although a young *protégée* of Carl Ebert, Ayhan Alnar, had sung Susanna in an Edinburgh *Figaro* in 1947—and she fulfilled every expectation. Thus, despite a rather heavy-handed production, the opera was a considerable success and was revived in 1968. The Cimarosa piece was also well received, despite the fact that Gui missed the first seven performances owing to the illness of his wife, who had been stricken by a particularly violent form of food poisoning on their way to England.

L'Heure espagnole, a one-acter by Ravel which shared—many people

101 Above, Design by Franco Zeffirelli for *L'elisir d'amore*
102 Below, Costume drawing by David Walker

103 and 104   Design by Henry Bardon: above, for *Werther* and below, for *La Bohème*

thought a little uneasily—a double bill with *Dido and Aeneas*, was chiefly memorable for its décor by Osbert Lancaster. This included a prodigious number of clocks, musical toys and performing automata—always an obsession with Ravel who introduces thin mechanical sounds repeatedly into the score. Some people found this distracting; on the other hand it was generally agreed that in the particular company in which it found itself, so slight a work needed all the help it could get. Fortunately, from Michel Sénéchal and Hugues Cuenod, it got it.

A good deal more interesting was the production of *Werther* that same year by Michael Redgrave, working for Glyndebourne for the first time since his performance in the wartime *Beggar's Opera* twenty-six years before. This was the first Massenet opera to be tackled, and indeed Glyndebourne's first excursion into nineteenth-century French romantic music of any kind—John Christie's well-known dislike of the *genre* having, during his lifetime, always been allowed to prevail when anything of the kind was proposed. Vocally it was not outstanding, Hélia T'Hezan making of Charlotte rather too well-conducted a person and being described by one French critic as being *plus maternelle qu'amoureuse*, while Jean Brazzi as Werther was condemned in an English paper as looking for all the world like a Corsican Elvis Presley. Redgrave's straightforward, unflashy production, however, which never came between the audience and the music—something which could not invariably be said of recent work at Glyndebourne—met with almost universal approval. In consequence of its success, he was engaged again the following year for *La Bohème*. This was Glyndebourne's first Puccini opera, and there were some patrons who openly professed themselves shocked that the management should even have considered putting on the work of a composer who was at that time still widely considered a lightweight, and a vulgar one at that. Alas, the production was once again let down by the singing—even though all the principals were Italian—and it was not for another eleven years that the Puccini-Glyndebourne combination was finally to be vindicated.

The real triumph of 1967 was a new offering by Raymond Leppard: his arrangement of *L'Ormindo*, by Francesco Cavalli. The obscurity of the composer—and perhaps some degree of caution following a disastrous 'production' (really little more than a concert performance in costume) of Handel's oratorio *Jephtha* the previous year—accounted for some initial timidity on the part of the audience; this was, however, totally dispelled after the first night, by which time it was obvious that Glyndebourne had another major hit on its hands. Although, so far as anyone knew, *L'Ormindo* had not been performed anywhere since 1644, it proved to be a glorious work, refreshingly unconventional and still free of the formal limitations that the dictates of *opera seria* were so soon to impose. As the *Observer* put it, the general flavour was 'nearer the Palladium than the Parthenon'. Cavalli, Raymond Leppard used to say, was the Schubert to his master Monteverdi's Beethoven; Günther Rennert's production—his last—seemed at times a little heavy-handed, and the black and white, pseudo-Moroccan sets by Erich Kondrak would have seemed a bit startling to seventeenth-century Venice; but the singing—especially by Peter-Christoph Runge and John Wakefield as the two

105 Above, Production conference: Moran Caplat, Henry Bardon and Sir Michael Redgrave discuss *La Bohème*

106 Below, Franco Enriquez, Pauline Grant, Moran Caplat and Emanuele Luzzati discuss *Don Giovanni*

107 *L'Ormindo*, 1967: Peter-Christoph Runge, Isabel Garcisanz, John Wakefield

male leads, by Anne Howells, who came into the cast as a replacement at the last moment and scored the first resounding success of her career, and by Hugues Cuenod in drag as the old nurse—could not have been bettered.

The last great surprise of the decade, where choice of opera was concerned, was Tchaikovsky's *Eugene Onegin* in 1968—Glyndebourne's first Russian opera apart from *The Rake's Progress* (which has an English libretto). It was, as we might have expected, sung in Russian, a foreign language to all ten of the principal singers—even though Elisabeth Söderström could claim a Russian mother. Equally predictably, there were complaints that the audience would not be able to understand it—though one wonders what percentage of Glyndebourne audiences fully understand even the Italian and German of the Mozart canon. In fact, none of this mattered a bit. The singing was exquisite, above all that of Miss Söderström herself as Tatyana and the Polish tenor Wieslaw Ochman as Lensky; and once again the show was nearly stolen by Hugues Cuenod—this time as the French tutor, Monsieur Triquet. Meanwhile an authentic Slav atmosphere had been assured by the Bulgarian producer Michael Hadjimischev of the Sofia Opera, whose father had been his country's Minister in London before the war and who spoke English and Russian equally well.

Of all the producers working at Glyndebourne during the 1960s, however, the one who left the most indelible imprint was Franco Enriquez. After his 1960 début with *I Puritani* he was not heard of again for three years; then, however, there came a most memorable *Magic Flute* designed by his fellow-Italian Emanuele Luzzati, which was destined to inaugurate a long and harmonious collaboration between them. But Luzzati sets were not without their dangers:

95

3 BOYS 1973

LEPORELLO

SELIM

114   Above, *Don Giovanni* design conference 1967: Emanuele Luzzati, Franco Enriquez and Moran Caplat

115   Below, Jani Strasser with Gianandrea Gavazzeni, 1965

in this particular production Glyndebourne came perhaps as near as it ever has to disaster on stage. The story is best told by Geoffrey Gilbertson, who was at that time Stage Director:

Luzzati had designed these columns that had men inside them so that they could trundle around the stage. The trouble was that they were about fifteen foot high, and pretty hard for the chaps to manoeuvre. In fact they had a hell of a job to stay upright. Well, I had contact with each column by radio, so as to give them their cues: 'Columns stand by', 'Columns go', that sort of thing. I suppose we were getting a bit over-confident, anyway during I think it was the twelfth performance I said 'Columns go' as usual and there was the most almighty crash, and I knew one of them had fallen over. I rushed to the wings to have a look, and not one but two of them had gone. Of course, once they were down, they couldn't possibly get up again by themselves. I was in my dinner jacket, but I crawled in on all fours and somehow got to the nearest one, and there was this white, frightened face looking up at me. The opera was still going on you see, with great crashes of thunder, and Papageno and Tamino were just about to come on to the stage—we couldn't possibly have stopped the show at that moment. Anyway I said are you OK and this white face just looked at me and said it wasn't my fault, it was the other one. I was furious. How dare you, I said, this is no time to start blaming others. But at that moment Papageno and Tamino arrived, and the two of them simply lifted the two columns bodily up on to their feet again, and as they did so one of them said in German, just as if it was part of the dialogue, 'Guinness gives you strength'. I can tell you, it brought the house down. A cheap laugh if you like, but just the thing to relieve the tension and get things going again.

The Magic Flute was followed the very next year by a new Enriquez-Luzzati *Macbeth*—in which even the superb performance in the title role by the Greek baritone Kostas Paskalis could not altogether console us for Enriquez's regrettable decision that Banquo's ghost should be invisible not only to those present at the feast but to the audience as well. Next came *Anna Bolena* and *Dido and Aeneas* (both designed by Ghiglia) and then three new Mozart productions in a row: *Don Giovanni* in 1967, *Die Entführung* in 1968 and *Così fan tutte* in 1969. The *Don Giovanni*—the first opera, incidentally, to be sponsored by the Peter Stuyvesant Foundation, which in 1966 provided a grant of £35,000 over seven years for the staging of Mozart operas—did not, it must be admitted, entirely escape criticism. It was difficult, then as now, to defend Enriquez when he made Don Giovanni have his supper *in* the cemetery, the statue never moving from its position and consequently never fastening him in its icy grip. (Such indeed were the protests over this that the scene was radically revised when the production was repeated two years later.) The Commendatore for his part had been obliged to fight his Act I duel in an ankle-length furry dressing-gown, so that it was no wonder that it ended the way it did. *Die Entführung*, on the other hand, was a huge success. It was given new spoken dialogue by Fritz Spiegl, in a simplified German ('*Ich hab' ein Idee!*') which was readily understandable by everyone, whether they spoke the language or not; and everyone also enjoyed the little snatch of *Rule Britannia* which accompanied Blonde's assertion that she was an Englishwoman, born to freedom. (She was in fact a Swede, Birgit Nordin.) Margaret Price—who had first distinguished

116   *Così fan tutte*, 1971 (designer
Emanuele Luzzati): Margaret Price,
Jerry Jennings, Edith Thallaug, Paolo
Montarsolo, Knut Skram

117   *Macbeth*, 1972 (designer Emanuele
Luzzati): Kostas Paskalis, Joyce
Barker, Rae Woodland, Keith Erwen

118   Jani Strasser with Anne Howells, 1969

herself two years before, in the ill-fated *Jephtha*—was a lovely Constanze, and the veteran Otakar Kraus spoke the part of Pasha Selim with a power and authority that few other singers could have matched.

The Enriquez-Luzzati *Così fan tutte* of 1969 was the only new production of that year and consequently the last of the decade. (Sadly, it also marked the end of their collaboration at Glyndebourne.) Luzzati's beige-and-yellow sets with their brilliantly-coloured tiles seemed to bring the whole warmth of the Mediterranean flooding on to the stage; Jane Berbié was an irresistible Despina; and the husband-and-wife team of Ryland Davies and Anne Howells won all hearts as Ferrando and Dorabella. Hanneke van Bork was the perfect Fiordiligi in her gentler moments, if a little short on the steel necessary for *Come scoglio*. As for the revival of *Don Giovanni*, it marked a considerable improvement on 1967, not just because of the changes in the last Act but above all thanks to the presence in the title role of Ruggiero Raimondi—a bass rather than a baritone, but surely the richest and most satisfying since Ezio Pinza himself.

Raimondi was twenty-seven at the time, and was by no means the only young singer to be heard during those years at Glyndebourne who subsequently became world-famous. Thus Mirella Freni—another of Gui's discoveries—sang Zerlina as early as 1960, the same year in which Heather Harper appeared as one of the Three Ladies in *The Magic Flute*; in 1962 Despina and Zerbinetta were sung by Reri Grist and Cherubino by Edith Mathis, and in 1964 the part of Ilia in *Idomeneo* went to Gundula Janowitz while that of Idamante was given to a virtually unknown young Italian named Luciano Pavarotti. Montserrat Caballé came to Sussex in 1965 to make her English début, singing the Marschallin in *Der Rosenkavalier* and the Countess in

119   *Idomeneo*, 1964: Richard Lewis, Luciano Pavarotti, Gundula Janowitz

Figaro.★ In 1966, it was hoped that the title role in *Werther* might be sung by the promising young Placido Domingo; unfortunately, due to unforeseen circumstances, he was unable to appear in time for his audition.

Still, it was an impressive record; and by the time that the company set out for Munich and the Flanders Festival in the autumn of 1969 there were unmistakable signs that Glyndebourne had emerged from its period of insecurity and indecision—not least among them being George Christie's newly-asserted leadership and his promotion of John Pritchard to be Music Director. The days of 'Counsellors' were over; the ship was on course again.

120   *Figaro* rehearsal, 1962: Carl Ebert and Mirella Freni

During the 1960s the BBC became distinctly less enthusiastic about Glyndebourne. Its productions were still televised from time to time—*Falstaff* in 1960, *L'elisir d'amore* in 1962, *The Magic Flute* in 1964 and *Dido and Aeneas* in 1965; but there was no regular annual broadcast as in the previous decade. In 1967 the recording vans were back again for *Don Giovanni*, but almost unbelievably, in the actual transmission the overture was omitted. It was not a good augury for the future.

This half-heartedness was perhaps partly, but certainly not entirely, due to the fall in Glyndebourne's own standards. The fact was that the competition was growing increasingly stiff. Covent Garden under Solti was improving beyond recognition; Sadler's Wells was preparing to move from Islington to the Coliseum as the English National Opera; while outside London the Scottish and Welsh national companies were also becoming forces to be reckoned with. Clearly, if Glyndebourne wished to extend its audiences beyond its own theatre—which, after many enlargements, still numbered only 844 seats—it must take an initiative of its own.

For some time already, George Christie had been turning over in his mind the idea of a regular Glyndebourne Touring Company. Not only, he realised, would this bring live opera to many cities and towns which had few if any opportunities of hearing any; it would also provide an opportunity for talented members of the chorus to take on solo parts and show what they could do. As a seasonal company that re-engaged its chorus every year rather than keeping it on a long-term contract, Glyndebourne had always been able to boast a quite exceptionally young and talented group of singers, the best of whom would be trained as understudies for the principal roles. Since, however, they hardly ever had the chance to go on stage in these roles, they were naturally tending more and more to take themselves off—with the training and expertise on which Glyndebourne had expended so much time and effort—to other companies. How much better it would be to send them on tour under the Glyndebourne banner—and how many stars might not thus be revealed?

And so the decision was taken, and in 1966 the young Brian Dickie, after only four years at Glyndebourne, was appointed Administrator of the new Touring Company, in the expectation of its launch in the following year. All

121   Myer Fredman and Brian Dickie during rehearsals for Glyndebourne Touring Opera's first season, 1968

★ She horrified everyone by arriving without knowing a single note of her part as the Marschallin, and promptly fell ill during the first week of rehearsals. Thanks to a Herculean effort by Gerald Gover and Martin Isepp of the Music Staff, she learnt the role in six days and was word perfect by the opening night; but she never returned to Glyndebourne

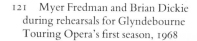

that was needed was the money. Sadly, the Arts Council could offer only £15,000—nowhere near enough—and the launch had to be postponed;* but George Christie was able to go to his old employers, the Gulbenkian Foundation, who agreed to contribute £30,000 over the next three years—a sum they subsequently increased by another £10,000, making £40,000 in all. With this, an improved Arts Council grant and some support from industry, the infant company was ready in 1968 to undertake its inaugural tour.

For the first four years, the tour took place not in the autumn as it does nowadays but in the early spring, before the main Glyndebourne season went into rehearsal. This meant that the Touring Company rehearsals began in midwinter—no picnic in a virtually unheated theatre—and the show got on the road at the beginning of March. For its opening season, the schedule was formidable indeed—to take *L'Ormindo*, *L'elisir d'amore*, *The Magic Flute* and *Don Giovanni* to Newcastle, Liverpool, Manchester, Sheffield and Oxford, doing seven performances a week with a Saturday matinée. The principal conductor was the Glyndebourne Chorus Master, Myer Fredman, but Raymond Leppard went along for *L'Ormindo* and Kenneth Montgomery for *L'elisir d'amore*. The orchestra was the Northern Sinfonia. Among the cast were Ryland Davies and Jill Gomez, both of whom had been understudies in 1967; Ian Wallace was singing Dulcamara, Richard Van Allan Osmano (in *L'Ormindo*) and Leporello.

The problems of this first tour were often nightmarish, not the least of them being a force ten gale which caused the police to close the road across the Pennines to all heavy goods vehicles on the very day that the company was travelling from Newcastle to Liverpool. The van with the costumes got through without too much difficulty, as did the artists, who went by train; but the sets and lighting equipment were delayed overnight and eventually arrived at the Royal Court Theatre only an hour or so before the audience. Unfortunately the opera scheduled for that evening, *The Magic Flute*, had the most complicated lighting programme of any of the four productions; there was no time to prepare it in advance, and Geoffrey Gilbertson, the company Manager and Stage Director, had to sit up on the lighting bridge with the electricians, giving them the cues and improvising the effects as he went along. The next day's press notices concentrated rather less on the quality of the production than on the *bravura* with which the company had surmounted its difficulties; but they were nothing if not enthusiastic, and the theatre was packed out for the rest of the run. The same opera gave trouble in Sheffield, where the Lyceum Theatre proved to be so steeply raked that Luzzati's columns kept falling over like ninepins; but by now the company seemed to have got used to that particular problem and to have taken it in its stride.

In 1969 it set off again, on a tour in which Leeds and Nottingham were substituted for Sheffield and Oxford. This time there were only three operas—*Macbeth*, *Die Entführung* and *Eugene Onegin*—but once more there were 'House Full' signs outside every theatre. The Touring Company had fully justified George Christie's hopes. It had become an institution, and was there to stay.

122–124   Scenes from some early GTO performances

122   Above right, Ian Wallace, Jill Gomez, Ryland Davies and Terence Sharpe in *L'elisir d'amore*, 1968

123   Above far right, Richard Van Allan as Osmin, 1969

124   Below right, *Eugene Onegin*, 1968 (designer Pier Luigi Pizzi), choreographer Pauline Grant

---

* Meanwhile, however, the main company managed a tour of Scandinavia instead.

PART FIVE

THE 1970s

THE GLYNDEBOURNE STYLE OF the 1970s bore above all the stamp of four men, two conductors and two producers. The conductors were John Pritchard and Bernard Haitink. John Pritchard had grown up with Glyndebourne. A member of the Music Staff since 1947, he had conducted at least one opera in every season since 1951. Now, as we have seen, he had at last assumed full responsibility for the musical direction of the company, and during the decade was to conduct no less than eighteen more, including nine new productions—figures which would doubtless have been more impressive still had he not left at the end of the 1977 season to take up a new appointment as Chief Conductor at Cologne.

In comparison with Pritchard, Bernard Haitink was a relative newcomer. Eight years younger—he was then forty-three and had already been Permanent Conductor of the Amsterdam Concertgebouw for the past eleven years—he made his first appearance at Glyndebourne with *Die Entführung* in 1972. Strangely enough in view of so distinguished a career, this was only the third opera that he had ever conducted, and only his second by Mozart. He was thus able to bring to the work an extraordinary freshness of approach—almost a feeling of wonder—which, combined with that astonishing attention to detail and subtlety of phrasing which Sussex audiences were to come to know so well in the years that followed, was an unforgettable experience for all who heard it. Before the decade was out he had added three more Mozart operas—*The Magic Flute* in 1973, *Don Giovanni* in 1977 and *Così fan tutte* in 1978—as well as *The Rake's Progress*, *Pelléas et Mélisande*, *Fidelio* and Haydn's *La fedeltà premiata*, and in 1978 he succeeded Pritchard as Musical Director.

Of the two producers, the first was John Cox. He had first come to Glyndebourne as assistant to Carl Ebert in 1959, and made his solo début at Glyndebourne in 1970—stepping in at a late date to replace Franco Enriquez, whose overall conception he had to follow—with an only moderately successful *Turco in Italia*, the most memorable feature of which was the return of Graziella Sciutti for the first time after eleven years; this he followed, however, in 1971 with a radiant *Ariadne auf Naxos* before being appointed Director of Production in 1972. By the end of the 1979 season he had ten more operas to his credit, ranging from Haydn to Gottfried von Einem. In the whole

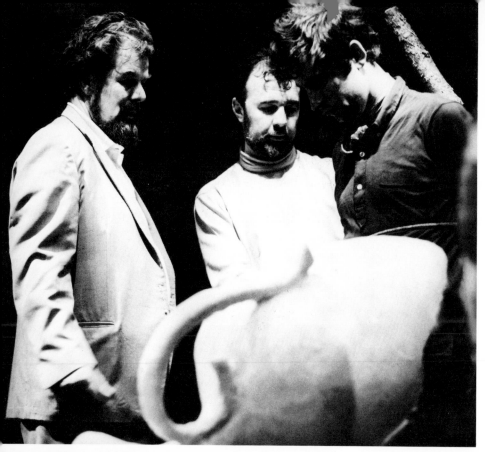

history of Glyndebourne, his present total of sixteen (up to and including the 1984 season) has been beaten only by Carl Ebert himself.

And so we come to the last of the four, Sir Peter Hall—who, in George Christie's words, 'gave Glyndebourne a new dimension'. Like Cox, he too began in 1970—with *La Calisto*, another of Raymond Leppard's superb seventeenth-century re-animations—following it two years later with yet another, Monteverdi's *Il ritorno d'Ulisse in patria*. Next came three new productions of the three Mozart/Da Ponte operas, the best that Glyndebourne has ever seen; and the decade ended with a glorious *Fidelio*, if anything even more majestic than Günther Rennert's immensely impressive conception of 1959.

Of the works produced during the second half of the decade, however, many would never have seen the light of day but for the group of sponsors who came to Glyndebourne's financial rescue. Up to 1973 or thereabouts, the company's policy had been to rely on box office receipts to cover some 80 per cent of the costs; when inflation took off in the following year, however, this was no longer remotely realistic. George Christie's solution was to set up a Finance Committee, subordinate to the Arts Trust, and to invite Sir Alex Alexander, at that time Chairman of Imperial Foods (and a Glyndebourne Trustee), to head it. The results were little short of spectacular: the Stuyvesant Foundation had of course blazed the trail in the 1960s, but it was now followed by Imperial Tobacco (working as a group through individual brand names, including John Player), and several other major firms, together with a number of private individuals—of whom special mention should be made of Mr Fred Kobler and Mr Ralph Corbett of Cincinnati. Had it not been for them, Glyndebourne's plight during the economic storms of the later 1970s would have been parlous indeed.

In its choice of repertoire, the company continued to strike what seemed to most of us the perfect balance between the familiar and the off-beat. Of the former, apart from the Mozart canon, we had a new *Macbeth* (produced by Michael Hadjimischev) John Cox's new *Rake's Progress* (designed by David Hockney), a new *Falstaff* and *Pelléas et Mélisande*, and a nearly new *Bohème*, with Cox re-using the 1967 costumes and sets for what was otherwise a completely original production. Of the latter, among the most enthusiastically received were the two offerings by Raymond Leppard mentioned above. The first, *La Calisto*, was an arrangement of a work by Cavalli which, as far as was known, had never been given since its first performance in 1651. Janet Baker sang with sublime beauty as the goddess Diana (and also as her father, Jupiter, disguised as his daughter); Ileana Cotrubas in the title role was turned into a bear—played by George and Mary Christie's daughter Louise—the various *dei ex machina* once again rose and descended precariously by means of magnificently obvious stage machinery, forests appeared and disappeared in the twinkling of an eye, fountains sprang water and Hugues Cuenod as usual came near to stealing the show as an elderly and somewhat bad-tempered tenor nymph. Dame Janet (as she later became) appeared again in *Il ritorno d'Ulisse*, scoring in the role of Penelope what one critic hailed as 'the greatest triumph of

130–132   *La Calisto* (designer John Bury)
  Above, The Prologue
  Below left, Ugo Trama, Ileana Cotrubas, Peter Gottlieb
  Below right, Federico Davià as Pan

133   Right, *Il ritorno d'Ulisse in patria*, 1972 (designer John Bury) . . . conference of the gods

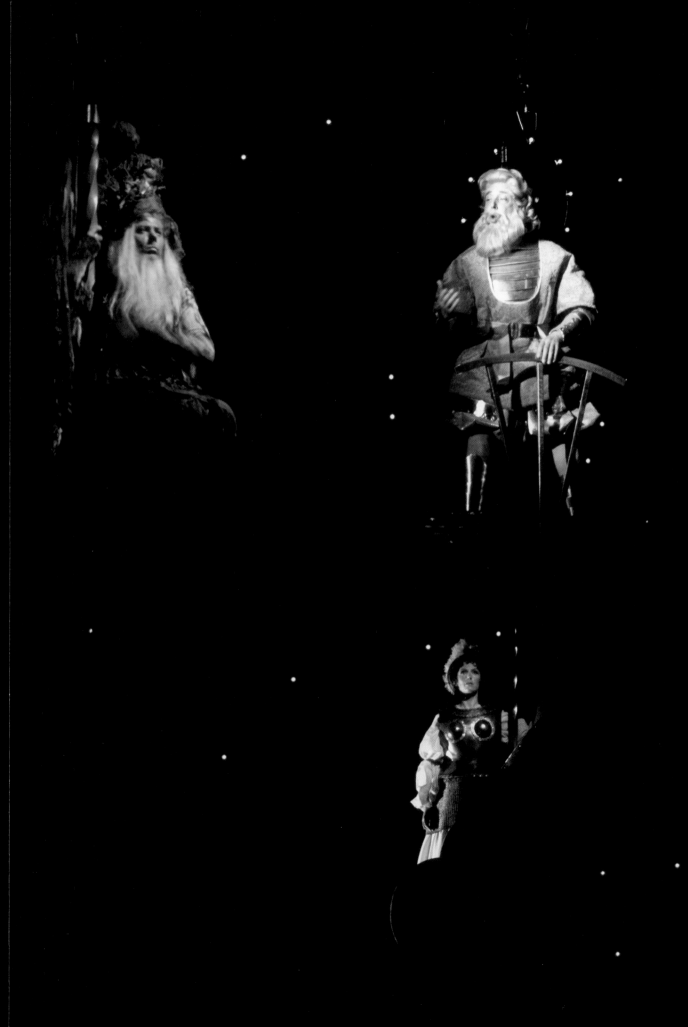

134 Above far left, *Il ritorno d'Ulisse in patria*, Janet Baker and Janet Hughes

135 Above left, *Il ritorno d'Ulisse in patria*, 1979, Anne Murray, Richard Lewis, Richard Stilwell

136 Below left, Benjamin Luxon and Janet Baker

her career', with a Ulysses in every respect worthy of her—and one cannot say more than that—in the person of Benjamin Luxon. Anne Howells was a lovely Minerva, Richard Lewis a gentle yet powerful Eumete and full use was once again made of the stage machinery by which, *inter alia*, ships were turned to stone and at one moment a gigantic eagle filled the sky.★

It was during a performance of this opera that one of the goddesses, obliged by the producer to remain invisibly suspended some forty feet above the stage while awaiting her next appearance, appealed urgently for a drink. As Geoffrey Gilbertson recalls it, 'I can see her now, swinging up there in the breeze, and this hand came out with a can of lager, and she swung backwards and forwards until she just managed to catch it. And down below there was Janet Baker, singing this wonderful second act lullaby. Any moment, I thought, that can was going to come crashing down into Janet's lap, and the Stage Manager would be over the Downs and far away . . .'

At the other end of the spectrum were the operas by living composers, beginning in 1970 with *The Rising of the Moon* by Nicholas Maw. This, the first opera ever to be specially commissioned by Glyndebourne, proved to be an elaborate and ambitious essay in romantic comedy—though with serious undertones—set in Ireland in 1875. It had a cast of thirteen, and was richly—perhaps over-richly—scored, with a triple wind section as in *Der Rosenkavalier*. Osbert Lancaster's sets contained just the right element of humour, and the conductor—to everyone's surprise—was Raymond Leppard, whom we had always thought of as a baroque or early eighteenth-century man but who proved every bit as much at home with Maw as he was with Monteverdi. This was followed in 1973 by the British première of Gottfried von Einem's *The Visit of the Old Lady*, an operatic version of Friedrich Dürrenmatt's play, which had been performed some years before on the London stage by Alfred Lunt and

137 and 138 Below, *The Rising of the Moon*, 1970: Johanna Peters, Dennis Wicks, Alexander Oliver, John Gibbs; Kerstin Meyer, Rae Woodland, Annon Lee Silver, Delia Wallis

★For more about Raymond Leppard's realisations for Glyndebourne, see his article in *Glyndebourne: A Celebration*.

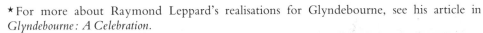

139   Kerstin Meyer as the Old Lady,
The Visit of the Old Lady, 1973
(designer Michael Annals – her dress
by Hardy Amies)

Lynn Fontanne under the simple title of *The Visit*. At the suggestion of the composer himself, Glyndebourne made one of its rare departures from its original-language rule and sang the work in English, the native tongue of all twenty-one members of the cast—except, unfortunately, Kerstin Meyer in the title role, who was all too often incomprehensible. The plot was a curious one, about a fabulously rich old lady who arrives in a village and offers it vast wealth if it will organise the murder of a local shopkeeper who had many years before made her pregnant and then deserted her. John Cox pulled out all the stops in his production, using a real vintage Ford car, a visibly revolving stage and a train hurtling through a station, but the music—which one critic described as being 'a bit Orff' and fell in fact somewhere about half-way between him and Richard Strauss—was generally felt to be not distinguished enough to carry so ambitious a piece. It was not, however, entirely unsuccessful and was revived in the following year.

Another recent work—it had been composed as lately as 1959—was Francis Poulenc's setting for a single soprano voice of Jean Cocteau's one-act monologue *La Voix humaine*. This was given in 1977 as a curtain-raiser to Janáček's *The Cunning Little Vixen*, which had been first produced (on its own) two years before. The composer described it as a *tragédie lyrique*: it is in fact a soliloquy in the form of a one-sided telephone conversation between a woman and the lover whom she is about to lose. The work was not entirely new to Glyndebourne, having been performed by the company at the 1960 Edinburgh Festival. On that occasion it had been sung by Denise Duval and designed and directed by Cocteau himself; this time it was both directed and sung—ravishingly—by Graziella Sciutti, in almost unaccented French. One was sorry in a way not to have the Cocteau sets, but there was an Art Déco *tour de force* by Martin Battersby that amply made up for them—and incidentally included a Cocteau drawing on the wall.

As to *The Cunning Little Vixen*, opinions were divided. Raymond Leppard, once again bursting his baroque bonds, made a brilliant job of the often perplexing score, but the audiences never really took Jonathan Miller's production to their hearts. Neither he nor they can altogether be blamed: the problem with any opera—or play for that matter—in which the majority of the characters are animals is the danger of slipping into cuteness, and in order to avoid this fate Dr Miller and his costume designer Rosemary Vercoe went perhaps rather too far in the opposite direction, making them all too human and giving them clothes which, while stylised, never really brought out the individual characteristics of the animals concerned. Patrick Robertson's scenery (relying heavily on back-projections) provided some degree of verisimilitude, while Norma Burrowes and Benjamin Luxon were both outstanding as the Vixen and the Forester respectively; but one left the theatre unconvinced.

This opera was sung in English—not even Glyndebourne dared attempt it in Czech. The success of the Russian-language *Eugene Onegin*, however, encouraged the company to consider another Tchaikovsky production and the result was, in 1971, *The Queen of Spades*. The producer and designer, Michael Hadjimischev and Pier Luigi Pizzi, were the same as before, and the cast once again numbered enough Slavs (five Bulgarians and a Pole) to ensure at least some degree of authenticity; but this time the formula somehow failed to work. Ghost stories need, above all things, dramatic tension; it simply was not there. The scalp never crept, the spine never tingled. There was some fine singing, notably from Virginia Popova as the old Countess and from Reni Penkova as Pauline, the latter impressing everyone sufficiently to get herself signed up for Dorabella in 1975 and for Meg Page in 1976 and 1977; but fine singing, this time, was not quite enough.

A good deal more successful was John Cox's production of *Ariadne auf Naxos* the same year. Quite apart from the outstandingly high standard of singing even by Glyndebourne standards (with Sylvia Geszty a sparkling Zerbinetta) it immediately captured the audience's imagination with the set for the first act. Instead of placing the actors on the stage of Monsieur Jourdain's private theatre the designer, Michael Annals, put them underneath it, amid a tangle of traps, pulleys and ropes. (The model, we were told, was the understage of the

140 Graziella Sciutti in *La Voix humaine*, 1977 (designer Martin Battersby)

141 and 142   Left, *The Cunning Little Vixen*, 1977 (designers Patrick Robertson and
Rosemary Vercoe). Above, Norma Burrowes and Michael Lewis. Below, the forest animals

143   Above, *Ariadne auf Naxos*, 1971 (designer Michael Annals): The Prologue

144   Below, Costume design by Rosemary Vercoe for *The Cunning Little Vixen*

eighteenth-century Swedish court theatre at Drottningholm.) Act II was
equally exciting, with a most spectacular transformation scene and the advance
of Bacchus's ship so far downstage that one felt serious concern for the
orchestra. As a final *bonne-bouche*, Glyndebourne continued the tradition,
begun in 1962, of actually staging the firework display promised by the Major-
Domo, while the audience were returning to their cars after the performance.
What other opera house, one wonders, could manage that particular trick? A
few, perhaps; but surely no other in the world would have had subsequently to
pacify the estate game-keeper, who arrived furiously one morning to complain
that all the newly-hatched pheasant chicks were dying of fright. (Since that
incident, 'bangers' have been banned. Fireworks now consist exclusively of
'whooshers', and the pheasants survive.)

   That 1971 *Ariadne* inaugurated what was almost an orgy of Strauss, who
received three more new productions (all by John Cox) during the decade and

145   Above, Costume design by
        Martin Battersby for the Countess in
        Capriccio
146   Below, Costume design by
        Michael Annals for *Ariadne auf Naxos*

was to be represented in every season except that of 1978. The first of the three was *Capriccio*, first heard at Glyndebourne in 1963 and now ten years later revived—and completely metamorphosed—by Cox. The central issue of the opera—which is essentially a conversation piece about whether music is superior to poetry or *vice versa*—is obviously as alive today as it was in the late eighteenth century, the period in which Strauss and his librettist, Clemens Krauss, chose to set the action. Cox therefore sought to stress its contemporaneity by bringing that setting forward, not to the present day (where the utterly different social conditions would make nonsense of the whole thing) but to the most recent period in which large-scale private patronage of the arts and a social life of leisured elegance still existed without undue self-consciousness. We accordingly now found ourselves in the same country house that Dennis Lennon had designed for the earlier production (and the same Elisabeth Söderström singing the Countess) but a hundred and fifty years later in time, with furniture and costumes of the 1920s and Braques and Marie Laurencins on the walls.

All this new decoration was the work of Martin Battersby, who was to do a still more thorough job—in which, this time, he was able to start from scratch—with *Intermezzo* in 1974. This to some people embarrassingly intimate revelation of the Strausses' domestic life was performed in English—Strauss himself having insisted in his introduction on the comprehensibility of the text—the composer's own libretto having been translated for the occasion by Andrew Porter. Here again, Battersby seemed to bring the 1920s effortlessly back to life, providing a perfect setting for Miss Söderström's virtuoso performance as the insufferable 'Christine'—an only faintly disguised portrait of Pauline Strauss herself.

The last Strauss production of the decade was *Die schweigsame Frau*, a light comedy whose libretto, by Stefan Zweig, was loosely based on Ben Jonson's *The Silent Woman*. This opera too was an attempt by the composer to poke fun at his own world of musicians and singers, its basic premise being the horror and disgust felt by an elderly admiral on discovering that his nephew is a professional singer and married to a soprano. John Cox turned it into a richly baroque romp, Michael Annals (who had given us that unforgettable Drottningholm *Ariadne*) provided the perfect late-eighteenth-century decor, and the youthful Andrew Davis caught every nuance of an old man's music.★

Mr Davis was, perhaps, a little less successful with his first Mozart opera at Glyndebourne, the 1978 *Magic Flute*, in which the sparkle of youth seemed a trifle lacking. One suspects, however, that for much of the time the audience's attention was taken up by David Hockney's sets. His opening scene was straight out of an Italian primitive, with stylised cypresses and palm-trees

★For more about these productions, see John Cox's article, 'The Strauss Operas' in *Glyndebourne: A Celebration*.

147   Above right, *Capriccio*, 1973 (designers Dennis Lennon and Martin Battersby): Eugenia Ratti,
        Ricardo Cassinelli, Marius Rintzler, Elisabeth Söderström, Kerstin Meyer
148   Below right, Elisabeth Söderström as Christine in *Intermezzo*, 1974 (designer Martin Battersby)

149–152   Designs by Martin Battersby for *Intermezzo*

149   Left, Costume design for a party-goer

150   Below left, The fancy dress party

151   Above right, Costume designs for Christine

152   Above far right, Felicity Lott as Christine

153   Below right, Christine consults her lawyer about a divorce

growing out of rocky clefts, while the dragon which so nearly demolishes the hero in the first minute of the opera proved to be a precise clone of that slain by Paolo Uccello's *St George* in the National Gallery. After that, however, we slipped smoothly back into Ancient Egypt, featuring *inter alia* a large number of distinctly unmonumental pyramids. The animals were enchanting as well as enchanted, and would have delighted Schikaneder—and, surely, Mozart himself; both, however, would have been horrified to see Papageno's cage full of *dead* birds. He was a bird catcher, not a bird killer and, as Spike Hughes felicitously put it, his job was to fill the Queen's aviary, not her deep freeze.

This *Magic Flute* was in fact the second opera which David Hockney had designed for Glyndebourne, having made his début with the new production of *The Rake's Progress* in 1975. The work had first been seen as early as 1953 at Edinburgh, whence it was brought to Glyndebourne in the following year. The designer then was Osbert Lancaster, who had deliberately set it in the very late eighteenth century in order not to clash with the Rex Whistler sets for the Sadler's Wells ballet on the identical theme, which was being performed at Edinburgh the same year. For this new production, however, Hockney not only went back half a century or so to Hogarth's own day but actually created a pastiche of his engravings for the designs—with, it must be said, remarkable effect. The auction scene in particular was little short of a triumph; opinions were more divided over the scene in Bedlam, where—to match the highly

154 Above, *Die Zauberflöte*, 1978 (designer David Hockney)

155 Above right, David Hockney's design for Baba the Turk

156 Below right, *The Rake's Progress*, 1975 (designer David Hockney): Donald Gramm and Leo Goeke

stylised music— the inmates were packed like battery hens in serried ranks of nesting-boxes, from which they would pop up to sing and then once again disappear from view. Leo Goeke as Tom and Jill Gomez as Anne were both ideal for their parts—though their laurels were very nearly stolen by Donald Gramm as Nick Shadow and Rosalind Elias as the bearded Baba the Turk—and Bernard Haitink conducted in a way which would have made the composer very happy indeed.

Haitink was also in the pit for two out of the three Mozart productions staged by Sir Peter Hall. The operas chosen were the three with libretti by Lorenzo da Ponte, and were taken in chronological order; the designer in each case was Peter Hall's regular collaborator since his Stratford days, John Bury. Thanks to his non-operatic background, Hall was able to bring an unusually open mind to all three works, going back to their earliest editions, looking at them with a fresh eye and running them virtually without cuts. The *Figaro* came first, with John Pritchard conducting; apart from one critic, who claimed that the whole approach was too serious (which it wasn't) just about everyone hailed it as a triumph. The sets were firmly realistic, the characters all carefully thought out: no pasteboard here either, but warm, breathing flesh and blood. The Countess was sung first by Elizabeth Harwood and later by Kiri te Kanawa, making her first appearance at Glyndebourne; Ileana Cotrubas— now, after an unforgettable 1969 Mélisande and a perfect 1970 Calisto, a regular Glyndebourne favourite—was a flawless Susanna, Knut Skram a virile Figaro, Benjamin Luxon a first-rate Almaviva, and as Cherubino the glowingly youthful Frederica von Stade won all hearts—including quite obviously that of the Countess herself, who made no secret of her infatuation with him, and quite right too.

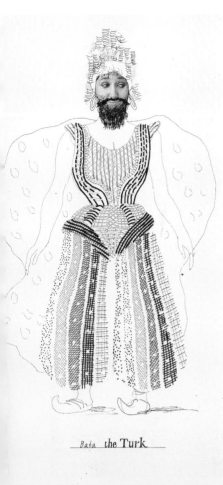

Baba the Turk

157–160   Designs by David Hockney
157 and 158   *The Rake's Progress*, 1975. Above, Bedlam; below, the Auction Scene

159 and 160   *Die Zauberflöte*, 1978

Next, in 1977, came *Don Giovanni*. Traditionally, as we know, this opera is set in the Seville of Philip II, although there is nothing in the libretto to say that it should be; Hall brought it forward to the days of Goya, which lent the whole thing a new sense of immediacy, as well as achieving a level of dramatic tension unique in the experience of most of us—especially at the end of Act I when, incidentally, Don Giovanni did not make his escape as he usually does, but remained to defy his enemies and their threatened 'thunder of vengeance'. Benjamin Luxon—despite a startling resemblance to the Prince Consort—made a magnificent Don before being succeeded after eleven performances by Thomas Allen; the Australian Joan Carden gave us an exquisite Donna Anna, and thanks to the stage presence—as well as the exquisite singing—of Leo Goeke, even Don Ottavio, no longer a lovesick youth but a distinctly paternal figure in late middle age, appeared a good deal less wet than he usually does. The two Leporellos were both ex-members of the Glyndebourne Chorus: in the earlier performances Stafford Dean, in the later Richard Van Allan. Meanwhile the Hall touch was everywhere evident: there was a marvellous moment, for example, when after the duel in Act I, Don Giovanni carefully wiped the blade of his sword on the Commendatore's cloak, then pulled a ring off the dead man's finger and pocketed it before slipping away into the shadows.

Finally, in 1978, came the *Così fan tutte*. Once again, Hall went back to the earliest available edition, thereby managing to avoid any number of the old clichés and restoring two arias (*Ah lo veggio* and *Rivolgete a lui lo sguardo*) which are almost invariably cut. The star of this production was unquestionably Maria Ewing, whose sense of comedy and impeccable timing impressed the audience almost as much as the sound of her voice. As Dorabella she proved irresistible, and no one who saw her can have been particularly surprised when, not very long afterwards, her producer corroborated this view. Now Lady Hall, she has appeared in three subsequent Glyndebourne productions and we can only hope for many more.

During the 1970s, thirteen complete Glyndebourne operas were televised. The BBC, returning after a three-year absence, broadcast *La Calisto* in 1971, after which the company concluded a most successful agreement with Southern Television; as a result twelve more operas were shown over the next eight years, including *Macbeth* (with Josephine Barstow taking over the lead), *Il ritorno d'Ulisse*, *Falstaff*, *The Rake's Progress* and *Fidelio*. The only disadvantage to this contract was that STV often had difficulty in persuading the Independent Television network to accept the programmes, so making them available to viewers in other parts of the country; fortunately the arrangement was not exclusive, and the BBC was able to return to do a superb *Capriccio* in 1976, as well as Peter Hall's *Così fan tutte* two years later.

Meanwhile the Glyndebourne Touring Company was going from strength to strength. Every year it visited five provincial centres, usually with three operas—the principal exception being 1971, when the decision was first taken to tour in the late summer rather than the early spring. This being the year of transition, there were in fact two 1971 tours: to Liverpool, Edinburgh and

Southampton in March and April and to Leeds, Norwich and Newcastle in September. (Much to George Christie's delight, he received two annual subsidies from the Arts Council instead of one.) In other years, the company also visited Manchester, Oxford, Nottingham, Southsea, Birmingham and Bristol.★ It would have cast its net wider still, could more provincial cities have provided adequate theatres; nevertheless, there was a wide geographical spread over the years, and many thousands of people were given their first experience of live opera, a large proportion of them returning regularly in later years for more of it. So much for the 'élitism' of which the ignorant or the envious have always accused Glyndebourne, and still occasionally attempt to do so.

Quality, however, has never deteriorated. During the decade the Touring Company regularly fielded artists of the calibre of Benjamin Luxon (Onegin in 1971), Elizabeth Gale (Susanna, Nannetta and Blonde), Linda Esther Gray (the Countess, Tatyana, Mimi and Agathe in *Der Freischütz*), Felicity Lott (Fiordiligi and the Countess in *Capriccio*), Rosalind Plowright (the Countess in *Figaro* and Donna Elvira) and Thomas Allen(Don Giovanni). And in 1975 *The Rake's Progress* was conducted by the twenty-year-old Simon Rattle, who had joined the company only the year before. Only once was there anything that could be described as a flop—with the single production conceived expressly for the Touring Company, *Der Freischütz* in 1975. Directed by John Cox and

★ There were trips abroad too: *The Rake's Progress* was seen at Angers in 1977 and Nancy in 1980, and *La fedeltà premiata* at Nancy in 1979.

164 *Così fan tutte*, 1976 (designer John Bury): Håkan Hagegård, Maria Ewing, Nan Christie, Bozena Betley, Max-René Cosotti, Stafford Dean

165 Felicity Lott and Elizabeth Gale in
     Intermezzo, 1983

with a first-rate cast that included Linda Esther Gray, Elizabeth Gale and John Rawnsley, it should have worked magnificently; the reviews, indeed, were surprisingly good. But it had been done on too low a budget, a fact which became increasingly obvious as the opera went on, and the audience failed to respond.

This is not, of course, to say that all the other productions worked perfectly every time. There was the occasion in Newcastle in 1970 when it was found that all the orchestral parts for *Così fan tutte* had been left behind in Oxford. They were despatched the 250 miles by taxi, and the curtain was delayed from 7 p.m. to 7.30, the audience being informed that if the music had not arrived by then the performance would be cancelled and they would receive their money back. At 7.29 precisely the taxi turned up, and the evening was saved. There was also the occasion in Manchester when the Opera House ran out of programmes. The opera for that evening, as bad luck would have it, was *Eugene Onegin*, which was sung in Russian; and at the end of the first Act the unfortunate House Manager found himself besieged by irate members of the audience demanding to know what was happening on stage. Once again Geoffrey Gilbertson came to the rescue, reading from the synopsis over the

166 *Falstaff* 1977 (designer Jean-Pierre Ponnelle): Max-René Cosotti and Elizabeth Gale

loud-speaker system—only to be greeted by one of the under-employed programme sellers at the end of the performance with the words: 'Ee, luv, that was luvly, just like "Listen with Muther!"'

Such, then, were the principal milestones along the road which Glyndebourne followed during the last complete decade in its history to date. Inevitably, each member of the audience will have his or her own special memories. For some it will be the gloriously funny *pas de deux* in John Cox's *Capriccio*; for others, the ravishing singing of the sixty-year-old Richard Lewis in the 1974 *Idomeneo*, as one Turner landscape faded into another on the cyclorama behind; for yet others, the haunting beauty of Elisabeth Söderström's Leonore in the Peter Hall *Fidelio*, she and Bernard Haitink seeming to inspire each other to ever greater heights as the opera progressed, or the way the evening fell on Hugh Casson's 'englischer Garten' at Eszterháza in *La fedeltà premiata* just as, one felt, it was simultaneously falling in the real Glyndebourne garden outside.

Lists of this kind can, of course, be extended almost indefinitely; everyone will have his own, and each will be different. Perhaps indeed it is the sum total of these little vignettes, remaining as they do so obstinately in the memory, that constitutes for us *aficionados* the real Glyndebourne experience. What is beyond

168 *La fedeltà premiata* 1979 (designer Hugh Casson): Kathleen Battle, Richard Van Allan, Sylvia Lindenstrand, James Atherton

question is that the 1970s provided them in their hundreds. And they provided something else too, every bit as important: proof positive that Glyndebourne, now on the threshold of its middle age, had no intention of sinking back into complacency. The balance between the old and the new, the traditional and the off-beat, the familiar and the unknown, was still being held; promising young artists with reputations yet to be made were singing alongside established stars and rising magnificently to the challenge. Meanwhile Glyndebourne, while always conscious of its duty to satisfy its patrons, was not afraid to stretch them a little too. Of course there were objections from time to time: any opera company that never receives a complaint must be a dull company indeed. But its popularity, and the loyalty of its regular supporters, never flagged; and it ended the decade with its own reputation higher than ever, its permanent place on the English musical scene still more firmly established and assured.

PART SIX

THE 1980s

AS THESE WORDS ARE being written, Glyndebourne is approaching the end of its 1984 season; very soon now, the 1980s will have run half their course. This section cannot therefore be more than a provisional and interim report. Nevertheless, on the basis of all that we have seen and heard over the past five years and of what we know of future plans, the current decade bids fair to equal—and even perhaps to surpass—its predecessor. Which, it need hardly be emphasised, is saying a good deal.

The period has seen two important changes at the top. With the end of the 1981 season, Moran Caplat retired from his post as General Administrator. He had been with Glyndebourne ever since his demobilisation from the Navy after the war, in 1949 taking over from Rudolf Bing as General Manager; he had thus effectively run the company for thirty-three years. Even now, his connection with it endures: he still lives only a mile or two away, and as a Director of Glyndebourne Productions Ltd still plays an active part in its deliberations. He has been succeeded by Brian Dickie, whose whole career—indeed, half of whose life—has been spent with Glyndebourne. He first arrived in 1962 as assistant to Jani Strasser, arranging the rehearsal schedules and music calls, and from there rose rapidly up the ladder. He was the first Administrator of the Touring Company, running it from its inception in 1968 until 1981, and in 1971 was additionally given the title of Opera Manager. No one understands Glyndebourne and its problems better than he, and no one was better qualified to succeed Moran Caplat at the helm. He and his wife Victoria have now become familiar and beloved Glyndebourne figures second only to George and Mary Christie themselves.

At much the same time as Brian Dickie took over as General Administrator, John Cox accepted the offer of a similar position with Scottish Opera and was consequently obliged to give up his post as Director of Production. Fortunately, however, he too has been able to maintain close links with Glyndebourne: we saw two Cox revivals in 1982, while in the years following he has actually found time to offer us two superlatively good new productions. Before discussing these, however, we must look briefly at what he did in 1980 and 1981, while still a member of the Glyndebourne team. He began, as the decade opened, with a new *Rosenkavalier*, which was perhaps noteworthy less

170 Above, Erté in his Paris apartment, 1980

171 Below, Erté's design for Mohammed

for the production (excellent though it was) than for the sets. These were by the French designer Erté, then eighty-seven years old. Largely, one suspects, because Erté felt more at home in the nineteenth century, the date of the production was advanced by nearly a hundred years to the 1860s, the place apparently transferred from Vienna to deepest Ruritania. Felicity Lott melted all hearts as Oktavian, Rachel Yakar was a moving Feldmarschallin and Donald Gramm gave us an Ochs without the usual coarseness, still relatively young and not altogether unattractive. With such characterisations the opera should have worked to perfection; for many of us, however, the décor—and in particular the costumes—tended to come between the artists and the audience; despite the beauty of Haitink's conducting there was always a lurking suspicion that we were not really at Glyndebourne at all, but at the Casino de Paris or the Folies-Bergère. Happier by far was the new *Barber of Seville* in 1981 under the young French conductor Sylvain Cambreling. William Dudley's sets with their vine-covered terraces and canopied penthouse (the latter equipped with a magnificent telescope for Dr Bartolo) struck precisely the right note, John Rawnsley made a fine Figaro and Maria Ewing once again showed us what an inspired comic actress she can be.

Two years later, returning from Glasgow as a guest, John Cox gave us an enchanting new production of *La Cenerentola*, now seen at Glyndebourne for the first time in twenty-three years. Rossini would have loved it. His score—this time entrusted to the young Italian Donato Renzetti, making his first appearance in Sussex—sparkled from start to finish, and Cox's production was every bit as effervescent. Quite rightly, he went all out for laughs—and he got them. The action may have been a little too manic for some tastes, but most people found it hilariously funny—and everyone must have enjoyed the splendid on-stage storm machine in Act II.

Cox's most recent production has been *Arabella* of 1984; this proved to be pure enchantment. Julia Trevelyan Oman gave us sets which—even during the cabmen's ball in the second act—somehow contrived never to look cluttered, Haitink drew every ounce of magic from Strauss's ravishing score, and as Arabella herself Ashley Putnam (who had previously sung Musetta in John Cox's *Bohème*) sounded as lovely as she looked, which was very lovely indeed. Her compatriot Gianna Rolandi—an American despite her name—was a perfect Zdenka, and if John Bröcheler as Mandryka could not quite efface memories of Fischer-Dieskau in the same part—well, who could? Of all the Strauss operas we have enjoyed at Glyndebourne over the years, this—together with the *Ariadne auf Naxos* productions of 1957 and 1971—was the most beautiful.

The vacancy left by John Cox was not immediately filled. It now seems to have been subsumed, however, within the new functions of Sir Peter Hall, who was appointed Artistic Director in 1984—the first since Carl Ebert. Hall's right to the title is of course not for a moment in doubt; what the appointment will actually mean in practice, on the other hand, remains to be seen. For the moment, the important thing is that the man who is perhaps the greatest director of our time has accepted this close relationship with Glyndebourne—and that, surely, must be good news for everyone.

172   Above, *Der Rosenkavalier*, 1980,
Robert Hume and Rachel Yakar

Peter Hall's productions in the 1980s began with his *Midsummer Night's Dream* in 1981. The *Sunday Times* described it as 'an unqualified delight', which is exactly what it was. The approach was straightforward, entirely without gimmickry—the sets (by John Bury) realistic, the costumes Elizabethan. And yet the 'wood near Athens' has never been more magical. Like John Piper before him, Bury eschewed the colour green altogether in the first two acts; he knew what most designers of the play always seem to forget—that there is no green under the moon. Everything should be—and was—black and silver. Only in Act III, when the sun began to rise, did green for the first time enter the spectrum. It is hard to remember any other occasion when such dramatic effect has been achieved by the use of colour alone. And the wood was not only magical: it was also alive. Every tree had someone inside it, someone who could keep its leaves trembling and even, very slowly and almost imperceptibly, move it across the stage. Thus everything was subtly changing, shifting, living a life of its own. The whole mood perfectly reflected Britten's music, from the moment that those first unearthly *glissandi* ushered us into fairyland. Ileana Cotrubas made an exquisite Tytania (and was followed half-way through the run by the equally lovely Lillian Watson) and Curt Appelgren a simply splendid Bottom. Apart from these two—and a Dutch Theseus in the person of Lieuwe Visser—all the cast were native English-speakers. James Bowman

173–176   *A Midsummer Night's Dream* (designer John Bury)

173   Above left, The Mechanicals

174   Below left, Ileana Cotrubas as Tytania and Curt Applegren as Bottom

175   Above right, James Bowman, Ileana Cotrubas and fairies

176   Below right, Costume design for Tytania, drawn by Elizabeth Bury

distanced himself from the foolish mortals with every note he sang (what a stroke of genius it was on Britten's part to give the role of Oberon to a counter-tenor) and Damien Nash, as an unashamedly cockney Puck, very nearly ran away with the show. Bernard Haitink conducted with all his usual meticulous sensitivity. Glyndebourne has often given us productions as perfectly con-ceived as this, but never, one suspects, anything better.

The second Hall production was Gluck's *Orfeo ed Euridice* of 1982, last heard at Glyndebourne, in a slightly different form, in 1947. The new version, arranged by Raymond Leppard, was sung in Italian and marked, sadly for us all, Dame Janet Baker's farewell to the operatic stage. She could hardly have left it on a more triumphant note. Peter Hall's (and John Bury's) conceptions of the celestial and infernal regions were to say the least intriguing—particularly the former, which proved agreeably sexier than most of us had supposed. One found oneself wondering whether Euridice was all that pleased to be taken away.

Then, in 1984, came Peter Hall's new production of *L'incoronazione di Poppea*. This opera had not lain dormant for so long as *Orfeo*—a mere twenty years, as opposed to thirty-five—but was clearly due for a revival. On this occasion we had the three goddesses (of Fortune, Virtue and Love) perched

high above the classical colonnades that formed the main part of John Bury's permanent set, constantly in view and themselves watching all that occurred on the earth below them. Maria Ewing displayed all her usual seductiveness as Poppea, and Cynthia Clarey—standing in at the last moment for an ailing Frederica von Stade—sang heroically (in both senses of the word) as Ottavia, her confident attack and rock-steady vocal line suggesting that she had been singing the part for years instead of learning it in the aeroplane on her way over.

Of the three other new productions of the 1980s, the first was the worst. It came in 1980, and was *Die Entführung*, in the third version to be seen at Glyndebourne. This time the producer was Peter Wood, the designer William Dudley. It looked exceedingly pretty in a rather fussy way, but the decor proved positively austere in comparison with the production. One critic gave it an excellent notice; for most people, however, the opera seemed to get lost in the plethora of stage business; Mozart was never allowed to speak for himself. Most irritating of all were the live birds that fluttered about everywhere, cooing incessantly through the arias. Valerie Masterson and Lillian Watson struggled manfully against this avian opposition, and Gustav Kuhn in the pit conducted with crispness; but none of them ever really had a chance. (It is only fair to add that the revival in 1983 was vastly improved and far more favourably received.)

By contrast, *L'Amour des Trois Oranges*★—which appeared in 1982, having been most appropriately sponsored by Cointreau—was a tumultuous success. The opera takes the form of a play within a play: a fairy tale performed by a troupe of travelling *commedia dell'arte* players, set in France soon after the Revolution. Thus far, we seemed to be in the world of Domenico Tiepolo; it was only when the performance of the fairy tale began that the designer, Maurice Sendak, came into his own. The result was a series of what must be among the most astonishing creations ever seen on the Glyndebourne stage, culminating in a huge animated figure, filling almost the entire proscenium, of a monstrous cook, concocting a hideous stew of dismembered limbs in a giant cauldron. It might have been argued—indeed, it *was*—that Prokofiev's music was almost literally smothered by Sendak's extraordinary and macabre powers of invention. Perhaps this is true; one can only say that few members of the audience seem to have minded. The producer, Frank Corsaro, was, like the designer, working for the first time at Glyndebourne; but their joint triumph seems to have started something. Sendak has already designed two more operas for the Company, adapted from his books *Where the Wild Things Are* and

182   Maurice Sendak

★ I use the French version of the title because this was the language in which the opera was sung—a decision which can be defended only on the shaky grounds that the Chicago première was performed (by a largely French Company) also in French in 1921. The original libretto was in Russian; Russian and English should therefore have been the only permissible alternatives. Let us hope that Tom Stoppard's admirable translation for the Touring Company will be used when the opera returns to Sussex.

183   Below, *L'Amour des Trois Oranges*, 1982 (designer Maurice Sendak)

184   Right, *Where the Wild Things Are*, 1984 (designer Maurice Sendak)

Higglety Pigglety Pop!; the music for both is by Oliver Knussen. Together they form a double bill which will be taken on tour in the autumn of 1984 and presented at Glyndebourne in the 1985 Festival.

And so, finally, we come to the only major new production of the past five years which has not yet been mentioned: the *Idomeneo* designed by John Napier and directed by Trevor Nunn. The opera had had its first performance at Glyndebourne (which was, as we have seen, its first professional performance in England) in 1951. Produced by Carl Ebert and with ravishingly beautiful sets by Oliver Messel, it had survived until 1964. Ten years later came John Cox's production, with Turneresque designs by Roger Butlin at the end of what appeared to be a vast Nissen hut; this, however, did not meet with popular favour and was never revived. The time had thus obviously come for a new one, and Nunn, who had never previously worked for Glyndebourne, was invited to take on the job for the 1983 season. There could not have been a happier choice. *Idomeneo* is set in Crete, and the new production borrowed various Minoan themes—notably great spreading bulls' horns—which proved enormously effective; with these, however, it combined a strong Japanese element, both in the decor and in the movement of the artists on the stage. The result was the creation of a seemingly new civilisation, with a strong and completely original character of its own. The singers—especially Philip Langridge as Idomeneo and the young American Carol Vaness as Electra— were superb and Bernard Haitink in the pit was at the very top of his form; but the greatest *tour de force* was indisputably the production itself, among the most distinguished in all Glyndebourne's fifty-year history. We can only hope that Mr Nunn will be invited to do a lot more work for the company—as much, indeed, as his time allows.

191   Bernard Haitink and Trevor Nunn discussing *Idomeneo*

192–195   *Idomeneo* in the 1970s and 1980s:

192   Designer Roger Butlin used Turner paintings as backcloths for John Cox's production in 1974

193   Above right, Costume design by John Napier, 1983

194   Above far right, Philip Langridge as Idomeneo, 1983

195   Below right, Philip Langridge (*seated*), Anthony Roden and Thomas Hemsley, 1983

196   Jane Glover in rehearsal, with Stefan Janski

The Glyndebourne Touring Company, it need hardly be said, entered the 1980s with a good deal more confidence and aplomb than—as a tentative two-year-old—it had the 1970s. Now in receipt of a £50,000-a-year grant from Barclays' Bank, it travels a good deal heavier than it did in those early days—scenery, costumes, props and lighting equipment fill ten huge articulated lorries—but it has kept all its freshness and enthusiasm, and its popularity seems to grow with every year that passes. Brian Dickie has been succeeded as Administrator by Anthony Whitworth-Jones, and the Musical Director since 1982 is Jane Glover. She too has had a meteoric Glyndebourne career, joining the Music Staff only in 1979, becoming Chorus Director in the following year—a post which she still holds—and conducting her first Glyndebourne opera (*Die Entführung*) on the 1980 tour. Since then she has been responsible for seven more; thus, despite her youth, she can already boast a formidable Glyndebourne record.

It has always been the policy of the Touring Company, just as it has always been at Glyndebourne itself, to present all operas in the original language. But just as we have seen three exceptions to this rule in Sussex—*The Visit of the Old Lady*, *The Cunning Little Vixen* and *Intermezzo*—so there have also been two on tour. The first was for the 1976 *Capriccio* and the second for the 1983 *Love of Three Oranges*, for which a brilliant English translation was specially made by Tom Stoppard. The tremendous success of this production wherever it went augurs well for *Where the Wild Things Are* and *Higglety Pigglety Pop!*—which will be visiting five provincial cities just as this book goes to press. The first part of this double bill has already been seen at the National Theatre, but the second will have its world première on the tour.

197   Geoffrey Gilbertson, Brian Dickie and Anthony Whitworth-Jones during the 1984 Festival

198   Trinity Boys Choir preparing for a performance of *A Midsummer Night's Dream*

Can Glyndebourne really be fifty years old? Certainly, the realisation that half a century had elapsed since John Christie first opened his miniature opera house amid the Sussex Downs came to many people as a considerable shock. But there could be no argument about it, and there was accordingly much cause for celebration—and for not a few tears—when on Monday 28 May 1984—precisely the same day and date as in 1934—the curtain rose again on *The Marriage of Figaro*, with Bernard Haitink conducting it, almost unbelievably, for the very first time. Between this performance and that of fifty years before, the opera had been given, in Sussex or by the Touring Company, 241 times; yet its brilliance and sparkle remained undimmed. John Christie and Audrey Mildmay, Fritz Busch and Carl Ebert and Jani Strasser were all in their graves, but George and Mary Christie and Brian Dickie, Bernard Haitink and Peter Hall—supported, let it never be forgotten, by a considerable number of loyal friends and sponsors—are carrying on the work with the same enthusiasm and the same success. All of these, thank heaven, are still young; George Christie, in the year that sees his own fiftieth birthday as well as Glyndebourne's, is still two years younger than his father was when it all began, and his colleagues are much the same age. Under their direction and guidance, the Festival's second half-century bids fair to be even more exciting than its first.

More ambitious too: to take only one example, the intention is that future Festivals should continue longer than they do at present, and that they should offer six full-length operas instead of five. Among these, before the 1980s have run their course, will be several works never yet heard at Glyndebourne: *Carmen* for instance, and *Simon Boccanegra*, and—in what promises to be a fascinating breakthrough into completely new territory—George Gershwin's *Porgy and Bess*. And so, just as we have innumerable past pleasures to be grateful for, so also is there any amount to look forward to in the years to come. And when the curtain goes up on *The Marriage of Figaro* on 28 May 2034—as I have no doubt whatever that it will—I greatly look forward, despite what will then be my own ripe old age of 104, to being trundled down to see it.

199 Above, George and Mary Christie on the occasion of their Silver Wedding, August 1983, with their children

200 Below, On 31 July 1984 Her Majesty the Queen attended the performance of *Arabella* to mark the Festival's fiftieth anniversary

OPERAS PERFORMED BY GLYNDEBOURNE FESTIVAL OPERA, 1934–1984

1934

Glyndebourne 28 May– 10 June: 12 performances

Conductor FRITZ BUSCH
Producer CARL EBERT
Music Staff HANS OPPENHEIM, ALBERTO EREDE, HANS STRASSER
Scenery Designer and Stage Manager HAMISH WILSON
Assistant Stage Manager B. HOWARD
Assistant Producer HANS PETER BUSCH
Manager ALFRED NIGHTINGALE
Costumes ANN LITHERLAND
Wardrobe Mistress JULIETTE MAGNY
Scenery Artist SIMPSON ROBINSON
Scenery Builders THE RINGMER BUILDING WORKS, Sussex
Engineer W. THORPE
Stage Foreman R. W. GOUGH
Wigs W. CLARKSON
Leader of the Orchestra GEORGE STRATTON

Così fan tutte

MOZART *6 performances*

Ferrando   Heddle Nash (*English*)
Guglielmo   Willi Domgraf-Fassbänder (*German*)
Don Alfonso   Vincenzo Bettoni (*Italian*)
Fiordiligi   Ina Souez (*British*)
Dorabella   Luise Helletsgruber (*Austrian*)
Despina   Irene Eisinger (*Austrian*)

Conductor   FRITZ BUSCH
Producer   CARL EBERT
Scenery   HAMISH WILSON
Costumes   ANN LITHERLAND

Le nozze di Figaro

MOZART *6 performances*

Figaro   Willi Domgraf-Fassbänder (*German*)
Susanna   Audrey Mildmay (*English*)
Bartolo   Norman Allin (*English*)
Marcellina   Constance Willis (*English*)
Cherubino   Luise Helletsgruber (*Austrian*) Lucie Manén (*German*)
Count Almaviva   Roy Henderson (*Scottish*)
Don Basilio   Heddle Nash (*English*)
The Countess   Aulikki Rautawaara (*Finnish*)
Antonio   Fergus Dunlop (*English*)
Barbarina   Winifred Radford (*English*)
Don Curzio   Morgan Jones (*Welsh*)

Conductor   FRITZ BUSCH
Producer   CARL EBERT
Scenery   HAMISH WILSON
Costumes   ANN LITHERLAND

201   Facing page, *Così fan tutte*, 1937
202   1934 (left to right) Chorister, Constance Willis, Lucie Manen, Herta Glatz, Carl Ebert, Audrey Mildmay, Winifred Radford, Fergus Dunlop, Fritz Busch, Ina Souez, Alberto Erede, Hans Oppenheim, Aulikki Rautawaara, Willi Domgraf-Fassbänder, Jani Strasser

1935

*Glyndebourne 27 May–
29 June: 25 performances*

Le nozze di Figaro

MOZART *7 performances*

Figaro   Willi Domgraf-Fassbänder
   (*German*)
Susanna   Audrey Mildmay (*English*)
Bartolo   Ronald Stear (*English*)
Marcellina   Constance Willis (*English*)
Cherubino   Luise Helletsgruber (*Austrian*)
Count Almaviva   Roy Henderson (*Scottish*)
Don Basilio   Heddle Nash (*English*)
The Countess   Aulikki Rautawaara (*Finnish*)
Antonio   Fergus Dunlop (*English*)
Barbarina   Winifred Radford (*English*)
Don Curzio   Morgan Jones (*Welsh*)

Conductors FRITZ BUSCH, HANS OPPENHEIM
Producer CARL EBERT
Scenery HAMISH WILSON
Costumes ANN LITHERLAND

Die Entführung aus dem Serail

MOZART *5 performances*

Belmonte   Walther Ludwig (*German*)
Osmin   Ivar Andrésen (*Norwegian*)
Pedrillo   Heddle Nash (*English*)
Pasha Selim   Carl Ebert (*German*)
   Willi Domgraf-Fassbänder (*German*)
Constanze   Noel Eadie (*English*)
Blonde   Irene Eisinger (*Austrian*)
Dumb Slave   Joseph Roger Childs (*English*)

Conductor FRITZ BUSCH
Producer CARL EBERT
Scenery HAMISH WILSON
Costumes ANN LITHERLAND

---

203   Left, *Le nozze di Figaro*, 1939: Audrey
   Mildmay, John Brownlee, Maria Markan
204   Right, *Così fan tutte*, 1934: Vincenzo
   Bettoni, Irene Eisinger, Willi Domgraf-
   Fassbänder, Heddle Nash, Ina Souez, Luise
   Helletsgruber

Die Zauberflöte

MOZART *8 performances*

Tamino   Walther Ludwig (*German*)
Three Ladies   Luise Helletsgruber (*Austrian*)
   Maria Selve (*English*)
   Sophie Schoenning (*Norwegian*)
Papageno   Willi Domgraf-Fassbänder
   (*German*)
   Roy Henderson (*Scottish*)
Queen of the Night   Míla Kočová (*Czech*)
   Noel Eadie (*English*)
Three Boys   Winifred Radford (*English*)
   Jean Beckwith (*English*)
   Molly Mitchell (*English*)
Monostatos   Edwin Ziegler (*American*)
Pamina   Aulikki Rautawaara (*Finnish*)
The Speaker (Act I)   John Brownlee
   (*Australian*)
   Ronald Stear (*English*)
The Speaker (Act II)   Carl Ebert (*German*)
Sarastro   Ivar Andrésen (*Norwegian*)
Priests and Men in Armour   D. Morgan Jones
   (*Welsh*)
   Gerald Kassen (*South African*)
Papagena   Irene Eisinger (*Austrian*)

Conductor FRITZ BUSCH
Producer CARL EBERT
Designer HAMISH WILSON

Così fan tutte

MOZART *5 performances*

Ferrando   Heddle Nash (*English*)
Guglielmo   Willi Domgraf-Fassbänder
   (*German*)
Don Alfonso   John Brownlee (*Australian*)
Fiordiligi   Ina Souez (*British*)
Dorabella   Luise Helletsgruber (*Austrian*)
Despina   Irene Eisinger (*Austrian*)

Conductor FRITZ BUSCH
Producer CARL EBERT
Scenery HAMISH WILSON
Costumes ANN LITHERLAND

1936

*Glyndebourne 29 May–
5 July: 32 performances*

Don Giovanni

MOZART *10 performances*

Leporello   Salvatore Baccaloni (*Italian*)
Donna Anna   Ina Souez (*British*)
Don Giovanni   John Brownlee (*Australian*)
The Commendatore   David Franklin
   (*English*)
Don Ottavio   Koloman von Pataky
   (*Hungarian*)
Donna Elvira   Luise Helletsgruber
   (*Austrian*)
Zerlina   Audrey Mildmay (*English*)
Masetto   Roy Henderson (*Scottish*)

Conductor FRITZ BUSCH
Producer CARL EBERT
Scenery HAMISH WILSON
Costumes HEIN HECKROTH

Le nozze di Figaro

MOZART *6 performances*

Figaro   Mariano Stabile (*Italian*)
Susanna   Audrey Mildmay (*English*)
Bartolo   Salvatore Baccaloni (*Italian*)
Marcellina   Constance Willis (*English*)
Cherubino   Luise Helletsgruber (*Austrian*)
Count Almaviva   John Brownlee
   (*Australian*)
Don Basilio   Heddle Nash (*English*)
The Countess   Aulikki Rautawaara (*Finnish*)
Antonio   Fergus Dunlop (*English*)
Barbarina   Winifred Radford (*English*)
Don Curzio   D. Morgan Jones (*Welsh*)

Conductor FRITZ BUSCH
Producer CARL EBERT
Scenery HAMISH WILSON
Costumes ANN LITHERLAND

1937

Die Entführung aus dem Serail

MOZART *4 performances*

Belmonte Koloman von Pataky (*Hungarian*)
Osmin Salvatore Baccaloni (*Italian*)
Pedrillo Heddle Nash (*English*)
Pasha Selim Carl Ebert (*German*)
  Erich Kunz (*Austrian*)
Constanze Julia Moor (*Swiss*)
Blonde Irma Beilke (*German*)
Dumb Slave Joseph Roger Childs (*English*)

Conductor FRITZ BUSCH
Producer CARL EBERT
Scenery HAMISH WILSON
Costumes ANN LITHERLAND

Così fan tutte

MOZART *4 performances*

Ferrando Heddle Nash (*English*)
Guglielmo Roy Henderson (*Scottish*)
Don Alfonso John Brownlee (*Australian*)
Fiordiligi Ina Souez (*British*)
Dorabella Luise Helletsgruber (*Austrian*)
Despina Tatiana Menotti (*Italian*)

Conductor FRITZ BUSCH
Producer CARL EBERT
Scenery HAMISH WILSON
Costumes ANN LITHERLAND

Die Zauberflöte

MOZART *8 performances*

Tamino Thorkild Noval (*Danish*)
Three Ladies Erika Storm (*German*)
  Sophie Schönning (*Norwegian*)
  Betsy de la Porte (*South African*)
Papageno Roy Henderson (*Scottish*)
Queen of the Night Noel Eadie (*English*)
  Julia Moor (*Swiss*)
Three Boys Winifred Radford (*English*)
  Jean Beckwith (*English*)
  Molly Mitchell (*English*)
Monostatos Paul Schwarz (*American*)
Pamina Aulikki Rautawaara (*Finnish*)
The Speaker (Act I) George Hancock
  (*English*)
The Speaker (Act II) Carl Ebert (*German*)
Sarastro Alexander Kipnis (*American*)
Priests and Men in Armour D. Morgan Jones
  (*Welsh*)
  David Franklin (*English*)
Papagena Lili Heinemann (*German*)

Conductors FRITZ BUSCH
  Hans Oppenheim
Producer CARL EBERT
Designer HAMISH WILSON

Glyndebourne 19 May–3 July: 35 performances

Don Giovanni

MOZART *10 performances*

Leporello Salvatore Baccaloni (*Italian*)
Donna Anna Ina Souez (*British*)
Don Giovanni John Brownlee (*Australian*)
The Commendatore Norman Walker
  (*English*)
Don Ottavio Dino Borgioli (*Italian*)
Donna Elvira Luise Helletsgruber
  (*Austrian*)
Zerlina Marita Farell (*Czech*)
Masetto Roy Henderson (*Scottish*)

Conductor FRITZ BUSCH
Producer CARL EBERT
Scenery HAMISH WILSON
Costumes HEIN HECKROTH

Die Entführung aus dem Serail

MOZART *3 performances*

Belmonte Eric Starling (*English*)
Osmin Herbert Alsen (*German*)
Pedrillo Heddle Nash (*English*)
Pasha Selim Carl Ebert (*German*)
Constanze Margherita Perras (*Greek*)
Blonde Irene Eisinger (*Austrian*)
Dumb Slave Joseph Roger Childs (*English*)

Conductor FRITZ BUSCH
Producer CARL EBERT
Scenery HAMISH WILSON
Costumes ANN LITHERLAND

Così fan tutte

MOZART *6 performances*

Ferrando Heddle Nash (*English*)
Guglielmo Willi Domgraf-Fassbänder
  (*German*)
  Roy Henderson (*Scottish*)
Don Alfonso John Brownlee (*Australian*)
  Salvatore Baccaloni (*Italian*)
Fiordiligi Ina Souez (*British*)
Dorabella Luise Helletsgruber (*Austrian*)
Despina Irene Eisinger (*Austrian*)

Conductor FRITZ BUSCH
Producer CARL EBERT
Scenery HAMISH WILSON
Costumes ANN LITHERLAND

Le nozze di Figaro

MOZART *8 performances*

Figaro Willi Domgraf-Fassbänder (*German*)
Susanna Irene Eisinger (*Austrian*)
Bartolo Salvatore Baccaloni (*Italian*)
Marcellina Constance Willis (*English*)
Cherubino Marita Farell (*Czech*)
Count Almaviva John Brownlee
  (*Australian*)
Don Basilio Heddle Nash (*English*)
The Countess Aulikki Rautawaara (*Finnish*)
Antonio Fergus Dunlop (*English*)
Barbarina Winifred Radford (*English*)
  Margaret Field-Hyde (*English*)
Don Curzio Eric Starling (*English*)

Conductor FRITZ BUSCH
Producer CARL EBERT
Scenery HAMISH WILSON
Costumes ANN LITHERLAND

Die Zauberflöte

MOZART *8 performances*

Tamino Thorkild Novai (*Danish*)
Three Ladies Luise Helletsgruber (*Austrian*)
  Marita Farell (*Czech*), Joyce Newton
  (*English*)
Papageno Roy Henderson (*Scottish*)
Queen of the Night Sinaïda Lissitschkina
  (*Nicaraguan*)
Three Boys Winifred Radford (*English*)
  Jean Beckwith (*English*), Molly Mitchell
  (*English*)
Monostatos Ernest Frank (*British*)
Pamina Aulikki Rautawaara (*Finnish*)
The Speaker (Act I) Norman Walker
  (*English*)
The Speaker (Act II) Carl Ebert (*German*)
Sarastro Herbert Alsen (*German*)
  David Franklin (*English*)
Priests and Men in Armour Eric Starling
  (*English*)
  Norman Walker (*English*)
Papagena Irene Eisinger (*Austrian*)
  Margaret Field-Hyde (*English*)

Conductor FRITZ BUSCH
Producer CARL EBERT
Designer HAMISH WILSON

1938

*Glyndebourne 21 May–
9 July: 36 performances*

Macbeth

VERDI *10 performances*
First professional production in England

Macbeth   Francesco Valentino (*American*)
Banquo   David Franklin (*English*)
Lady Macbeth   Vera Schwarz (*Jugoslavian*)
Gentlewoman   Elisabeth Abercrombie
   (*English*)
Macduff   David Lloyd (*Welsh*)
Malcolm   Eric Starling (*English*)
Doctor   Fergus Dunlop (*Scottish*)
Servant   Cuthbert Matthews (*Australian*)
Murderer   Robert Rowell (*English*)
Fleance   Ian Hunter (*English*)

Conductor   FRITZ BUSCH
Producer   CARL EBERT
Designer   CASPAR NEHER

Don Giovanni

MOZART *7 performances*

Leporello   Salvatore Baccaloni (*Italian*)
Donna Anna   Ina Souez (*British*)
Don Giovanni   John Brownlee (*Australian*)
The Commendatore   David Franklin
   (*English*)
Don Ottavio   Dino Borgioli (*Italian*)
Donna Elvira   Luise Helletsgruber
   (*Austrian*)
   Hilde Konetzni (*Austrian*)
Zerlina   Marita Farell (*Czech*)
   Winifred Radford (*English*)
Masetto   Roy Henderson (*Scottish*)

Conductors   FRITZ BUSCH, ALBERTO EREDE
Producer   CARL EBERT
Scenery   HAMISH WILSON
Costumes   ANN LITHERLAND

Così fan tutte

MOZART *5 performances*

Ferrando   Heddle Nash (*English*)
Guglielmo   Roy Henderson (*Scottish*)
Don Alfonso   John Brownlee (*Australian*)
Fiordiligi   Ina Souez (*British*)
Dorabella   Luise Helletsgruber (*Austrian*)
Despina   Irene Eisinger (*Austrian*)

Conductor   FRITZ BUSCH
Producer   CARL EBERT
Scenery   HAMISH WILSON
Costumes   ANN LITHERLAND

Le nozze di Figaro

MOZART *9 performances*

Figaro   Mariano Stabile (*Italian*)
Susanna   Audrey Mildmay (*English*)
   Irene Eisinger (*Austrian*)
Bartolo   Salvatore Baccaloni (*Italian*)
Marcellina   Constance Willis (*English*)
Cherubino   Marita Farell (*Czech*)
Count Almaviva   John Brownlee
   (*Australian*)
Don Basilio   Heddle Nash (*English*)
The Countess   Aulikki Rautawaara (*Finnish*)
Antonio   Fergus Dunlop (*Scottish*)
Barbarina   Irene Eisinger (*Austrian*)
   Winifred Radford (*English*)
Don Curzio   Eric Starling (*English*)

Conductors   FRITZ BUSCH, ALBERTO EREDE
Producer   CARL EBERT
Scenery   HAMISH WILSON
Costumes   ANN LITHERLAND

Don Pasquale

DONIZETTI *5 performances*

Don Pasquale   Salvatore Baccaloni (*Italian*)
Dr Malatesta   Mariano Stabile (*Italian*)
Ernesto   Dino Borgioli (*Italian*)
Norina   Audrey Mildmay (*English*)
Notary   Fergus Dunlop (*Scottish*)

Conductor   FRITZ BUSCH
Producer   CARL EBERT
Scenery   HAMISH WILSON
Costumes   KENNETH GREEN

1939

*Glyndebourne 1 June–
15 July: 38 performances*

Don Giovanni

MOZART *7 performances*

Leporello   Salvatore Baccaloni (*Italian*)
Donna Anna   Ina Souez (*British*)
Don Giovanni   John Brownlee (*Australian*)
The Commendatore   David Franklin
   (*English*)
Don Ottavio   David Lloyd (*Welsh*)
   Dino Borgioli (*Italian*)
Donna Elvira   Hella Toros (*British*)
Zerlina   Audrey Mildmay (*English*)
Masetto   Roy Henderson (*Scottish*)

Conductors   FRITZ BUSCH, ALBERTO EREDE
Producer   CARL EBERT
Scenery   HAMISH WILSON
Costumes   HEIN HECKROTH

Don Pasquale

DONIZETTI *4 performances*

Don Pasquale   Salvatore Baccaloni (*Italian*)
Dr Malatesta   Mariano Stabile (*Italian*)
Ernesto   Luigi Fort (*Italian*)
Norina   Audrey Mildmay (*English*)
Notary   David Franklin (*English*)

Conductor   FRITZ BUSCH
Producer   CARL EBERT
Scenery   HAMISH WILSON
Costumes   KENNETH GREEN

205   *Le nozze di Figaro*, 1939, curtain call

Macbeth

VERDI *10 performances*

Macbeth Francesco Valentino (*American*)
Banquo David Franklin (*English*)
Lady Macbeth Margherita Grandi
  (*Tasmanian*)
Gentlewoman Constance Willis (*English*)
Macduff David Lloyd (*Welsh*)
Malcolm Eric Starling (*English*)
Doctor Robert Rowell (*English*)
Servant Cuthbert Matthews (*Australian*)
Murderer Nicholas Harrison (*English*)

Conductor FRITZ BUSCH
Producer CARL EBERT
Designer CASPAR NEHER

Così fan tutte

MOZART *7 performances*

Ferrando Gino del Signore (*Italian*)
Guglielmo Roy Henderson (*Scottish*)
Don Alfonso John Brownlee (*Australian*)
Fiordiligi Ina Souez (*British*)
Dorabella Risë Stevens (*American*)
Despina Irene Eisinger (*Austrian*)

Conductor FRITZ BUSCH
Producer CARL EBERT
Scenery HAMISH WILSON
Costumes ANN LITHERLAND

Le nozze di Figaro

MOZART *10 performances*

Figaro Mariano Stabile (*Italian*)
Susanna Audrey Mildmay (*English*)
  Irene Eisinger (*Austrian*)
Bartolo Salvatore Baccaloni (*Italian*)
Marcellina Constance Willis (*English*)
Cherubino Risë Stevens (*American*)
Count Almaviva John Brownlee
  (*Australian*)
Don Basilio Eric Starling (*English*)
The Countess Maria Markan (*Icelandic*)
Antonio Fergus Dunlop (*Scottish*)
Barbarina Irene Eisinger (*Austrian*)
  Rose Hill (*English*)
Don Curzio Maldwyn Thomas (*Welsh*)

Conductors FRITZ BUSCH, ALBERTO EREDE
Producer CARL EBERT
Scenery HAMISH WILSON
Costumes ANN LITHERLAND

1940

After tour of BRIGHTON, CARDIFF, LIVERPOOL,
MANCHESTER, GLASGOW and EDINBURGH

Theatre Royal, Haymarket 16 January–25 May: 126 performances

The Beggar's Opera

JOHN GAY *arr.* Frederic Austin

Peachum Roy Henderson
Lockit Joseph Farrington
Macheath Michael Redgrave
Filch Bruce Flegg
Mrs Peachum Constance Willis
  Elsie French
Polly Peachum Audrey Mildmay
  Irene Eisinger
Lucy Lockit Linda Gray
Diana Trapes Alys Brough

Conductors FREDERIC AUSTIN, ANTHONY
  BERNARD, MICHAEL MUDIE
Producer JOHN GIELGUD
Décor by MOTLEY

206 Left, Costume fitting for Kathleen
    Ferrier as Lucretia
207 Right, Kathleen Ferrier and Peter Pears
    in Edinburgh, 1947

1946

Glyndebourne 12–27 July: 14 performances

On tour: 67 performances

The Rape of Lucretia

BENJAMIN BRITTEN *World première*

Male Chorus Peter Pears
  Aksel Schiötz
Female Chorus Joan Cross
  Flora Nielson
Collatinus Norman Walker
  Owen Brannigan
Junius Edmund Donlevy
  Frederick Sharp
Tarquinius Otakar Kraus
  Frank Rogier
Lucretia Kathleen Ferrier
  Nancy Evans
Bianca Anna Pollak
  Catherine Lawson
Lucia Margaret Ritchie
  Lesley Duff

Conductors ERNEST ANSERMET, REGINALD
  GOODALL, HANS OPPENHEIM, BENJAMIN
  BRITTEN
Producer ERIC CROZIER
Designer JOHN PIPER

1947

*Glyndebourne 19 June–12 July:
18 performances*

Orfeo

GLUCK *9 performances*

Orfeo   Kathleen Ferrier (*English*)
Euridice   Ann Ayars (*American*)
Amor   Zoë Vlachopoulos (*Greek*)
THE SOUTHERN PHILHARMONIC ORCHESTRA

Conductor FRITZ STIEDRY
Producer CARL EBERT
Designer JOSEPH CARL

English Opera Group at Glyndebourne

Albert Herring

BENJAMIN BRITTEN *9 performances*
World première

Lady Billows   Joan Cross
Florence Pike   Gladys Parr
Miss Wordsworth   Margaret Ritchie
The Vicar   William Parsons
The Mayor   Roy Ashton
The Superintendent of Police   Norman
   Lumsden
   Bruce Clark
Sid   Frederick Sharp
   Denis Dowling
Albert Herring   Peter Pears
Nancy   Nancy Evans
   Catherine Lawson
Emmie   Lesley Duff
Cis   Anne Sharp
   Elisabeth Parry
Harry   David Spenser

Conductors BENJAMIN BRITTEN, IVAN CLAYTON
Producer FREDERICK ASHTON
Designer JOHN PIPER

*Edinburgh 24 July–
13 September: 18 performances*

Macbeth

VERDI *9 performances*

Macbeth   Francesco Valentino (*American*)
Banquo   Italo Tajo (*Italian*)
   Owen Brannigan (*English*)
Lady Macbeth   Margherita Grandi
   (*Tasmanian*)
Gentlewoman   Vera Terry (*Australian*)
Macduff   Walter Midgley (*English*)
Malcolm   Andrew McKinley (*American*)
Doctor   André Orkin (*English*)
Servant   Robert Vivian (*English*)
Murderer   Edward Thomas (*English*)
Fleance   George Christie (*English*)

THE SCOTTISH ORCHESTRA

Conductor BERTHOLD GOLDSCHMIDT
Producer CARL EBERT
Designer CASPAR NEHER

Le nozze di Figaro

MOZART *9 performances*

Figaro   Italo Tajo (*Italian*)
Susanna   Tatiana Menotti (*Italian*)
   Ayhan Alnar (*Turkish*)
Bartolo   Owen Brannigan (*English*)
Marcellina   Catherine Lawson (*English*)
Cherubino   Giulietta Simionato (*Italian*)
Count Almaviva   John Brownlee
   (*Australian*)
Don Basilio   Bruce Flegg (*English*)
The Countess   Eleanor Steber (*American*)
Antonio   Ernest Frank (*British*)
Barbarina   Barbara Trent (*English*)
Don Curzio   Gwent Lewis (*Welsh*)

Conductors WALTER SUSSKIND, RENATO
   CELLINI
Producer CARL EBERT
Scenery HAMISH WILSON
Costumes ANN LITHERLAND

1948

*Edinburgh 22 July–
12 September: 18 performances*

Don Giovanni

MOZART *9 performances*

Leporello   Vito de Taranto (*Italian*)
Donna Anna   Ljuba Welitsch (*Bulgarian*)
Don Giovanni   Paolo Silveri (*Italian*)
The Commendatore   David Franklin
   (*English*)
Don Ottavio   Richard Lewis (*English*)
Donna Elvira   Christina Carroll (*American*)
Zerlina   Ann Ayars (*American*)
   Hilde Güden (*Austrian*)
Masetto   Ian Wallace (*Scottish*)

Conductor RAFAEL KUBELIK
Producer CARL EBERT
Scenery HAMISH WILSON
Costumes HEIN HECKROTH

Così fan tutte

MOZART *9 performances*

Ferrando   Petre Munteanu (*Rumanian*)
Guglielmo   Erich Kunz (*Austrian*)
Don Alfonso   Mariano Stabile (*Italian*)
Fiordiligi   Suzanne Danco (*Belgian*)
Dorabella   Eugenia Zareska (*British*)
Despina   Hilde Güden (*Austrian*)

Conductor VITTORIO GUI
Producer CARL EBERT
Designer ROLF GÉRARD

On previous pages:
208   Above left, Outside the King's Theatre
   at the first Edinburgh Festival: Carl Ebert,
   Ljuba Welitsch, David Poleri
209   *The Rape of Lucretia*, 1946. Above
   right, Margaret Ritchie, Frank Rogier,
   Kathleen Ferrier. Below, Joan Cross,
   Kathleen Ferrier, Otakar Kraus
210   Opposite, Kathleen Ferrier in *Orfeo*, 1947

1949

Edinburgh 21 August—
11 September: 18 performances

Un ballo in maschera

VERDI *11 performances*

Riccardo	Mirto Picchi (*Italian*)
	William Horne (*American*)
Renato	Paolo Silveri (*Italian*)
Amelia	Ljuba Welitsch (*Bulgarian*)
	Margherita Grandi (*Tasmanian*)
Ulrica	Jean Watson (*Canadian*)
	Amalia Pini (*Italian*)
Oscar	Alda Noni (*Italian*)
Samuele	Ian Wallace (*Scottish*)
Tommaso	Hervey Alan (*English*)
Silvio	Francis Loring (*English*)

Conductors VITTORIO GUI, HANS OPPENHEIM
Producer CARL EBERT
Designer CASPAR NEHER

211 Sena Jurinac in her dressing room

Così fan tutte

MOZART *7 performances*

Ferrando	Petre Munteanu (*Rumanian*)
Guglielmo	Marko Rothmüller (*Jugoslavian*)
Don Alfonso	John Brownlee (*Australian*)
Fiordiligi	Suzanne Danco (*Belgian*)
Dorabella	Sena Jurinac (*Jugoslavian*)
Despina	Irene Eisinger (*Austrian*)

Conductors VITTORIO GUI, HANS OPPENHEIM
Producer CARL EBERT
Designer ROLF GÉRARD

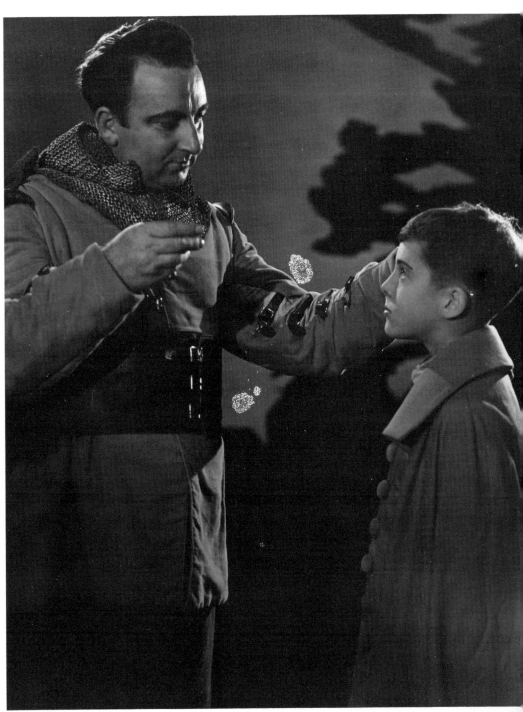

212 Owen Brannigan and George Christie (as Fleance) in *Macbeth*, Edinburgh, 1947

1950

Glyndebourne 6–23 July: 14 performances

Die Entführung aus dem Serail

MOZART *7 performances*

Belmonte   Richard Holm (*German*)
Osmin   Endre Koréh (*Hungarian*)
Pedrillo   Murray Dickie (*Scottish*)
Pasha Selim   Anton Walbrook (*German*)
Constanze   Ilse Hollweg (*German*)
Blonde   Alda Noni (*Italian*)
Sailor   Michael Hayes (*English*)

Conductor FRITZ BUSCH
Producer CARL EBERT
Designer ROLF GÉRARD

Così fan tutte

MOZART *7 performances*

Ferrando   Richard Lewis (*English*)
Guglielmo   Erich Kunz (*Austrian*)
    Geraint Evans (*Welsh*)
Don Alfonso   Mario Borriello (*Italian*)
Fiordiligi   Sena Jurinac (*Jugoslavian*)
Dorabella   Blanche Thebom (*American*)
Despina   Alda Noni (*Italian*)

Conductor FRITZ BUSCH
Producer CARL EBERT
Designer ROLF GÉRARD

Edinburgh 20 August– 9 September: 18 performances

Le nozze di Figaro

MOZART *9 performances*

Figaro   George London (*American*)
Susanna   Elfride Troetschel (*German*)
Bartolo   Ian Wallace (*Scottish*)
Marcellina   Jean Watson (*Canadian*)
Cherubino   Sena Jurinac (*Jugoslavian*)
Count Almaviva   Marko Rothmüller
    (*Jugoslavian*)
Don Basilio   Murray Dickie (*Scottish*)
The Countess   Clara Ebers (*German*)
Antonio   Dennis Wicks (*English*)
Barbarina   April Cantelo (*English*)
Don Curzio   Leslie Fyson (*English*)

Conductor FERENÇ FRICSAY
Producer CARL EBERT
Designer ROLF GÉRARD

Ariadne auf Naxos
(First Version)

RICHARD STRAUSS *9 performances*

Le Bourgeois Gentilhomme

M. Jourdain   Miles Malleson
Dorante   David King-Wood
Dorimène   Tatiana Leven
Professor of Philosophy   Harold Scott

Ariadne auf Naxos

Najade   Maureen Springer (*English*)
Dryade   Marjorie Thomas (*English*)
Echo   April Cantelo (*English*)
Ariadne   Hilde Zadek (*Austrian*)
Harlekin   Douglas Craig (*English*)
Zerbinetta   Ilse Hollweg (*German*)
Brighella   Murray Dickie (*Scottish*)
Truffaldino   Bruce Dargavel (*Welsh*)
Scaramuccio   Alexander Young (*English*)
Bacchus   Peter Anders (*German*)

Conductor SIR THOMAS BEECHAM
Producer CARL EBERT
Designer OLIVER MESSEL

213   Sena Jurinac as Cherubino, Edinburgh 1950

1951

Glyndebourne 20 June–21 July: 25 performances

Idomeneo

MOZART *6 performances*
First professional production in England
(*The original edited for performance by Hans Gal*)

Ilia   Sena Jurinac (*Jugoslavian*)
Idamante   Léopold Simoneau (*Canadian*)
Arbace   Alfred Poell (*Austrian*)
Electra   Birgit Nilsson (*Swedish*)
Idomeneo   Richard Lewis (*English*)
High Priest   Alexander Young (*English*)
Voice of Neptune   Bruce Dargavel (*Welsh*)

Conductors FRITZ BUSCH, JOHN PRITCHARD
Producer CARL EBERT
Designer OLIVER MESSEL

Le nozze di Figaro

MOZART *7 performances*

Figaro   Alois Pernerstorfer (*Austrian*)
Susanna   Genevieve Warner (*American*)
Bartolo   Owen Brannigan (*English*)
Marcellina   Janet Howe (*Scottish*)
Cherubino   Dorothy MacNeil (*American*)
Count Almaviva   Alfred Poell (*Austrian*)
Don Basilio   Murray Dickie (*Scottish*)
    Alexander Young (*English*)
The Countess   Lisa Della Casa (*Swiss*)
Antonio   Dennis Wicks (*English*)
Barbarina   April Cantelo (*English*)
Don Curzio   Leslie Fyson (*English*)

Conductors FRITZ BUSCH, JOHN PRITCHARD
Producer CARL EBERT
Scenery HUTCHINSON SCOTT
Costumes ROLF GÉRARD

Così fan tutte

MOZART *6 performances*

Ferrando   Richard Lewis (*English*)
Guglielmo   Marko Rothmüller (*Jugoslavian*)
Don Alfonso   Sesto Bruscantini (*Italian*)
Fiordiligi   Sena Jurinac (*Jugoslavian*)
Dorabella   Alice Howland (*American*)
Despina   Isa Quensel (*Swedish*)

Conductors FRITZ BUSCH, JOHN PRITCHARD
Producer CARL EBERT
Designer ROLF GÉRARD

1952

Don Giovanni

MOZART *6 performances*

Leporello   Alois Pernerstorfer (*Austrian*)
Donna Anna   Hilde Zadek (*Austrian*)
Don Giovanni   Mario Petri (*Italian*)
The Commendatore   Bruce Dargavel
   (*Welsh*)
Don Ottavio   Léopold Simoneau (*Canadian*)
Donna Elvira   Suzanne Danco (*Belgian*)
Zerlina   Genevieve Warner (*American*)
Masetto   Geraint Evans (*Welsh*)

Conductors FRITZ BUSCH, JOHN PRITCHARD
Producer CARL EBERT
Designer JOHN PIPER

Edinburgh 20 August– 9 September: 18 performances

La forza del destino

VERDI *9 performances*

Marquis   Stanley Mason (*English*)
Leonora   Walburga Wegner (*German*)
Curra   Bruna Maclean (*Scottish*)
Don Alvaro   David Poleri (*American*)
Don Carlo   Marko Rothmüller
   (*Jugoslavian*)
Alcade   Dennis Wicks (*English*)
Trabuco   Robert Thomas (*Welsh*)
Preziosilla   Mildred Miller (*American*)
Fra Melitone   Owen Brannigan (*English*)
Padre Guardiano   Bruce Dargavel (*Welsh*)
Surgeon   Philip Lewtas (*English*)

Conductor FRITZ BUSCH
Producer CARL EBERT
Designer LESLIE HURRY

Don Giovanni

MOZART *9 performances*

Leporello   Alois Pernerstorfer (*Austrian*)
   Owen Brannigan (*English*)
Donna Anna   Hilde Zadek (*Austrian*)
Don Giovanni   Mario Petri (*Italian*)
The Commendatore   Bruce Dargavel
   (*Welsh*)
Don Ottavio   Léopold Simoneau (*Canadian*)
Donna Elvira   Dorothy MacNeil (*American*)
Zerlina   Genevieve Warner (*American*)
   Roxane Houston (*Irish*)
   Pierrette Alarie (*Canadian*)
Masetto   Geraint Evans (*Welsh*)

Conductors FRITZ BUSCH, JOHN PRITCHARD
Producer CARL EBERT
Designer JOHN PIPER

Glyndebourne 15 June–20 July: 28 performances

Idomeneo

MOZART *8 performances*

Ilia   Sena Jurinac (*Jugoslavian*)
Idamante   Léopold Simoneau (*Canadian*)
Arbace   John Cameron (*Australian*)
Electra   Maria Kinasiewicz (*Polish*)
Idomeneo   Richard Lewis (*English*)
High Priest   Alexander Young (*English*)
Voice of Neptune   Hervey Alan (*English*)

Conductor JOHN PRITCHARD
Producer CARL EBERT
Designer OLIVER MESSEL

La Cenerentola

ROSSINI *9 performances*

Don Ramiro   Juan Oncina (*Spanish*)
Dandini   Sesto Bruscantini (*Italian*)
Don Magnifico   Ian Wallace (*Scottish*)
Clorinda   Alda Noni (*Italian*)
Tisbe   Fernanda Cadoni (*Italian*)
Cenerentola   Marina de Gabarain (*Spanish*)
Alidoro   Hervey Alan (*English*)

Conductor VITTORIO GUI
Producer CARL EBERT
Designer OLIVER MESSEL

Così fan tutte

MOZART *3 performances*

Ferrando   Richard Lewis (*English*)
Guglielmo   Sesto Bruscantini (*Italian*)
Don Alfonso   Dezsö Ernster (*Hungarian*)
Fiordiligi   Sena Jurinac (*Jugoslavian*)
Dorabella   Anna Pollak (*English*)
Despina   Alda Noni (*Italian*)

Conductor VITTORIO GUI
Producer CARL EBERT
Designer ROLF GÉRARD

Macbeth

VERDI *8 performances*

Macbeth   Marko Rothmüller (*Jugoslavian*)
Banquo   Frederick Dalberg (*South African*)
Lady Macbeth   Dorothy Dow (*American*)
Gentlewoman   Patricia Bartlett (*Australian*)
Macduff   James Johnston (*Irish*)
Malcolm   John Kentish (*English*)
Doctor   Dennis Wicks (*English*)

Conductor VITTORIO GUI
Producer CARL EBERT
Designer CASPAR NEHER

---

214   *Le Bourgeois Gentilhomme*, 1950: David
   King-Wood, Tatiana Leven, Miles
   Malleson

1953

Glyndebourne 7 June–26 July: 37 performances

Alceste

GLUCK *8 performances*

Herald   Dennis Wicks (*English*)
Evander   Alexander Young (*English*)
Alceste   Magda Laszlo (*Hungarian*)
High Priest   John Cameron (*Australian*)
Admète   Richard Lewis (*English*)
Hercules   Thomas Hemsley (*English*)
Voice of Tanato   Hervey Alan (*English*)
Apollo   John Cameron (*Australian*)

Conductor VITTORIO GUI
Producer CARL EBERT
Scenery HUGH CASSON
Costumes ROSEMARY VERCOE
Statue of Apollo CHRISTOPHER IRONSIDE

La Cenerentola

ROSSINI *9 performances*

Don Ramiro   Juan Oncina (*Spanish*)
Dandini   Sesto Bruscantini (*Italian*)
Don Magnifico   Ian Wallace (*Scottish*)
Clorinda   Alda Noni (*Italian*)
Tisbe   Fernanda Cadoni (*Italian*)
Cenerentola   Marina de Gabarain (*Spanish*)
Alidoro   Hervey Alan (*English*)

Conductor VITTORIO GUI
Producer CARL EBERT
Designer OLIVER MESSEL

Ariadne auf Naxos
(Second Version)

RICHARD STRAUSS *8 performances*

Composer   Sena Jurinac (*Jugoslavian*)
Music Master   Sesto Bruscantini (*Italian*)
Dancing Master   Murray Dickie (*Scottish*)
Zerbinetta   Mattiwilda Dobbs (*American*)
Ariadne   Dorothy Dow (*American*)
Harlekin   Kurt Gester (*German*)
Scaramuccio   Alexander Young (*English*)
Truffaldino   Fritz Ollendorf (*German*)
Brighella   Murray Dickie (*Scottish*)
Najade   Edna Graham (*New Zealand*)
Dryade   Marjorie Thomas (*English*)
Echo   April Cantelo (*English*)
Bacchus   Carlos Guichandut (*Argentinian*)

Conductor JOHN PRITCHARD
Producer CARL EBERT
Designer OLIVER MESSEL

Die Entführung aus dem Serail

MOZART *6 performances*

Belmonte   Helmut Krebs (*German*)
Osmin   Fritz Ollendorf (*German*)
Pedrillo   Murray Dickie (*Scottish*)
Pasha Selim   Carl Ebert (*German*)
      David Franklin (*English*)
Constanze   Sari Barabas (*Hungarian*)
Blonde   Emmy Loose (*Czech*)
      April Cantelo (*English*)

Conductor ALFRED WALLENSTEIN
Producer CARL EBERT
Designer ROLF GÉRARD

Così fan tutte

MOZART *6 performances*

Ferrando   Juan Oncina (*Spanish*)
      Alexander Young (*English*)
Guglielmo   Geraint Evans (*Welsh*)
Don Alfonso   Sesto Bruscantini (*Italian*)
Fiordiligi   Sena Jurinac (*Jugoslavian*)
      Rita McKerrow (*English*)
Dorabella   Anna Pollak (*English*)
Despina   Alda Noni (*Italian*)

Conductor JOHN PRITCHARD
Producer CARL EBERT
Designer ROLF GÉRARD

Edinburgh 23 August– 12 November: 18 performances

La Cenerentola

ROSSINI *7 performances*

Don Ramiro   Juan Oncina (*Spanish*)
Dandini   Sesto Bruscantini (*Italian*)
Don Magnifico   Ian Wallace (*Scottish*)
Clorinda   Alda Noni (*Italian*)
Tisbe   Fernanda Cadoni (*Italian*)
Cenerentola   Marina de Gabarain (*Spanish*)
Alidoro   Hervey Alan (*English*)

Conductor VITTORIO GUI
Producer CARL EBERT
Designer OLIVER MESSEL

The Rake's Progress

STRAVINSKY *5 performances*
First stage performance in Britain

Anne   Elsie Morison (*Australian*)
Tom Rakewell   Richard Lewis (*English*)
Trulove   Hervey Alan (*English*)
Nick Shadow   Jerome Hines (*American*)
Mother Goose   Mary Jarred (*English*)
Baba the Turk   Nan Merriman (*American*)
Sellem   Murray Dickie (*Scottish*)
Keeper of the Madhouse   Dennis Wicks
      (*English*)

Conductor ALFRED WALLENSTEIN
Producer CARL EBERT
Designer OSBERT LANCASTER

Idomeneo

MOZART *6 performances*

Ilia   Sena Jurinac (*Jugoslavian*)
Idamante   Helmut Krebs (*German*)
Arbace   John Cameron (*Australian*)
Electra   Jennifer Vyvyan (*English*)
Idomeneo   Richard Lewis (*English*)
High Priest   John Carolan (*Irish*)
Voice of Neptune   Hervey Alan (*English*)

Conductor JOHN PRITCHARD
Producer CARL EBERT
Designer OLIVER MESSEL

215   *Alceste*, 1953: Magda Laszlo and
      Richard Lewis

1954

Glyndebourne 10 June–27 July: 36 performances

Il barbiere di Siviglia

ROSSINI *9 performances*

Count Almaviva   Juan Oncina (*Spanish*)
Figaro   Sesto Bruscantini (*Italian*)
Rosina   Graziella Sciutti (*Italian*)
Bartolo   Ian Wallace (*Scottish*)
Basilio   Antonio Cassinelli (*Italian*)
Fiorello   Gwyn Griffiths (*Welsh*)
Berta   Noreen Berry (*South African*)
Ambrogio   Harold Williams (*English*)
Officer   David Kelly (*Scottish*)
Notary   Daniel McCoshan (*Scottish*)

Conductor   VITTORIO GUI
Producer   CARL EBERT
Designer   OLIVER MESSEL

Alceste

GLUCK *6 performances*

Herald   Thomas Hemsley (*English*)
Evander   Paul Asciak (*Maltese*)
Alceste   Magda Laszlo (*Hungarian*)
High Priest   Raimundo Torres (*Spanish*)
Admète   Richard Lewis (*English*)
Hercules   Thomas Hemsley (*English*)
Voice of Tanato   James Atkins (*English*)
Apollo   Raimundo Torres (*Spanish*)

Conductors   VITTORIO GUI, BRYAN BALKWILL
Producer   CARL EBERT
Scenery   HUGH CASSON
Costumes   ROSEMARY VERCOE

Arlecchino

BUSONI *6 performances*
First stage production in Britain

Ser Matteo   Ian Wallace (*Scottish*)
Arlecchino   Kurt Gester (*German*)
Abbate Cospicuo   Geraint Evans (*Welsh*)
Doctor Bombasto   Fritz Ollendorf (*German*)
Colombina   Elaine Malbin (*American*)
Leandro   Murray Dickie (*Scottish*)

Conductor   JOHN PRITCHARD
Producer   PETER EBERT
Designer   PETER RICE

Ariadne auf Naxos
(Second Version)

RICHARD STRAUSS *6 performances*

Composer   Sena Jurinac (*Jugoslavian*)
Music Master   Geraint Evans (*Welsh*)
Dancing Master   Murray Dickie (*Scottish*)
Zerbinetta   Mattiwilda Dobbs (*American*)
   Ilse Hollweg (*German*)
Ariadne   Lucine Amara (*American*)
Harlekin   Kurt Gester (*German*)
Scaramuccio   Juan Oncina (*Spanish*)
Truffaldino   Fritz Ollendorf (*German*)
Brighella   Murray Dickie (*Scottish*)
Najade   Maureen Springer (*English*)
Dryade   Noreen Berry (*South African*)
Echo Elaine Malbin (*American*)
Bacchus Richard Lewis (*English*)

Conductor   JOHN PRITCHARD
Producer   CARL EBERT
Designer   OLIVER MESSEL

Don Giovanni

MOZART *9 performances*

Leporello   Benno Kusche (*German*)
Donna Anna   Margaret Harshaw (*American*)
Don Giovanni   James Pease (*American*)
The Commendatore   Hervey Alan (*English*)
Don Ottavio   Léopold Simoneau (*Canadian*)
Donna Elvira   Sena Jurinac (*Jugoslavian*)
Zerlina   Anny Schlemm (*German*)
Masetto   Thomas Hemsley (*English*)

Conductor   GEORG SOLTI
Producer   CARL EBERT
Designer   JOHN PIPER

The Rake's Progress

STRAVINSKY *6 performances*

Anne   Elsie Morison (*Australian*)
Tom Rakewell   Richard Lewis (*English*)
Trulove   Hervey Alan (*English*)
Nick Shadow   Marko Rothmüller
   (*Jugoslavian*)
Mother Goose   Mary Jarred (*English*)
Baba the Turk   Marina de Gabarain
   (*Spanish*)
Sellem   Hugues Cuenod (*Swiss*)
Keeper of the Madhouse   David Kelly
   (*Scottish*)

Conductors   PAUL SACHER, BRYAN BALKWILL
Producer   CARL EBERT
Designer   OSBERT LANCASTER

216   Alison Edwards, Harry Kellard and
   Rosemary Wilkins in the Wardrobe
   Room during the making of Mattiwilda
   Dobbs's costume for *Die Entführung*; and
   Mattiwilda Dobbs as Constanze, wearing
   the costume

Edinburgh 22 August–
11 September: 18 performances

Le Comte Ory

ROSSINI *7 performances*

Raimbaud   Sesto Bruscantini (*Italian*)
Ory   Juan Oncina (*Spanish*)
Alice   Halinka de Tarczynska (*Australian*)
Ragonde   Monica Sinclair (*English*)
Isolier   Fernanda Cadoni (*Italian*)
Le Gouverneur   Ian Wallace (*Scottish*)
Adèle   Sari Barabas (*Hungarian*)

Conductor   VITTORIO GUI
Producer   CARL EBERT
Designer   OLIVER MESSEL

Ariadne auf Naxos
(Second Version)

RICHARD STRAUSS *6 performances*

Composer   Sena Jurinac (*Jugoslavian*)
Music Master   Geraint Evans (*Welsh*)
Dancing Master   Murray Dickie (*Scottish*)
Zerbinetta   Mattiwilda Dobbs (*American*)
Ariadne   Lucine Amara (*American*)
Harlekin   Kurt Gester (*German*)
Scaramuccio   Juan Oncina (*Spanish*)
Truffaldino   Fritz Ollendorf (*German*)
Brighella   Murray Dickie (*Scottish*)
Najade   Maureen Springer (*English*)
Dryade   Noreen Berry (*South African*)
Echo   Elaine Malbin (*American*)
Bacchus   Richard Lewis (*English*)

Conductor   JOHN PRITCHARD
Producer   CARL EBERT
Designer   OLIVER MESSEL

Così fan tutte

MOZART *5 performances*

Ferrando   Juan Oncina (*Spanish*)
   Richard Lewis (*English*)
Guglielmo   Geraint Evans (*Welsh*)
Don Alfonso   Sesto Bruscantini (*Italian*)
Fiordiligi   Sena Jurinac (*Jugoslavian*)
Dorabella   Magda Laszlo (*Hungarian*)
Despina   Alda Noni (*Italian*)

Conductors   VITTORIO GUI, JOHN PRITCHARD
Producer   CARL EBERT
Scenery   ROLF GÉRARD
Costumes   ROSEMARY VERCOE

The Soldier's Tale

STRAVINSKY *4 performances*

Princess   Moira Shearer
Devil   Robert Helpmann
Soldier   Terence Longdon
Narrator   Anthony Nicholls

Conductor   HANS SCHMIDT-ISSERSTEDT
Producer   GÜNTHER RENNERT
Designer   ALFRED MAHLAU

IN ASSOCIATION WITH THE EDINBURGH
   FESTIVAL SOCIETY

Berlin 25–26 September:
2 performances

La Cenerentola

ROSSINI *2 performances*

Don Ramiro   Juan Oncina (*Spanish*)
Dandini   Sesto Bruscantini (*Italian*)
Don Magnifico   Ian Wallace (*Scottish*)
Clorinda   Alda Noni (*Italian*)
   Halinka de Tarczynska (*Australian*)
Tisbe   Fernanda Cadoni (*Italian*)
Cenerentola   Marina de Gabarain (*Spanish*)
Alidoro   Hervey Alan (*English*)

Conductor   JOHN PRITCHARD
Producer   CARL EBERT
Designer   OLIVER MESSEL

217   John Piper with Wardrobe Mistress
   Rosemary Vercoe

1955
Glyndebourne 8 June–26 July:
37 performances

Le nozze di Figaro

MOZART *9 performances*

Figaro   Sesto Bruscantini (*Italian*)
Susanna   Elena Rizzieri (*Italian*)
Bartolo   Ian Wallace (*Scottish*)
Marcellina   Monica Sinclair (*English*)
Cherubino   Frances Bible (*American*)
   Risë Stevens (*American*)
Count Almaviva   Franco Calabrese (*Italian*)
Don Basilio   Hugues Cuenod (*Swiss*)
The Countess   Sena Jurinac (*Jugoslavian*)
Antonio   Gwyn Griffiths (*Welsh*)
Barbarina   Jeannette Sinclair (*English*)
Don Curzio   Daniel McCoshan (*Scottish*)

Conductor   VITTORIO GUI
Producer   CARL EBERT
Designer   OLIVER MESSEL

Le Comte Ory

ROSSINI *6 performances*

Raimbaud   Giuseppe Valdengo (*Italian*)
Ory   Juan Oncina (*Spanish*)
Alice   Halinka de Tarczynska (*Australian*)
Ragonde   Monica Sinclair (*English*)
Isolier   Fernanda Cadoni (*Italian*)
Le Gouverneur   Ian Wallace (*Scottish*)
Adèle   Sari Barabas (*Hungarian*)

Conductor   VITTORIO GUI
Producer   CARL EBERT
Designer   OLIVER MESSEL

Don Giovanni

MOZART *9 performances*

Leporello   Geraint Evans (*Welsh*)
Donna Anna   Sena Jurinac (*Jugoslavian*)
Don Giovanni   Giuseppe Valdengo (*Italian*)
The Commendatore   Hervey Alan (*English*)
Don Ottavio   Richard Lewis (*English*)
Donna Elvira   Lucine Amara (*American*)
Zerlina   Genevieve Warner (*American*)
Masetto   Thomas Hemsley (*English*)

Conductor   JOHN PRITCHARD
Producer   CARL EBERT
Staged by   PETER EBERT
Designer   JOHN PIPER

1956

Il barbiere di Siviglia

ROSSINI *9 performances*

Count Almaviva Juan Oncina (*Spanish*)
Figaro Sesto Bruscantini (*Italian*)
Rosina Gianna d'Angelo (*American*)
Bartolo Ian Wallace (*Scottish*)
Basilio Cristiano Dalamangas (*Greek*)
Fiorello Gwyn Griffiths (*Welsh*)
Berta Monica Sinclair (*English*)
Ambrogio Harold Williams (*English*)
Officer David Kelly (*Scottish*)
Notary Daniel McCoshan (*Scottish*)

Conductors VITTORIO GUI, BRYAN BALKWILL
Producer CARL EBERT
Designer OLIVER MESSEL

The Rake's Progress

STRAVINSKY *4 performances*

Anne Elsie Morison (*Australian*)
Tom Rakewell Richard Lewis (*English*)
Trulove Hervey Alan (*English*)
Nick Shadow Marko Rothmüller
  (*Jugoslavian*)
Mother Goose Mary Jarred (*English*)
Baba the Turk Marina de Gabarain
  (*Spanish*)
Sellem John Kentish (*English*)
Keeper of the Madhouse David Kelly
  (*Scottish*)

Conductor PAUL SACHER
Producer CARL EBERT
Designer OSBERT LANCASTER

Edinburgh 21 August–
10 September : 18 performances

Il barbiere di Siviglia

ROSSINI *6 performances*

Count Almaviva Juan Oncina (*Spanish*)
Figaro Sesto Bruscantini (*Italian*)
Rosina Gianna d'Angelo (*American*)
Bartolo Ian Wallace (*Scottish*)
Basilio Cristiano Dalamangas (*Greek*)
Fiorello Gwyn Griffiths (*Welsh*)
Berta Monica Sinclair (*English*)
Ambrogio Harold Williams (*English*)
Officer David Kelly (*Scottish*)
Notary Daniel McCoshan (*Scottish*)

Conductor ALBERTO EREDE
Producer CARL EBERT
Designer OLIVER MESSEL

Falstaff

VERDI *6 performances*

Falstaff Fernando Corena (*Swiss*)
Dr Caius Dermot Troy (*Irish*)
Bardolph Daniel McCoshan (*Scottish*)
Pistol Marco Stefanoni (*Italian*)
Meg Page Fernanda Cadoni (*Italian*)
Alice Ford Anna Maria Rovere (*Italian*)
Mistress Quickly Oralia Dominguez
  (*Mexican*)
Nannetta Eugenia Ratti (*Italian*)
Fenton Juan Oncina (*Spanish*)
  Kevin Miller (*Australian*)
Ford Walter Monachesi (*Italian*)

Conductor CARLO MARIA GIULINI
Producer CARL EBERT
Designer OSBERT LANCASTER

La forza del destino

VERDI *6 performances*

Marquis David Kelly (*Scottish*)
Leonora Sena Jurinac (*Jugoslavian*)
Curra Monica Sinclair (*English*)
Don Alvaro David Poleri (*American*)
Don Carlo Marko Rothmüller
  (*Jugoslavian*)
Alcade James Atkins (*English*)
Trabuco John Carolan (*Irish*)
Preziosilla Marina de Gabarain (*Spanish*)
Fra Melitone Ian Wallace (*Scottish*)
Padre Guardiano Hervey Alan (*English*)
Surgeon Niven Miller (*Scottish*)

Conductor JOHN PRITCHARD
Producer PETER EBERT
Designer LESLIE HURRY

218 Costume design by Leslie Hurry for *La
forza del destino*

Glyndebourne 14 June–
14 August : 48 performances

Idomeneo

MOZART *7 performances*

Ilia Elisabeth Grümmer (*German*)
Idamante William McAlpine (*Scottish*)
Arbace James Milligan (*Canadian*)
Electra Lucille Udovick (*American*)
Idomeneo Richard Lewis (*English*)
High Priest David Galliver (*Welsh*)
Voice of Neptune Hervey Alan (*English*)

Conductor JOHN PRITCHARD
Producer CARL EBERT
Designer OLIVER MESSEL

Die Entführung aus dem Serail

MOZART *8 performances*

Belmonte Ernst Haefliger (*Swiss*)
Osmin Arnold van Mill (*Dutch*)
Pedrillo Kevin Miller (*Australian*)
Pasha Selim Leo Bieber (*German*)
Constanze Mattiwilda Dobbs (*American*)
Blonde Lisa Otto (*German*)
Sailor James Atkins (*English*)

Conductors PAUL SACHER, PETER GELLHORN
Producer CARL EBERT
Staged by PETER EBERT
Designer OLIVER MESSEL

Die Zauberflöte

MOZART *8 performances*

Tamino Ernst Haefliger (*Swiss*)
Three Ladies Joan Sutherland (*Australian*)
  Cora Canne-Meijer (*Dutch*)
  Monica Sinclair (*English*)
Papageno Geraint Evans (*Welsh*)
Queen of the Night Mattiwilda Dobbs
  (*American*)
Three Boys Belva Boroditsky (*Canadian*)
  Jeannette Sinclair (*English*)
  Vera Kinrade (*English*)
Monostatos Kevin Miller (*Australian*)
Pamina Pilar Lorengar (*Spanish*)
The Speaker Thomas Hemsley (*English*)
Sarastro Frederick Guthrie (*American*)
  Drago Bernadic (*Jugoslavian*)
Priests and Men in Armour John Carolan
  (*Irish*), David Kelly (*Scottish*)
Papagena Maureen Springer (*English*)
  Naida Labay (*Bulgarian*)

Conductor VITTORIO GUI
Producer CARL EBERT
Designer OLIVER MESSEL

Così fan tutte

MOZART 7 *performances*

Ferrando   Richard Lewis (*English*)
   Juan Oncina (*Spanish*)
Guglielmo   Sesto Bruscantini (*Italian*)
Don Alfonso   Ivan Sardi (*Hungarian*)
Fiordiligi   Sena Jurinac (*Jugoslavian*)
Dorabella   Nan Merriman (*American*)
Despina   Elena Rizzieri (*Italian*)

Conductors   VITTORIO GUI, JOHN PRITCHARD
Producer   CARL EBERT
Scenery   ROLF GÉRARD
Costumes   ROSEMARY VERCOE

Don Giovanni

MOZART 9 *performances*

Leporello   Geraint Evans (*Welsh*)
Donna Anna   Sena Jurinac (*Jugoslavian*)
Don Giovanni   Kim Borg (*Finnish*)
The Commendatore   Hervey Alan (*English*)
Don Ottavio   Richard Lewis (*English*)
Donna Elvira   Elisabeth Lindermeier
   (*German*), Doreen Watts (*English*)
Zerlina   Elsie Morison (*Australian*)
Masetto   Thomas Hemsley (*English*)

Conductor   JOHN PRITCHARD
Producer   CARL EBERT
Staged by   PETER EBERT
Designer   JOHN PIPER

Le nozze di Figaro

MOZART 9 *performances*

Figaro   Sesto Bruscantini (*Italian*)
Susanna   Elena Rizzieri (*Italian*)
Bartolo   Ian Wallace (*Scottish*)
Marcellina   Monica Sinclair (*English*)
Cherubino   Cora Canne-Meijer (*Dutch*)
Count Almaviva   Michel Roux (*French*)
Don Basilio   Hugues Cuenod (*Swiss*)
The Countess   Elisabeth Grümmer (*German*)
   Joan Sutherland (*Australian*)
Antonio   Gwyn Griffiths (*Welsh*)
Barbarina   Jeannette Sinclair (*English*)
Don Curzio   Daniel McCoshan (*Scottish*)

Conductors   VITTORIO GUI, MAURITS SILLEM
Producer   CARL EBERT
Designer   OLIVER MESSEL

Liverpool 10–22 September: 12 performances

Le nozze di Figaro

MOZART 4 *performances*

Figaro   Sesto Bruscantini (*Italian*)
Susanna   Elena Rizzieri (*Italian*)
Bartolo   Ian Wallace (*Scottish*)
Marcellina   Monica Sinclair (*English*)
Cherubino   Cora Canne-Meijer (*Dutch*)
Count Almaviva   Michel Roux (*French*)
Don Basilio   Hugues Cuenod (*Swiss*)
The Countess   Joan Sutherland (*Australian*)
Antonio   Gwyn Griffiths (*Welsh*)
Barbarina   Jeannette Sinclair (*English*)
Don Curzio   Daniel McCoshan (*Scottish*)

Conductors   VITTORIO GUI, JOHN PRITCHARD
Producer   CARL EBERT
Designer   OLIVER MESSEL

Don Giovanni

MOZART 4 *performances*

Leporello   Geraint Evans (*Welsh*)
Donna Anna   Sena Jurinac (*Jugoslavian*)
Don Giovanni   Kim Borg (*Finnish*)
The Commendatore   Hervey Alan (*English*)
Don Ottavio   Juan Oncina (*Spanish*)
Donna Elvira   Elisabeth Lindermeier
   (*German*)
Zerlina   Elsie Morison (*Australian*)
Masetto   Thomas Hemsley (*English*)

Conductors   JOHN PRITCHARD, BRYAN
   BALKWILL
Producer   CARL EBERT
Staged by   PETER EBERT
Designer   JOHN PIPER

La Cenerentola

ROSSINI 4 *performances*

Don Ramiro   Juan Oncina (*Spanish*)
Dandini   Sesto Bruscantini (*Italian*)
Don Magnifico   Ian Wallace (*Scottish*)
Clorinda   Cora Canne-Meijer (*Dutch*)
Tisbe   Gianna d'Angelo (*American*)
Cenerentola   Marina de Gabarain (*Spanish*)
Alidoro   Hervey Alan (*English*)

Conductors   VITTORIO GUI, JOHN PRITCHARD
Producer   CARL EBERT
Designer   OLIVER MESSEL

LIVERPOOL PHILHARMONIC ORCHESTRA

219 Above left, Geraint Evans
and Pilar Lorengar in *Die
Zauberflöte*, 1956

220 Below left, *Don Giovanni*,
Hervey Alan and James Pease

221 *The Rake's Progress*
(designer Osbert Lancaster):
The Auction Scene, Hugues
Cuenod as Sellem

222 BBC Television
transmission of *The Rake's
Progress*, August 1958: the final
scene – Bedlam. Richard
Lewis as Tom and Elsie
Morison as Anne

1957

Glyndebourne 11 June–
13 August: 49 performances

L'italiana in Algeri

ROSSINI *8 performances*

Elvira   Antonietta Pastori (*Italian*)
Zulma   Josephine Veasey (*English*)
Mustafa   Paolo Montarsolo (*Italian*)
Haly   Thomas Hemsley (*English*)
Lindoro   Juan Oncina (*Spanish*)
Isabella   Oralia Dominguez (*Mexican*)
Taddeo   Marcello Cortis (*Austrian*)

Conductor   VITTORIO GUI
Producer   PETER EBERT
Designer   OSBERT LANCASTER

Le Comte Ory

ROSSINI *8 performances*

Raimbaud   Heinz Blankenburg (*American*)
Ory   Juan Oncina (*Spanish*)
Alice   Jeannette Sinclair (*English*)
Ragonde   Monica Sinclair (*English*)
Isolier   Fernanda Cadoni (*Italian*)
Le Gouverneur   Peter Lagger (*Swiss*)
Adèle   Sari Barabas (*Hungarian*)

Conductor   VITTORIO GUI
Producer   CARL EBERT
Designer   OLIVER MESSEL

Der Schauspieldirektor

MOZART *8 performances*

Herr Frank   Peter Lagger (*Swiss*)
Herr Vogelsang   Alexander Young (*English*)
Mme Herz   Joan Sutherland (*Australian*)
Mlle Silberklang   Naida Labay (*Bulgarian*)
Herr Buff   Gwyn Griffiths (*Welsh*)

Conductor   BRYAN BALKWILL
Producer   ANTHONY BESCH
Designer   PETER RICE

Ariadne auf Naxos
(Second Version)

RICHARD STRAUSS *8 performances*

Composer   Elisabeth Söderström (*Swedish*)
Music Master   Thomas Hemsley (*English*)
Dancing Master   Hugues Cuenod (*Swiss*)
Zerbinetta   Mimi Coertse (*South African*)
   Sari Barabas (*Hungarian*)
Ariadne   Lucine Amara (*American*)
Harlekin   Heinz Blankenburg (*American*)
Scaramuccio   Kevin Miller (*Australian*)
Truffaldino   Peter Lagger (*Swiss*)
Brighella   Edward Byles (*Welsh*)
Najade   Rosl Schwaiger (*Austrian*)
Dryade   Monica Sinclair (*English*)
Echo   Pilar Lorengar (*Spanish*)
Bacchus   David Lloyd (*American*)

Conductor   JOHN PRITCHARD
Producer   CARL EBERT
Designer   OLIVER MESSEL

Falstaff

VERDI *9 performances*

Falstaff   Geraint Evans (*Welsh*)
Dr Caius   Hugues Cuenod (*Swiss*)
Bardolph   John Lewis (*Welsh*)
Pistol   Hervey Alan (*English*)
Meg Page   Fernanda Cadoni (*Italian*)
Alice Ford   Orietta Moscucci (*Italian*)
Mistress Quickly   Oralia Dominguez
   (*Mexican*)
Nannetta   Antonietta Pastori (*Italian*)
Fenton   Juan Oncina (*Spanish*)
Ford   Antonio Boyer (*Italian*)

Conductor   VITTORIO GUI
Producer   CARL EBERT
Designer   OSBERT LANCASTER

Die Entführung aus dem Serail

MOZART *8 performances*

Belmonte   Ernst Haefliger (*Swiss*)
Osmin   Mihály Székely (*Hungarian*)
Pedrillo   Kevin Miller (*Australian*)
Pasha Selim   Leo Bieber (*German*)
Constanze   Wilma Lipp (*Austrian*)
Blonde   Rosl Schwaiger (*Austrian*)
Sailor   James Atkins (*English*)

Conductor   PAUL SACHER
Producer   CARL EBERT
Staged by   PETER EBERT
Designer   OLIVER MESSEL

Die Zauberflöte

MOZART *8 performances*

Tamino   David Lloyd (*American*)
Three Ladies   Heather Harper (*Irish*)
   Nancy Evans (*English*)
   Monica Sinclair (*English*)
Papageno   Geraint Evans (*Welsh*)
   Heinz Blankenburg (*American*)
Queen of the Night   Margareta Hallin
   (*Swedish*)
Three Boys   Belva Boroditsky (*Canadian*)
   Jeannette Sinclair (*English*)
   Helen Watts (*English*)
Monostatos   Kevin Miller (*Australian*)
Pamina   Pilar Lorengar (*Spanish*)
The Speaker   Thomas Hemsley (*English*)
   Walter Hertner (*German*)
Sarastro   Mihály Székely (*Hungarian*)
Priests and Men in Armour   John Carolan
   (*Irish*), James Atkins (*English*)
Papagena   Rosl Schwaiger (*Austrian*)
   Naida Labay (*Bulgarian*)

Conductors   PAUL SACHER, PETER GELLHORN
Producer   CARL EBERT
Designer   OLIVER MESSEL

223   Vittorio Gui

1958
Paris 8–16 May: 8 performances

Le Comte Ory
ROSSINI *4 performances*

Raimbaud Heinz Blankenburg (*American*)
Ory Juan Oncina (*Spanish*)
Alice Mary Illing (*English*)
Ragonde Monica Sinclair (*English*)
Isolier Fernanda Cadoni (*Italian*)
Le Gouverneur Xavier Depraz (*French*)
Adèle Sari Barabas (*Hungarian*)

Conductor VITTORIO GUI
Producer CARL EBERT
Designer OLIVER MESSEL

Falstaff
VERDI *4 performances*

Falstaff Geraint Evans (*Welsh*)
Dr Caius Hugues Cuenod (*Swiss*)
Bardolph Mario Carlin (*Italian*)
Pistol Marco Stefanoni (*Italian*)
Meg Page Fernanda Cadoni (*Italian*)
Alice Ford Ilva Ligabue (*Italian*)
Mistress Quickly Oralia Dominguez
  (*Mexican*)
Nannetta Graziella Sciutti (*Italian*)
Fenton Juan Oncina (*Spanish*)
Ford Mario Borriello (*Italian*)

Conductor VITTORIO GUI
Producer CARL EBERT
Designer OSBERT LANCASTER

Glyndebourne 27 May– 1 August: 51 performances

Falstaff
VERDI *9 performances*

Falstaff Geraint Evans (*Welsh*)
Dr Caius Hugues Cuenod (*Swiss*)
Bardolph Mario Carlin (*Italian*)
Pistol Marco Stefanoni (*Italian*)
Meg Page Fernanda Cadoni (*Italian*)
Alice Ford Ilva Ligabue (*Italian*)
Mistress Quickly Oralia Dominguez
  (*Mexican*)
Nannetta Graziella Sciutti (*Italian*)
Fenton Juan Oncina (*Spanish*)
Ford Mario Borriello (*Italian*)

Conductor VITTORIO GUI
Producer CARL EBERT
Designer OSBERT LANCASTER

Alceste
GLUCK *8 performances*

Herald Gwyn Griffiths (*Welsh*)
Evander David Holman (*Canadian*)
Alceste Consuelo Rubio (*Spanish*)
High Priest Robert Massard (*French*)
Admète Richard Lewis (*English*)
Hercules Robert Massard (*French*)
Voice of Tanato Dennis Wicks (*English*)
Apollo Heinz Blankenburg (*American*)

Conductor VITTORIO GUI
Producer CARL EBERT
Scenery HUGH CASSON
Costumes ROSEMARY VERCOE

Le nozze di Figaro
MOZART *9 performances*

Figaro Geraint Evans (*Welsh*)
Susanna Graziella Sciutti (*Italian*)
Bartolo Mihály Székely (*Hungarian*)
Marcellina Monica Sinclair (*English*)
Cherubino Teresa Berganza (*Spanish*)
Count Almaviva Michel Roux (*French*)
Don Basilio Hugues Cuenod (*Swiss*)
The Countess Pilar Lorengar (*Spanish*)
Antonio Gwyn Griffiths (*Welsh*)
Barbarina Mary Illing (*English*)
Don Curzio John Kentish (*English*)

Conductor HANS SCHMIDT-ISSERSTEDT
Producer CARL EBERT
Designer OLIVER MESSEL

The Rake's Progress
STRAVINSKY *7 performances*

Anne Elsie Morison (*Australian*)
Tom Rakewell Richard Lewis (*English*)
Trulove David Ward (*English*)
Nick Shadow Otakar Kraus (*Czech*)
Mother Goose Tamara Chumakova
  (*Russian*)
Baba the Turk Gloria Lane (*American*)
Sellem Hugues Cuenod (*Swiss*)
  John Kentish (*English*)
Keeper of the Madhouse Gwyn Griffiths
  (*Welsh*)

Conductor PAUL SACHER
Producer CARL EBERT
Designer OSBERT LANCASTER

Le Comte Ory
ROSSINI *10 performances*

Raimbaud Heinz Blankenburg (*American*)
Ory Juan Oncina (*Spanish*)
Alice Mary Illing (*English*)
Ragonde Monica Sinclair (*English*)
Isolier Fernanda Cadoni (*Italian*)
Le Gouverneur Xavier Depraz (*French*)
Adèle Sari Barabas (*Hungarian*)

Conductor JOHN PRITCHARD
Producer CARL EBERT
Designer OLIVER MESSEL

Il segreto di Susanna
WOLF-FERRARI *8 performances*

Gil Michel Roux (*French*)
Countess Mary Costa (*American*)
Sante Heinz Blankenburg (*American*)

Conductor JOHN PRITCHARD
Producer PETER EBERT
Designer CARL TOMS

Ariadne auf Naxos
(Second Version)

RICHARD STRAUSS *8 performances*

Composer Helga Pilarczyk (*German*)
Music Master Geraint Evans (*Welsh*)
Dancing Master Hugues Cuenod (*Swiss*)
Zerbinetta Rita Streich (*German*)
Ariadne Lucine Amara (*American*)
Harlekin Heinz Blankenburg (*American*)
Scaramuccio John Kentish (*English*)
Truffaldino John Holmes (*English*)
Brighella Duncan Robertson (*Scottish*)
Najade Jacqueline Delman (*English*)
Dryade Monica Sinclair (*English*)
Echo Pilar Lorengar (*Spanish*)
Bacchus Richard Lewis (*English*)

Conductor JOHN PRITCHARD
Producer CARL EBERT
Designer OLIVER MESSEL

Over page:
224 Left, Geraint Evans as Falstaff
225 Right, Joan Sutherland as Donna Anna

1959

Twenty-fifth Anniversary Season

Artistic Director CARL EBERT (1934)
General Manager MORAN CAPLAT (1945)
Conductors VITTORIO GUI (1948)
    LEOPOLD LUDWIG (1959)
    JOHN PRITCHARD (1947)
    PETER MAAG (1959)
Head of Music Staff JANI STRASSER (1934)
Associate Conductor and Chorus Master
    PETER GELLHORN (1954)
Assistant Conductors and Coaches JOHN
    BARKER (1958), GEORGE COOP (1950),
    RHOSLYN DAVIES (1959), MYER FREDMAN
    (1959), ERNA GAL (1950), PAUL HAMBURGER
    (1956), MARTIN ISEPP (1957), JAMES
    LOCKHART (1957), EVELYN TURNER-INMAN
    (1951)
Librarian HOWARD WICKS (1951)
Producers CARL EBERT (1934), PETER EBERT
    (1947), GÜNTHER RENNERT (1959)
Assistant Producers RICHARD DOUBLEDAY
    (1955), JOHN COX (1959)
Assistant to Günther Rennert: ANTHONY
    BESCH (1951)
Designers ROLF GÉRARD (1948), ITA
    MAXIMOWNA (1959), OLIVER MESSEL (1950),
    ROSEMARY VERCOE (1951)
Choreographer ROBERT HARROLD (1951)
Ballet Mistress SILVIA ASHMOLE (1947)
Stage Director JUNE DANDRIDGE (1951)
Stage Managers ANN DUFFY (1954), DAVID
    GAULD (1953), GEOFFREY GILBERTSON (1957)
Chief Technician R. W. (JOCK) GOUGH (1934)
Assistant Technician S. HUGGETT (1936)
Lighting Manager FRANCIS REID (1959)
Lighting Assistant T. FAULKNER (1959)
Wardrobe Manager ROSEMARY WILKINS
    (1951)
Cutters DOREEN BROWN (1957), HILARY
    CORBETT (1957)
Chief Dresser NELLIE AYRE (1947)
Maintenance BERTHA CUMMINS (1953)
Perruquière ALISON EDWARDS (1951)
Property Manager HARRY KELLARD (1947)
Head Gardener F. HARVEY (1934)
Assistant General Manager DOUGLAS CRAIG
    (1950)
Personal Assistant to the General Manager
    JANET MOORES (1934)
Regulating Secretary ELLEN MORGENTHAU
    (1950)
Treasurer ERIC WHITEHORN (1953)
Press Officer BERNARD MCNABB (1953)
Chief Telephonist KAY ARNOLD (1950)
Catering by The Four Seasons Hotel &
    Catering Co Ltd, under the direction of
    VERNON HERBERT (1956)

THE ROYAL PHILHARMONIC ORCHESTRA (1948)

(Dates in parenthesis indicate the year of first
    Glyndebourne engagement)

Glyndebourne 28 May– 16 August: 68 performances

Der Rosenkavalier

RICHARD STRAUSS *13 performances*

Oktavian Elisabeth Söderström (*Swedish*)
Feldmarschallin Régine Crespin (*French*)
Ochs Oscar Czerwenka (*Austrian*)
Valzacchi John Kentish (*English*)
Annina Nancy Evans (*English*)
Faninal Willy Ferenz (*Austrian*)
Sophie Anneliese Rothenberger (*German*)
Duenna Elizabeth Crook (*English*)
Singer William McAlpine (*Scottish*)
Landlord Duncan Robertson (*Scottish*)
Police Inspector Hervey Alan (*English*)

Conductor LEOPOLD LUDWIG
Producer CARL EBERT
Designer OLIVER MESSEL

Idomeneo

MOZART *9 performances*

Ilia Sylvia Stahlman (*American*)
Idamante William McAlpine (*Scottish*)
Arbace Lauri Payne (*Australian*)
Electra Angela Vercelli (*Italian*)
Idomeneo Richard Lewis (*English*)
High Priest Duncan Robertson (*Scottish*)
Voice of Neptune Hervey Alan (*English*)

Conductors JOHN PRITCHARD, PETER GELLHORN
Producer CARL EBERT
Designer OLIVER MESSEL

Così fan tutte

MOZART *12 performances*

Ferrando Juan Oncina (*Spanish*)
Guglielmo Geraint Evans (*Welsh*)
Don Alfonso Carlos Feller (*Argentinian*)
Fiordiligi Ilva Ligabue (*Italian*)
Dorabella Gloria Lane (*American*)
Despina Graziella Sciutti (*Italian*)

Conductor JOHN PRITCHARD
Producer CARL EBERT
Scenery ROLF GÉRARD
Costumes ROSEMARY VERCOE

Fidelio

BEETHOVEN *12 performances*

Jaquino Duncan Robertson (*Scottish*)
Marzelline Elsie Morison (*Australian*)
Rocco Mihály Székely (*Hungarian*)
Leonore Gré Brouwenstijn (*Dutch*)
Pizarro Kim Borg (*Finnish*)
First Prisoner John Kentish (*English*)
Second Prisoner Derick Davies (*Welsh*)
Florestan Richard Lewis (*English*)
Don Fernando David Kelly (*Scottish*)
    Lauri Payne (*Australian*)

Conductor VITTORIO GUI
Producer GÜNTHER RENNERT
Designer ITA MAXIMOWNA

La Cenerentola

ROSSINI *12 performances*

Don Ramiro Juan Oncina (*Spanish*)
Dandini Sesto Bruscantini (*Italian*)
Don Magnifico Ian Wallace (*Scottish*)
Clorinda Silvana Zanolli (*Italian*)
Tisbe Miti Truccato Pace (*Italian*)
Cenerentola Teresa Berganza (*Spanish*)
    Anna Maria Rota (*Italian*)
Alidoro Hervey Alan (*English*)

Conductors VITTORIO GUI, PETER GELLHORN
Producer CARL EBERT
Staged by PETER EBERT
Designer OLIVER MESSEL

Le nozze di Figaro

MOZART *10 performances*

Figaro Carlos Feller (*Argentinian*)
    Geraint Evans (*Welsh*)
Susanna Elisabeth Söderström (*Swedish*)
Bartolo Mihály Székely (*Hungarian*)
Marcellina Johanna Peters (*Scottish*)
Cherubino Josephine Veasey (*English*)
Count Almaviva Michel Roux (*French*)
Don Basilio Hugues Cuenod (*Swiss*)
The Countess Pilar Lorengar (*Spanish*)
Antonio Gwyn Griffiths (*Welsh*)
Barbarina Mary Illing (*English*)
Don Curzio John Kentish (*English*)

Conductor PETER MAAG
Producer CARL EBERT
Designer OLIVER MESSEL

1960

Glyndebourne 24 May– 16 August: 70 performances

I Puritani

BELLINI *11 performances*

Sir Bruno Robertson   John Kentish (*English*)
Elvira   Joan Sutherland (*Australian*)
Arturo   Nicola Filacuridi (*Italian*)
Giorgio   Giuseppe Modesti (*Italian*)
Riccardo   Ernest Blanc (*French*)
Lord Walton   David Ward (*English*)
Queen Henrietta   Monica Sinclair (*English*)

Conductors VITTORIO GUI, BRYAN BALKWILL
Producer FRANCO ENRIQUEZ
Designer DESMOND HEELEY

Falstaff

VERDI *11 performances*

Falstaff   Geraint Evans (*Welsh*)
Dr Caius   Hugues Cuenod (*Swiss*)
Bardolph   Mario Carlin (*Italian*)
Pistol   Marco Stefanoni (*Italian*)
Meg Page   Anna Maria Rota (*Italian*)
Alice Ford   Ilva Ligabue (*Italian*)
Mistress Quickly   Oralia Dominguez
  (*Mexican*)
Nannetta   Mariella Adani (*Italian*)
Fenton   Juan Oncina (*Spanish*)
Ford   Sesto Bruscantini (*Italian*)

Conductor VITTORIO GUI
Producer CARL EBERT
Designer OSBERT LANCASTER

Der Rosenkavalier

RICHARD STRAUSS *13 performances*

Oktavian   Regina Sarfaty (*American*)
Feldmarschallin   Régine Crespin (*French*)
  Claire Watson (*American*)
Ochs   Oscar Czerwenka (*Austrian*)
Valzacchi   John Kentish (*English*)
Annina   Nancy Evans (*English*)
Faninal   Willy Ferenz (*Austrian*)
Sophie   Anneliese Rothenberger (*German*)
Duenna   Elizabeth Crook (*English*)
Singer   William McAlpine (*Scottish*)
Landlord   Duncan Robertson (*Scottish*)
Police Inspector   Hervey Alan (*English*)

Conductor LEOPOLD LUDWIG
Producer CARL EBERT
Rehearsed by RICHARD DOUBLEDAY
Designer OLIVER MESSEL

Don Giovanni

MOZART *13 performances*

Leporello   Geraint Evans (*Welsh*)
  Sesto Bruscantini (*Italian*)
Donna Anna   Joan Sutherland (*Australian*)
Don Giovanni   Ernest Blanc (*French*)
The Commendatore   Marco Stefanoni
  (*Italian*)
Don Ottavio   Richard Lewis (*English*)
Donna Elvira   Ilva Ligabue (*Italian*)
Zerlina   Mirella Freni (*Italian*)
Masetto   Leonardo Monreale (*Italian*)

Conductors JOHN PRITCHARD, PETER GELLHORN
Producer GÜNTHER RENNERT
Designer ITA MAXIMOWNA

Die Zauberflöte

MOZART *10 performances*

Tamino   Richard Lewis (*English*)
Three Ladies   Heather Harper (*Irish*)
  Catherine Wilson (*English*)
  Monica Sinclair (*English*)
Papageno   Geraint Evans (*Welsh*)
Queen of the Night   Margareta Hallin
  (*Swedish*)
Three Boys   Emily Maire (*Scottish*)
  Elizabeth Harwood (*English*)
  Theresia Bester (*South African*)
Monostatos   Gwyn Griffiths (*Welsh*)
Pamina   Pilar Lorengar (*Spanish*)
The Speaker   Carlos Feller (*Argentinian*)
Sarastro   Mihály Székely (*Hungarian*)
Priests and Men in Armour   James Conrad
  (*South African*), David Read (*English*)
Papagena   Dodi Protero (*Canadian*)

Conductor COLIN DAVIS
Producer CARL EBERT
Staged by ANTHONY BESCH
Designer OLIVER MESSEL

La Cenerentola

ROSSINI *12 performances*

Don Ramiro   Juan Oncina (*Spanish*)
Dandini   Sesto Bruscantini (*Italian*)
Don Magnifico   Ian Wallace (*Scottish*)
Clorinda   Silvana Zanolli (*Italian*)
Tisbe   Miti Truccato Pace (*Italian*)
Cenerentola   Anna Maria Rota (*Italian*)
Alidoro   Hervey Alan (*English*)

Conductors JOHN PRITCHARD, PETER GELLHORN
Producer CARL EBERT
Staged by PETER EBERT
Designer OLIVER MESSEL

Edinburgh 23 August– 10 September: 17 performances

Falstaff

VERDI *7 performances*

Falstaff   Geraint Evans (*Welsh*)
Dr Caius   Hugues Cuenod (*Swiss*)
Bardolph   Mario Carlin (*Italian*)
Pistol   Marco Stefanoni (*Italian*)
Meg Page   Anna Maria Rota (*Italian*)
Alice Ford   Ilva Ligabue (*Italian*)
Mistress Quickly   Oralia Dominguez
  (*Mexican*)
Nannetta   Mariella Adani (*Italian*)
Fenton   Juan Oncina (*Spanish*)
Ford   Sesto Bruscantini (*Italian*)

Conductor VITTORIO GUI
Producer CARL EBERT
Staged by PETER EBERT
Designer OSBERT LANCASTER

I Puritani

BELLINI *6 performances*

Sir Bruno Robertson   John Kentish (*English*)
Elvira   Joan Sutherland (*Australian*)
Arturo   Nicola Filacuridi (*Italian*)
Giorgio   Giuseppe Modesti (*Italian*)
Riccardo   Ernest Blanc (*French*)
Lord Walton   David Ward (*English*)
Queen Henrietta   Monica Sinclair (*English*)

Conductors VITTORIO GUI, BRYAN BALKWILL
Producer FRANCO ENRIQUEZ
Designer DESMOND HEELEY

226 Left, Oralia Dominguez in *L'incoronazione di Poppea*
227 Below left, *L'incoronazione di Poppea*, 1962: the final scene

228–230 *Pelléas et Mélisande* (designer Beni Montresor)
228 Above right, Set design
229 Below right, Henri Gui and Denise Duval
230 Below far right, The death of Mélisande

TRIPLE BILL : *4 performances*

Il segreto di Susanna

WOLF–FERRARI

Gil   Sesto Bruscantini (*Italian*)
Countess   Mariella Adani (*Italian*)
Sante   Heinz Blankenburg (*American*)

Conductor   JOHN PRITCHARD
Producer   PETER EBERT
Designer   CARL TOMS

La Voix humaine

POULENC

Elle   Denise Duval (*French*)

Conductor   JOHN PRITCHARD
Producer and Designer   JEAN COCTEAU

Arlecchino

BUSONI

Ser Matteo   Ian Wallace (*Scottish*)
Arlecchino   Heinz Blankenburg (*American*)
Abbate Cospicuo   Gwyn Griffiths (*Welsh*)
Doctor Bombasto   Carlos Feller (*Argentinian*)
Colombina   Helga Pilarczyk (*German*)
Leandro   Dermot Troy (*Irish*)

Conductor   JOHN PRITCHARD
Producer   PETER EBERT
Designer   PETER RICE

1961

Glyndebourne 24 May– 20 August: 72 performances

L'elisir d'amore

DONIZETTI *14 performances*

Adina   Eugenia Ratti (*Italian*)
Nemorino   Luigi Alva (*Peruvian*)
Belcore   Enzo Sordello (*Italian*)
Dulcamara   Carlo Badioli (*Italian*)
Giannetta   Emily Maire (*Scottish*)

Conductor   CARLO PELICE CILLARIO
Producer and Designer   FRANCO ZEFFIRELLI

Die Entführung aus dem Serail

MOZART *15 performances*

Belmonte   Heinz Hoppe (*German*)
Osmin   Mihály Székely (*Hungarian*)
   Michael Langdon (*English*)
Pedrillo   Duncan Robertson (*Scottish*)
Pasha Selim   Robert Speaight (*English*)
Constanze   Mattiwilda Dobbs (*American*)
Blonde   Dorit Hanak (*Austrian*)
Sailor   Derick Davies (*Welsh*)

Conductor   PETER GELLHORN
Producer   PETER EBERT
Designer   OLIVER MESSEL

Fidelio

BEETHOVEN *12 performances*

Jaquino   Duncan Robertson (*Scottish*)
Marzelline   Elsie Morison (*Australian*)
Rocco   Mihály Székely (*Hungarian*)
Leonore   Gré Brouwenstijn (*Dutch*)
Pizarro   Herbert Fliether (*German*)
First Prisoner   John Kentish (*English*)
Second Prisoner   Derick Davies (*Welsh*)
Florestan   Richard Lewis (*English*)
Don Fernando   Thomas Hernsley (*English*)

Conductor   VITTORIO GUI
Producer   GÜNTHER RENNERT
Assistant Producer   ANTHONY BESCH
Designer   ITA MAXIMOWNA

---

231   Costume design by Jean Cocteau for
   La Voix humaine

Elegy for Young Lovers

HANS WERNER HENZE *8 performances*
World première in original language

Hilda Mack   Dorothy Dorow (*English*)
Carolina   Kerstin Meyer (*Swedish*)
Dr Reischmann   Thomas Hemsley (*English*)
Toni Reischmann   André Turp (*Canadian*)
Gregor Mittenhofer   Carlos Alexander
   (*American*)
Elizabeth Zimmer   Elisabeth Söderström
   (*Swedish*)
Josef Mauer   John Kentish (*English*)

Conductors   JOHN PRITCHARD, HANS WERNER
   HENZE
Producer   GÜNTHER RENNERT
Designer   LILA DE NOBILI

Don Giovanni

MOZART *13 performances*

Leporello   Geraint Evans (*Welsh*)
Donna Anna   Gerda Scheyrer (*Austrian*)
Don Giovanni   György Melis (*Hungarian*)
The Commendatore   Michael Langdon
   (*English*)
Don Ottavio   Richard Lewis (*English*)
Donna Elvira   Ilva Ligabue (*Italian*)
Zerlina   Mirella Freni (*Italian*)
Masetto   Leonardo Monreale (*Italian*)

Conductors   JOHN PRITCHARD, PETER GELLHORN
Producer   GÜNTHER RENNERT
Associate Producer   ANTHONY BESCH
Designer   ITA MAXIMOWNA

Il barbiere di Siviglia

ROSSINI *10 performances*

Count Almaviva   Juan Oncina (*Spanish*)
Figaro   Sesto Bruscantini (*Italian*)
Rosina   Alberta Valentini (*Italian*)
Bartolo   Ian Wallace (*Scottish*)
Basilio   Carlo Cava (*Italian*)
Fiorello   Duncan Robertson (*Scottish*)
Berta   Laura Sarti (*Italian*)
Ambrogio   Harold Williams (*English*)
Officer   John Evans (*Welsh*)

Conductor   VITTORIO GUI
Producer   CARL EBERT
Staged by   PETER EBERT
Designer   OLIVER MESSEL

1962

Glyndebourne 21 May– 19 August: 70 performances

Pelléas et Mélisande

DEBUSSY *10 performances*

Pelléas   Henri Gui (*French*)
Mélisande   Denise Duval (*French*)
Golaud   Michel Roux (*French*)
Geneviève   Kerstin Meyer (*Swedish*)
   Anna Reynolds (*English*)
Arkel   Guus Hoekman (*Dutch*)
Yniold   Rosine Brédy (*French*)
Doctor   John Shirley-Quirk (*English*)

Conductor VITTORIO GUI
Producer CARL EBERT
Designer BENI MONTRESSOR

Le nozze di Figaro

MOZART *16 performances*

Figaro   Heinz Blankenburg (*American*)
Susanna   Mirella Freni (*Italian*)
Bartolo   Carlo Cava (*Italian*)
Marcellina   Johanna Peters (*Scottish*)
Cherubino   Edith Mathis (*Swiss*)
   Maureen Keetch (*English*)
Count Almaviva   Gabriel Bacquier (*French*)
Don Basilio   Hugues Cuenod (*Swiss*)
The Countess   Leyla Gencer (*Turkish*)
Antonio   Derick Davies (*Welsh*)
Barbarina   Maria Zeri (*Greek*)
Don Curzio   John Kentish (*English*)

Conductors SILVIO VARVISO, JOHN PRITCHARD
Producer CARL EBERT
Designer OLIVER MESSEL

Così fan tutte

MOZART *15 performances*

Ferrando   Loren Driscoll (*American*)
Guglielmo   Ingvar Wixell (*Swedish*)
Don Alfonso   Michel Roux (*French*)
Fiordiligi   Antigone Sgourda (*Greek*)
Dorabella   Stefania Malagù (*Italian*)
Despina   Reri Grist (*American*)

Conductor JOHN PRITCHARD
Producer CARL EBERT
Scenery ROLF GÉRARD
Costumes BERNARD NEVILL

L'incoronazione di Poppea

MONTEVERDI *12 performances*
(*arr Raymond Leppard*)
First professional production in England

Ottone   Walter Alberti (*Italian*)
Poppea   Magda Laszlo (*Hungarian*)
Nerone   Richard Lewis (*English*)
Arnalta   Oralia Dominguez (*Mexican*)
   Jean Allister (*Irish*)
Ottavia   Frances Bible (*American*)
Damigella   Soo-Bee Lee (*Chinese*)
Seneca   Carlo Cava (*Italian*)
Valetto   Duncan Robertson (*Scottish*)
Drusilla   Lydia Marimpietri (*Italian*)
Lucano   Hugues Cuenod (*Swiss*)
First Soldier   Dennis Brandt (*English*)
Second Soldier   Gerald English (*English*)
Pallade   Josephine Allen (*English*)
Liberto   John Shirley-Quirk (*English*)
Amor   Marta Sellas (*Scottish*)
Lictor   Dennis Wicks (*English*)

Conductor JOHN PRITCHARD
Producer GÜNTHER RENNERT
Scenery HUGH CASSON
Costumes CONWY EVANS

Ariadne auf Naxos
(*First Version*)

RICHARD STRAUSS *11 performances*

Le Bourgeois Gentilhomme

M. Jourdain   Miles Malleson
Dorante   Richard Gale
Dorimène   Marion Mathie
Professor of Philosophy   Walter Hudd

Ariadne auf Naxos

Najade   Day McAusland (*Scottish*)
Dryade   Jean Allister (*Irish*)
Echo   Morag Noble (*Scottish*)
Ariadne   Enriqueta Tarrés (*Spanish*)
Harlekin   Heinz Blankenburg (*American*)
Zerbinetta   Gianna d'Angelo (*American*)
   Reri Grist (*American*)
Brighella   Duncan Robertson (*Scottish*)
Truffaldino   Dennis Wicks (*English*)
Scaramuccio   Adrian de Peyer (*English*)
Bacchus   Richard Lewis (*English*)
   William McAlpine (*Scottish*)

Conductor SILVIO VARVISO
Producer CARL EBERT
Staged by PETER EBERT
Designer OLIVER MESSEL

L'elisir d'amore

DONIZETTI *6 performances*

Adina   Mirella Freni (*Italian*)
Nemorino   Luigi Alva (*Peruvian*)
Belcore   Enzo Sordello (*Italian*)
Dulcamara   Sesto Bruscantini (*Italian*)
Giannetta   Emily Maire (*Scottish*)

Conductor CARLO FELICE CILLARIO
Producer and Designer FRANCO ZEFFIRELLI
Assistant Producer MICHAEL GELIOT

232   Above, Mirella Freni and Luigi Alva in
   L'elisir d'amore
233   Below, Carlo Cava as Dr Bartolo

1963

Glyndebourne 22 May–
18 August: 70 performances

Capriccio

RICHARD STRAUSS *10 performances*

Flamand   Horst Wilhelm (*German*)
Olivier   Raymond Wolansky (*American*)
La Roche   Benno Kusche (*German*)
The Countess   Elisabeth Söderström
   (*Swedish*)
The Count   Tom Krause (*Finnish*)
Clairon   Sona Cervena (*Czech*)
Italian Tenor   Pierre Duval (*Canadian*)
Italian Soprano   Alberta Valentini (*Italian*)
Major-Domo   John Shirley-Quirk (*English*)
Monsieur Taupe   Hugues Cuenod (*Swiss*)

Conductors JOHN PRITCHARD, BRYAN
   BALKWILL
Producer GÜNTHER RENNERT
Scenery DENNIS LENNON
Costumes ANTHONY POWELL

Fidelio

BEETHOVEN *8 performances*

Jaquino   Duncan Robertson (*Scottish*)
Marzelline   April Cantelo (*English*)
   Maureen Keetch (*English*)
Rocco   Victor de Narké (*Argentinian*)
Leonore   Gré Brouwenstijn (*Dutch*)
Pizarro   Herbert Fliether (*German*)
First Prisoner   John Kentish (*English*)
Second Prisoner   Derick Davies (*Welsh*)
Florestan   Richard Lewis (*English*)
Don Fernando   Benno Kusche (*German*)

Conductor BRYAN BALKWILL
Producer GÜNTHER RENNERT
Assistant Producer JOHN COX
Designer ITA MAXIMOWNA

Pelléas et Mélisande

DEBUSSY *10 performances*

Pelléas   Hans Wilbrink (*Dutch*)
Mélisande   Denise Duval (*French*)
Golaud   Michel Roux (*French*)
Geneviève   Anna Reynolds (*English*)
Arkel   Guus Hoekman (*Dutch*)
Yniold   Rosine Brédy (*French*)
Doctor   John Shirley-Quirk (*English*)

Conductor VITTORIO GUI
Producer CARL EBERT
Designer BENI MONTRESOR

Le nozze di Figaro

MOZART *10 performances*

Figaro   Heinz Blankenburg (*American*)
Susanna   Liliane Berton (*French*)
Bartolo   Carlo Cava (*Italian*)
   Michael Langdon (*English*)
Marcellina   Rosa Laghezza (*Italian*)
Cherubino   Edith Mathis (*Swiss*)
Count Almaviva   Michel Roux (*French*)
Don Basilio   Hugues Cuenod (*Swiss*)
The Countess   Leyla Gencer (*Turkish*)
Antonio   Derick Davies (*Welsh*)
Don Curzio   John Kentish (*English*)
Barbarina   Maria Zeri (*Greek*)

Conductors SILVIO VARVISO, MYER FREDMAN
Producer CARL EBERT
Staged by PETER EBERT
Designer OLIVER MESSEL

The Rake's Progress

STRAVINSKY *9 performances*

Anne   Heather Harper (*Irish*)
Tom Rakewell   Richard Lewis (*English*)
Trulove   Dennis Wicks (*English*)
Nick Shadow   Delme Bryn Jones (*Welsh*)
   Hermann Uhde (*German*)
Mother Goose   Tamara Chumakova (*Russian*)
Baba the Turk   Gloria Lane (*American*)
Sellem   Hugues Cuenod (*Swiss*)
Keeper of the Madhouse   Derick Davies
   (*Welsh*)

Conductor PAUL SACHER
Producer CARL EBERT
Staged by PETER EBERT
Designer OSBERT LANCASTER

L'incoronazione di Poppea

MONTEVERDI *10 performances*
(arr Raymond Leppard)

Ottone   Walter Alberti (*Italian*)
Poppea   Magda Laszlo (*Hungarian*)
Nerone   Richard Lewis (*English*)
Arnalta   Oralia Dominguez (*Mexican*)
   Jean Allister (*Irish*)
Ottavia   Frances Bible (*American*)
Damigella   Soo-Bee Lee (*Chinese*)
Seneca   Carlo Cava (*Italian*)
Valetto   Duncan Robertson (*Scottish*)
Drusilla   Lydia Marimpietri (*Italian*)
Lucano   Hugues Cuenod (*Swiss*)
   Gerald English (*English*)
First Soldier   Dennis Brandt (*English*)
Second Soldier   Gerald English (*English*)
Pallade   Elizabeth Bainbridge (*English*)
Liberto   John Shirley-Quirk (*English*)
Amor   Annon Lee Silver (*Canadian*)
Lictor   Dennis Wicks (*English*)

Conductor JOHN PRITCHARD
Producer GÜNTHER RENNERT
Scenery HUGH CASSON
Costumes CONWY EVANS

Die Zauberflöte

MOZART *13 performances*

Tamino   Ragnar Ulfung (*Norwegian*)
Three Ladies   Antigone Sgourda (*Greek*)
   Maureen Keetch (*English*)
   Elizabeth Bainbridge (*English*)
Papageno   Heinz Blankenburg (*American*)
Queen of the Night   Claudine Arnaud (*Belgian*)
Three Boys   Margaret Neville (*English*)
   Anne Pashley (*English*)
   Pauline Darroll (*English*)
Monostatos   Duncan Robertson (*Scottish*)
Pamina   Judith Raskin (*American*)
The Speaker   Donald Bell (*Canadian*)
Sarastro   Carlo Cava (*Italian*)
Priests and Men in Armour   Dennis Brandt
   (*English*)
   Dennis Wicks (*English*)
Papagena   Maria Zeri (*Greek*)

Conductor VITTORIO GUI
Producer FRANCO ENRIQUEZ
Designer EMANUELE LUZZATI

234   Edith Mathis as Cherubino

1964

Glyndebourne 21 May–
16 August: 72 performances

Macbeth

VERDI *12 performances*

Macbeth   Kostas Paskalis (*Greek*)
Banquo   Plinio Clabassi (*Italian*)
Lady Macbeth   Marta Pender (*American*)
Gentlewoman   Rae Woodland (*English*)
Macduff   John Wakefield (*English*)
Malcolm   Dennis Brandt (*English*)
Doctor   Derick Davies (*Welsh*)
   Emyr Green (*Welsh*)
Servant   Peter Lehmann Bedford (*English*)
Murderer   Erich Vietheer (*Australian*)

Conductor LAMBERTO GARDELLI
Producer FRANCO ENRIQUEZ
Designer EMANUELE LUZZATI

L'incoronazione di Poppea

MONTEVERDI *12 performances*
(arr Raymond Leppard)

Ottone   Walter Alberti (*Italian*)
Poppea   Saramae Endich (*American*)
Nerone   Richard Lewis (*English*)
Arnalta   Oralia Dominguez (*Mexican*)
Ottavia   Kerstin Meyer (*Swedish*)
   Dorothy Wilson (*English*)
Damigella   Soo-Bee Lee (*Chinese*)
Seneca   Carlo Cava (*Italian*)
Valetto   Duncan Robertson (*Scottish*)
Drusilla   Margaret Neville (*English*)
Lucano   Hugues Cuenod (*Swiss*)
   Gerald English (*English*)
First Soldier   Dennis Brandt (*English*)
Second Soldier   Gerald English (*English*)
Pallade   Elizabeth Bainbridge (*English*)
Liberto   Neilson Taylor (*English*)
Amor   Annon Lee Silver (*Canadian*)
Lictor   Stafford Dean (*English*)

Conductor RAYMOND LEPPARD
Producer GÜNTHER RENNERT
Associate Producer JOHN COX
Scenery HUGH CASSON
Costumes CONWY EVANS

La pietra del paragone

ROSSINI *13 performances*

Fabrizio   David Hartley (*English*)
Pacuvio   Heinz Blankenburg (*American*)
Ortensia   Anna Reynolds (*English*)
Fulvia   Alberta Valentini (*Italian*)
Asdrubale   Ugo Trama (*Italian*)
Giocondo   Umberto Grilli (*Italian*)
Clarice   Josephine Veasey (*English*)
Macrobio   Michel Roux (*French*)

Conductors JOHN PRITCHARD, MYER FREDMAN
Producer GÜNTHER RENNERT
Designer OSBERT LANCASTER

Capriccio

RICHARD STRAUSS *11 performances*

Flamand   Horst Wilhelm (*German*)
Olivier   Raymond Wolansky (*American*)
La Roche   Benno Kusche (*German*)
   Derick Davies (*Welsh*)
   Otto Wiener (*Austrian*)
The Countess   Elisabeth Söderström
   (*Swedish*)
The Count   George Fortune (*American*)
Clairon   Sona Cervena (*Czech*)
Italian Tenor   Amadeo Casanovas (*Spanish*)
Italian Soprano   Alberta Valentini (*Italian*)
Major-Domo   Stafford Dean (*English*)
Monsieur Taupe   Hugues Cuenod (*Swiss*)

Conductors JOHN PRITCHARD, BRYAN
   BALKWILL
Producer GÜNTHER RENNERT
Assistant Producer DENNIS MAUNDER
Scenery DENNIS LENNON
Costumes ANTHONY POWELL

Idomeneo

MOZART *12 performances*

Ilia   Gundula Janowitz (*Austrian*)
   ★Lorna Elias (*1 perf*)
Idamante   Luciano Pavarotti (*Italian*)
Arbace   Neilson Taylor (*English*)
Electra   Enriqueta Tarrés (*Spanish*)
Idomeneo   Richard Lewis (*English*)
High Priest   David Hughes (*Welsh*)
Voice of Neptune   Dennis Wicks (*English*)

Conductor JOHN PRITCHARD
Producer PETER EBERT
Designer OLIVER MESSEL

★role performed as understudy

235   Luciano Pavarotti and Gundula
   Janowitz in *Idomeneo*

Die Zauberflöte

MOZART *12 performances*

Tamino   Ragnar Ulfung (*Norwegian*)
Three Ladies   Margherita Kalmus (*English*)
   Anna Reynolds (*English*)
   Elizabeth Bainbridge (*English*)
Papageno   Heinz Blankenburg (*American*)
Queen of the Night Claudine Arnaud (*Belgian*)
Three Boys   Margaret Neville (*English*)
   Dorothy Wilson (*English*)
   Pauline Darroll (*English*)
Monostatos   Duncan Robertson (*Scottish*)
Pamina   Judith Raskin (*American*)
The Speaker   Delme Bryn Jones (*Welsh*)
Sarastro   Carlo Cava (*Italian*)
Priests and Men in Armour   Dennis Brandt
   (*English*)
   Dennis Wicks (*English*)
Papagena   Maria Zeri (*Greek*)

Conductors VITTORIO GUI, BRYAN BALKWILL
Producer FRANCO ENRIQUEZ
Associate Producer JOHN COX
Designer EMANUELE LUZZATI

1965

Glyndebourne 16 May–
15 August: 74 performances

Il matrimonio segreto

CIMAROSA *13 performances*

Paolino   Pietro Bottazzo (*Italian*)
Carolina   Margherita Rinaldi (*Italian*)
Geronimo   Carlo Badioli (*Italian*)
Elisetta   Alberta Valentini (*Italian*)
Fidalma   Rosa Laghezza (*Italian*)
Count Robinson   Federico Davià (*Italian*)

Conductors   VITTORIO GUI, MYER FREDMAN
Producer   FRANK HAUSER
Designer   DESMOND HEELEY

Der Rosenkavalier

RICHARD STRAUSS *15 performances*

Oktavian   Teresa Zylis-Gara (*Polish*)
   Josephine Veasey (*English*)
Feldmarschallin   Montserrat Caballé
   (*Spanish*)
   Erika Schmidt (*German*)
Ochs   Manfred Jungwirth (*Austrian*)
   Otto Edelmann (*Austrian*)
Valzacchi   David Hughes (*Welsh*)
Annina   Anna Reynolds (*English*)
Faninal   John Modenos (*American*)
Sophie   Edith Mathis (*Swiss*)
   Liselotte Hammers (*German*)
Duenna   Angela Jenkins (*English*)
Singer   Jon Andrews (*New Zealand*)
Landlord   David Lennox (*English*)
Police Inspector   Richard Golding (*English*)

Conductor   JOHN PRITCHARD
Producer   HANS NEUGEBAUER
Designer   OLIVER MESSEL

Anna Bolena

DONIZETTI *12 performances*

Giovanna   Patricia Johnson (*English*)
Anna   Leyla Gencer (*Turkish*)
   *Gwenyth Annear (1 perf)
Smeton   Maureen Morelle (*English*)
Enrico   Carlo Cava (*Italian*)
Rochefort   Don Garrard (*Canadian*)
Riccardo   Juan Oncina (*Spanish*)
Hervey   Lloyd Strauss Smith (*English*)

Conductors   GIANANDREA GAVAZZENI, MYER
   FREDMAN
Producer   FRANCO ENRIQUEZ
Designer   LORENZO GHIGLIA

*role performed as understudy

Le nozze di Figaro

MOZART *13 performances*

Figaro   Walter Alberti (*Italian*)
Susanna   Lydia Marimpietri (*Italian*)
Bartolo   Federico Davià (*Italian*)
Marcellina   Rosa Laghezza (*Italian*)
Cherubino   Biancamaria Casoni (*Italian*)
Count Almaviva   Gérard Souzay (*French*)
   John Kitchiner (*English*)
   Michel Roux (*French*)
Don Basilio   Hugues Cuenod (*Swiss*)
The Countess   Montserrat Caballé (*Spanish*)
   Lorna Elias (*Welsh*)
   Joan Carlyle (*English*)
Antonio   Derick Davies (*Welsh*)
Barbarina   Audrey Attwood (*English*)
Don Curzio   David Lennox (*English*)

Conductors   VITTORIO GUI, MYER FREDMAN
Producer   DANIEL LEVEUGLE
Designer   OLIVER MESSEL

Macbeth

VERDI *9 performances*

Macbeth   Kostas Paskalis (*Greek*)
Banquo   Michael Langdon (*English*)
Lady Macbeth   Gunilla af Malmborg
   (*Swedish*)
Gentlewoman   Margaret Curphey (*English*)
Macduff   David Hughes (*Welsh*)
Malcolm   Lloyd Strauss Smith (*English*)
Doctor   Derick Davies (*Welsh*)
Servant   Peter Lehmann Bedford (*English*)
Murderer   Paschal Allen (*English*)

Conductor   LAMBERTO GARDELLI
Producer   FRANCO ENRIQUEZ
Associate Producer   DENNIS MAUNDER
Designer   EMANUELE LUZZATI

La pietra del paragone

ROSSINI *12 performances*

Fabrizio   David Hartley (*English*)
Pacuvio   Heinz Blankenburg (*American*)
Ortensia   Anna Reynolds (*English*)
Fulvia   Alberta Valentini (*Italian*)
Asdrubale   Ugo Trama (*Italian*)
Giocondo   Umberto Grilli (*Italian*)
Clarice   Josephine Veasey (*English*)
Macrobio   Michel Roux (*French*)

Conductor   JOHN PRITCHARD
Producer   GÜNTHER RENNERT
Associate Producer   JOAN DOWNES
Designer   OSBERT LANCASTER

Glyndebourne for BBC
Television

L'Heure espagnole

RAVEL *1 performance*

Ramiro   Pierre Le Hémonet (*French*)
Torquemada   Hugues Cuenod (*Swiss*)
Concepcion   Lee Venora (*American*)
Gonzalve   Michel Sénéchal (*French*)
Gomez   Victor Autran (*French*)

Conductor   JOHN PRITCHARD
Producer   PETER EBERT
Designer   OSBERT LANCASTER

Arlecchino

BUSONI *1 performance*

Arlecchino   Heinz Blankenburg (*American*)
Ser Matteo   Ian Wallace (*Scottish*)
Abbate Cospicuo   John Modenos (*American*)
Doctor Bombasto   Dennis Wicks (*English*)
Leandro   Murray Dickie (*Scottish*)
Colombina   Lee Venora (*American*)
Annunziata   Silvia Ebert (*English*)

Conductor   JOHN PRITCHARD
Producer   PETER EBERT
Choreographer   PAULINE GRANT
Designer   PETER RICE

Dido and Aeneas

PURCELL *1 performance*
(*arr Benjamin Britten and Imogen Holst*)

Dido   Janet Baker (*English*)
Aeneas   Thomas Hemsley (*English*)
Belinda   Elizabeth Robson (*English*)
Sorceress   Yvonne Minton (*English*)
Sailor   Ryland Davies (*Welsh*)
2nd Woman   Lorna Elias (*Welsh*)
1st Witch and Voice of Mercury   Clare
   Walmesley (*English*)
2nd Witch   Elizabeth Bainbridge (*English*)

Conductor   JOHN PRITCHARD
Producer   FRANCO ENRIQUEZ
Choreographer   PAULINE GRANT
Designer   LORENZO GHIGLIA

1966

Glyndebourne *29 May–31 July*: 67 performances

DOUBLE BILL *13 performances*

Dido and Aeneas

PURCELL
(*arr Benjamin Britten and Imogen Holst*)

Belinda   Sheila Armstrong (*English*)
Dido   Janet Baker (*English*)
Second Lady   Angela Hickey (*English*)
Aeneas   Thomas Hemsley (*English*)
Sorceress   Patricia Johnson (*English*)
First Witch and Voice of Mercury   Clare
   Walmesley (*English*)
Second Witch   Jean Allister (*Irish*)
   Pamela Bowden (*English*)
Sailor   Ryland Davies (*Welsh*)

Conductor JOHN PRITCHARD
Original production FRANCO ENRIQUEZ
Staged by PAULINE GRANT & ALISON BROWNE
Designer LORENZO GHIGLIA
Choreographer PAULINE GRANT

Werther

MASSENET *13 performances*

The Bailiff   Stafford Dean (*English*)
Johann   Anthony Raffell (*English*)
Schmidt   Adrian de Peyer (*English*)
Sophie   Françoise Doué (*French*)
Werther   Jean Brazzi (*French*)
Charlotte   Hélia T'Hezan (*French*)
Albert   Peter Gottlieb (*Brazilian*)
   Pierre Le Hémonet (*French*)

Conductor CARLO FELICE CILLARIO
Producer MICHAEL REDGRAVE
Scenery HENRY BARDON
Costumes DAVID WALKER

L'Heure espagnole

RAVEL

Ramiro   Pierre Le Hémonet (*French*)
Torquemada   Hugues Cuenod (*Swiss*)
Concepcion   Isabel Garcisanz (*Spanish*)
Gonzalve   Michel Sénéchal (*French*)
Gomez   Victor Autran (*French*)

Conductor JOHN PRITCHARD
Producer DENNIS MAUNDER
Designer OSBERT LANCASTER

Die Zauberflöte

MOZART *16 performances*

Tamino   George Shirley (*American*)
Three Ladies   Margaret Kingsley (*English*)
   Anne Pashley (*English*)
   Ann Cooper (*English*)
Papageno   Peter-Christoph Runge (*German*)
   Heinz Blankenburg (*American*)
Queen of the Night   Rae Woodland (*English*)
Three Boys   Annon Lee Silver (*Canadian*)
   Anne Howells (*English*)
   Janet Kenny (*New Zealand*)
Monostatos   Hugues Cuenod (*Swiss*)
Pamina   Arlene Saunders (*American*)
The Speaker   Thomas Hemsley (*English*)
   Brian Donlan (*English*)
Sarastro   Victor de Narké (*Argentinian*)
Priests and Men in Armour   Ryland Davies
   (*Welsh*)
   Richard Van Allan (*English*)
Papagena   Sheila Armstrong (*English*)

Conductors HANS GIERSTER, MYER FREDMAN
Original production FRANCO ENRIQUEZ
Staged by DENNIS MAUNDER
Designer EMANUELE LUZZATI

Jephtha

HANDEL *12 performances*
(*Oratorio in two parts realized for scenic performance by Caspar Neher and Günther Rennert*)

Zebul   Don Garrard (*Canadian*)
Jephtha   Richard Lewis (*English*)
Storgè   Patricia Johnson (*English*)
Hamor   Calvin Marsh (*American*)
Iphis   Heather Harper (*Irish*)
Angel   Margaret Price (*Welsh*)

Conductors LEOPOLD LUDWIG, MYER FREDMAN
Producer and Choreographer GÜNTHER
   RENNERT
Original designs CASPAR NEHER
Realized by ERICH KONDRAK
Sponsored by the Peter Stuyvesant Foundation

---

236   *Werther*: Hélia T'Hezan and Jean
Brazzi

1967

Glyndebourne 21 May–31 July: 60 performances

La Bohème

PUCCINI 16 performances

Marcello Attilio D'Orazi (*Italian*)
Rodolfo Ottavio Garaventa (*Italian*)
Colline Federico Davià (*Italian*)
Schaunard Enrico Fissore (*Italian*)
Benoît/Alcindoro Carlo Badioli (*Italian*)
Mimì Anna Novelli (*Italian*)
Musetta Alberta Valentini (*Italian*)
Parpignol Alastair Newlands (*Scottish*)
Sergeant Brian Donlan (*English*)
Customs Officer James Christiansen
  (*English*)

Conductors JOHN PRITCHARD, MYER FREDMAN
Producer MICHAEL REDGRAVE
Scenery HENRY BARDON
Costumes DAVID WALKER

L'elisir d'amore

DONIZETTI 15 performances

Adina Adriana Maliponte (*Italian*)
Nemorino Ugo Benelli (*Italian*)
Belcore Zsolt Bende (*Hungarian*)
Dulcamara Carlo Badioli (*Italian*)
Giannetta Sheila Armstrong (*English*)

Conductors CARLO FELICE CILLARIO, KENNETH
  MONTGOMERY
Producer DENNIS MAUNDER
Designer FRANCO ZEFFIRELLI

L'Ormindo

CAVALLI 15 performances
(arr Raymond Leppard)

Ormindo John Wakefield (*English*)
Amida Peter-Christoph Runge (*German*)
Nerillo Isabel Garcisanz (*Spanish*)
Sicle Irmgard Stadler (*German*)
Melide Maureen Lehane (*English*)
Erice Hugues Cuenod (*Swiss*)
Erisbe Anne Howells (*English*)
Mirinda Jane Berbié (*French*)
King Ariadeno Federico Davià (*Italian*)
Osmano Richard Van Allan (*English*)

Conductor RAYMOND LEPPARD
Producer GÜNTHER RENNERT
Designer ERICH KONDRAK

Don Giovanni

MOZART 14 performances

Leporello Paolo Montarsolo (*Italian*)
Donna Anna Althea Bridges (*Australian*)
Don Giovanni Kostas Paskalis (*Greek*)
The Commendatore Marius Rintzler
  (*Rumanian*)
Don Ottavio Sven Olof Eliasson
  (*Norwegian*) Richard Lewis (*English*)
Donna Elvira Teresa Zylis-Gara (*Polish*)
Zerlina Sheila Armstrong (*English*)
Masetto Leonardo Monreale (*Italian*)

Conductors JOHN PRITCHARD, MYER FREDMAN
Producer FRANCO ENRIQUEZ
Associate Producer DENNIS MAUNDER
Designer EMANUELE LUZZATI
Choreographer ŒNONE TALBOT
Sponsored by the Peter Stuyvesant Foundation

Scandinavian tour 6–22 September: 14 performances Drottningholm, Oslo, Gothenberg, Copenhagen

Don Giovanni

MOZART 7 performances

Leporello Paolo Montarsolo (*Italian*)
Donna Anna Althea Bridges (*Australian*)
Don Giovanni Kostas Paskalis (*Greek*)
The Commendatore Marius Rintzler
  (*Rumanian*)
Don Ottavio Richard Lewis (*English*)
Donna Elvira Luisa Bosabalian (*Lebanese*)
Zerlina Sheila Armstrong (*English*)
Masetto Leonardo Monreale (*Italian*)

Conductors JOHN PRITCHARD, MYER FREDMAN
Producer FRANCO ENRIQUEZ
Associate Producer DENNIS MAUNDER
Designer EMANUELE LUZZATI
Lighting FRANCIS REID
Choreographer ŒNONE TALBOT

Il matrimoni segreto

CIMAROSA 7 performances

Paolino Pietro Bottazzo (*Italian*)
Carolina Margherita Rinaldi (*Italian*)
Geronimo Carlo Badioli (*Italian*)
Elisetta Alberta Valentini (*Italian*)
Fidalma Rosa Laghezza (*Italian*)
Count Robinson Federico Davià (*Italian*)

Conductors JOHN PRITCHARD, MYER FREDMAN
Original Producer FRANK HAUSER
Associate Producer DENNIS MAUNDER
Designer DESMOND HEELEY
Lighting FRANCIS REID

1968

Glyndebourne 23 May– 4 August: 58 performances

Eugene Onegin

TCHAIKOVSKY 17 performances

Larina Pamela Bowden (*English*)
Tatyana Elisabeth Söderström (*Swedish*)
Olga Gertrude Jahn (*German*)
Filippyevna Virginia Popova (*Bulgarian*)
Onegin Assen Selimsky (*Bulgarian*)
Lensky Wieslaw Ochman (*Polish*)
Prince Gremin Kim Borg (*Finnish*)
Petrovich Anthony Williams (*English*)
Zaretsky Richard Van Allan (*English*)
Monsieur Triquet Hugues Cuenod (*Swiss*)

Conductors JOHN PRITCHARD, MYER FREDMAN
Producer MICHAEL HADJIMISCHEV
Designer PIER LUIGI PIZZI
Choreographer PAULINE GRANT

Anna Bolena

DONIZETTI 12 performances

Giovanna Patricia Johnson (*English*)
Anna Milla Andrew (*Canadian*)
Smeton Janet Coster (*English*)
Enrico Marius Rintzler (*Rumanian*)
Rochefort Stafford Dean (*English*)
Riccardo George Shirley (*American*)
Hervey Peter Baillie (*New Zealand*)

Conductor LAMBERTO GARDELLI
Producer FRANCO ENRIQUEZ
Designer LORENZO GHIGLIA

Die Entführung aus dem Serail

MOZART 17 performances

Belmonte Richard Van Vrooman
  (*American*)
  Ryland Davies (*Welsh*)
Osmin Paolo Montarsolo (*Italian*)
  Dmiter Petkov (*Bulgarian*)
Pedrillo Karl-Ernst Mercker (*German*)
Pasha Selim Otakar Kraus (*Czech*)
Constanze Margaret Price (*Welsh*)
Blonde Birgit Nordin (*Swedish*)

Conductors JOHN PRITCHARD, MYER FREDMAN
Producer FRANCO ENRIQUEZ
Designer EMANUELE LUZZATI
Sponsored by the Peter Stuyvesant Foundation

L'Ormindo

CAVALLI *12 performances*
(arr Raymond Leppard)

Ormindo John Wakefield (*English*)
Amida Peter-Christoph Runge (*German*)
Nerillo Isabel Garcisanz (*Spanish*)
Sicle Hanneke van Bork (*Dutch*)
Elizabeth Tippett (*Australian*)
Melide Jean Allister (*Irish*)
Erice Hugues Cuenod (*Swiss*)
Erisbe Anne Howells (*English*)
Mirinda Jane Berbié (*French*)
King Ariadeno Federico Davià (*Italian*)
Osmano Richard Van Allan (*English*)

Conductors RAYMOND LEPPARD, KENNETH
MONTGOMERY
Producer GÜNTHER RENNERT
Associate Producer CHARLES HAMILTON
Designer ERICH KONDRAK

237 Below, Costume design by Lorenzo
Ghiglia for Henry VIII in *Anna Bolena*
238 Above right, *Die Entführung aus dem
Serail*: Margaret Price and Otakar Kraus
239 Below right, *Anna Bolena*, 1968: Milla
Andrew, Marius Rintzler, Patricia
Johnson

1969

Glyndebourne 25 May– 4 August: 60 performances

Così fan tutte

MOZART *19 performances*

Ferrando   Ryland Davies (*Welsh*)
Guglielmo   Knut Skram (*Norwegian*)
Don Alfonso   Paolo Montarsolo (*Italian*)
   Michel Roux (*French*)
Fiordiligi   Hanneke van Bork (*Dutch*)
Dorabella   Anne Howells (*English*)
   ★Rosanne Creffield (*1 perf*)
Despina   Jane Berbié (*French*)
   Maria Casula (*Italian*)

Conductors JOHN PRITCHARD
   MYER FREDMAN
Producer FRANCO ENRIQUEZ
Designer EMANUELE LUZZATI
Sponsored by the Peter Stuyvesant Foundation

★role performed as understudy

240   Costume design by David Walker for Werther

Don Giovanni

MOZART *15 performances*

Leporello   Paolo Montarsolo (*Italian*)
   Richard Van Allan (*English*)
Donna Anna   Phyllis Curtin (*American*)
Don Giovanni   Ruggero Raimondi (*Italian*)
The Commendatore   Marius Rintzler
   (*Rumanian*)
Don Ottavio   Wieslaw Ochman (*Polish*)
Donna Elvira   Irmgard Stadler (*German*)
Zerlina   Sheila Armstrong (*English*)
Masetto   Leonardo Monreale (*Italian*)

Conductor REINHARD PETERS
Producer FRANCO ENRIQUEZ
Designer EMANUELE LUZZATI
Choreographer ŒNONE TALBOT
Sponsored by the Peter Stuyvesant Foundation

Pelléas et Mélisande

DEBUSSY *9 performances*

Pelléas   Peter-Christoph Runge (*German*)
Mélisande   Ileana Cotrubas (*Rumanian*)
   Jill Gomez (*Trinidadian*)
Golaud   Jacques Mars (*French*)
Geneviève   Jocelyn Taillon (*French*)
   Margaret Lensky (*English*)
Arkel   Guus Hoekman (*Dutch*)
Yniold   Anne-Marie Blanzat (*French*)
Doctor   Richard Van Allan (*English*)

Conductor JOHN PRITCHARD
Producer PIERRE MÉDECIN
Designer BENI MONTRESOR

Werther

MASSENET *17 performances*

The Bailiff   Stafford Dean (*English*)
Johann   Richard Van Allan (*English*)
Schmidt   Hugues Cuenod (*Swiss*)
Sophie   Annon Lee Silver (*Canadian*)
   ★Wendy Eathorne (*1 perf*)
Werther   Jean Brazzi (*French*)
Charlotte   Josephine Veasey (*English*)
Albert   Peter Gottlieb (*French*)

Conductor MYER FREDMAN
Producer MICHAEL REDGRAVE
Scenery HENRY BARDON
Costumes DAVID WALKER

★role performed as understudy

1970

Glyndebourne 25 May– 9 August: 66 performances

Die Zauberflöte

MOZART *17 performances*

Tamino   Wieslaw Ochman (*Polish*)
Three Ladies   Teresa Cahill (*English*)
   Rosanna Creffield (*English*)
   Patricia Conti (*English*)
   Gwenyth Annear (*Australian*)
   Yvonne Fuller (*English*)
   Marjory McMichael (*Scottish*)
Papageno   Heinz Blankenburg (*American*)
   Knut Skram (*Norwegian*)
   John Gibbs (*English*)
Queen of the Night   Urszula Koszut (*Polish*)
   Louise Lebrun (*Canadian*)
Three Boys   Wendy Eathorne (*English*)
   Valerie Baulard (*English*)
   Sylvia Eaves (*English*)
Monostatos   Alexander Oliver (*Scottish*)
Pamina   Sheila Armstrong (*English*)
   Ileana Cotrubas (*Rumanian*)
The Speaker   Richard Van Allan (*English*)
Sarastro   Hans Sotin (*German*)
Priests and Men in Armour   Keith Erwen
   (*Welsh*)
   Michael Rippon (*English*)
Papagena   Norma Burrowes (*Irish*)

Conductors REINHARD PETERS, MYER FREDMAN
Producer FRANCO ENRIQUEZ
Designer EMANUELE LUZZATI

La Calisto

CAVALLI *9 performances*
(*arr Raymond Leppard*)

La Natura   Enid Hartle (*English*)
L'Eternità   Margaret Lensky (*English*)
   Sarah Walker (*English*)
Il Destino   Louise Lebrun (*Canadian*)
Giove   Ugo Trama (*Italian*)
Mercurio   Peter Gottlieb (*French*)
Calisto   Ileana Cotrubas (*Rumanian*)
   Jill Gomez (*Trinidadian*)
Endimione   James Bowman (*English*)
Diana   Janet Baker (*English*)
   Sarah Walker (*English*)
Linfea   Hugues Cuenod (*Swiss*)
Satirino   Janet Hughes (*English*)
Pane   Federico Davià (*Italian*)
Silvano   Owen Brannigan (*English*)
Giunone   Irmgard Stadler (*German*)

Conductor RAYMOND LEPPARD
Producer PETER HALL
Designer JOHN BURY

The Rising of the Moon

NICHOLAS MAW *8 performances*
World première

Brother Timothy   Alexander Oliver
  (*Scottish*)
Cathleen Sweeney   Anne Howells (*English*)
Donal O'Dowd   John Gibbs (*English*)
Lord Francis Jowler   Richard Van Allan
  (*English*)
  ★Wyndham Parfitt (*1 perf*)
Captain Lillywhite   John Fryatt (*English*)
Major Max von Zastrow   Peter Gottlieb
  (*French*)
Lady Eugenie Jowler   Rae Woodland
  (*English*)
Frau Elisabeth von Zastrow   Kerstin Meyer
  (*Swedish*)
Miss Atalanta Lillywhite   Annon Lee Silver
  (*Canadian*)
Corporal Haywood   Brian Donlan (*English*)
Cornet John Stephen Beaumont   John
  Wakefield (*English*)
Widow Sweeney   Johanna Peters (*English*)
Mr Lynch   Dennis Wicks (*English*)

Conductor   RAYMOND LEPPARD
Producer   COLIN GRAHAM
Designer   OSBERT LANCASTER

★role performed as understudy

Eugene Onegin

TCHAIKOVSKY *16 performances*

Larina   Pamela Bowden (*English*)
Tatyana   Katja Usunov (*Austro-Bulgarian*)
Olga   Alexandrina Milcheva (*Bulgarian*)
Filippyevna   Virginia Popova (*Bulgarian*)
Onegin   Nikola Vassilev (*Bulgarian*)
Lensky   Wieslaw Ochman (*Polish*)
Prince Gremin   Dmiter Petkov (*Bulgarian*)
Petrovich   William Elvin (*Scottish*)
Zaretsky   Richard Van Allan (*English*)
Monsieur Triquet   Hugues Cuenod (*Swiss*)

Conductors   JOHN PRITCHARD, MYER FREDMAN
Producer   MICHAEL HADJIMISCHEV
Designer   PIER LUIGI PIZZI
Choreographer   PAULINE GRANT

Il turco in Italia

ROSSINI *16 performances*

Zaida   Isabel Garcisanz (*Spanish*)
Albazar   John Fryatt (*English*)
The Poet   Michel Roux (*French*)
Don Geronio   Elfego Esparza (*American*)
Fiorilla   Graziella Sciutti (*Italian*)
  Sheila Armstrong (*English*)
Selim   Paolo Montarsolo (*Italian*)
Narciso   Ugo Benelli (*Italian*)

Conductors   JOHN PRITCHARD, MYER FREDMAN
Producer   JOHN COX
Designer   EMANUELE LUZZATI
Sponsored by the Peter Stuyvesant Foundation

Brussels 8 and 9 September

Pelléas et Mélisande

DEBUSSY *2 concert performances*

Pelléas   Peter-Christoph Runge (*German*)
Mélisande   Ileana Cotrubas (*Rumanian*)
Golaud   Jacques Mars (*French*)
Arkel   Guus Hoekman (*Dutch*)
Yniold   Sylvia Eaves (*English*)
Geneviève   Jocelyne Taillon (*French*)
Doctor   Richard Van Allan (*English*)

Conductor   JOHN PRITCHARD
LIEGE SYMPHONY ORCHESTRA

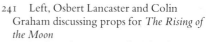

241   Left, Osbert Lancaster and Colin
  Graham discussing props for *The Rising of
  the Moon*
242   Right, John Fryatt and Richard Van
  Allan in *The Rising of the Moon*

243 Above, *Ariadne auf Naxos*, 1971: Dennis Wicks, Maurice Arthur, John Fryatt, John Gibbs, Sylvia Geszty
244 Below, *Falstaff*, 1976: At Herne's Oak: Richard Stilwell as Ford and Donald Gramm as Falstaff
On facing page:
245 Above left, *Le nozze di Figaro*, 1973: Frederica von Stade and Ileana Cotrubas
246 Above right, *The Queen of Spades*
247 Below, *Le nozze di Figaro* (designer John Bury): Frederica von Stade, Benjamin Luxon, Britta Möllerström

1971

*Glyndebourne 23 May–
3 August: 60 performances*

The Queen of Spades

TCHAIKOVSKY *16 performances*

Hermann   Maurice Maievsky (*French*)
  Gheorghi Sapoundjiev (*Bulgarian*)
Count Tomsky   Pavel Guerdjikov
  (*Bulgarian*)
Prince Yeletsky   Assen Selimsky (*Bulgarian*)
Officers   Anthony Roden (*Australian*)
  Michael Rippon (*English*)
  Gavin Walton (*English*)
Chaplitsky   Maurice Arthur (*English*)
Narumov   Brian Donlan (*English*)
The Countess   Virginia Popova (*Bulgarian*)
Lisa   Teresa Kubiak (*Polish*)
Pauline   Reni Penkova (*Bulgarian*)
Governess   Enid Hartle (*English*)
Prilepa   Angela Bostock (*English*)
Master of Ceremonies   Terry Jenkins
  (*English*)
Masha   Kathleen Smales (*English*)

Conductor   JOHN PRITCHARD
Producer   MICHAEL HADJIMISCHEV
Designer   PIER LUIGI PIZZI
Choreographer   PAULINE GRANT

The Rising of the Moon

NICHOLAS MAW *8 performances*

Brother Timothy   Alexander Oliver
  (*Scottish*)
Cathleen Sweeney   Anne Howells (*English*)
  Delia Wallis (*English*)
Donal O'Dowd   John Gibbs (*English*)
Lord Francis Jowler   Richard Van Allan
  (*English*)
Captain Lillywhite   John Fryatt (*English*)
Major Max von Zastrow   Peter Gottlieb
  (*French*)
Lady Eugenie Jowler   Rae Woodland
  (*English*)
Frau Elisabeth von Zastrow   Kerstin Meyer
  (*Swedish*)
Miss Atalanta Lillywhite   Wendy Eathorne
  (*English*), Sara de Javelin (*English*)
Corporal Haywood   Brian Donlan (*English*)
Cornet John Stephen Beaumont   John
  Wakefield (*English*)
Widow Sweeney   Johanna Peters (*English*)
Mr Lynch   Dennis Wicks (*English*)

Conductor   MYER FREDMAN
Producer   COLIN GRAHAM
Assistant Producer   PATRICK LIBBY
Designer   OSBERT LANCASTER

La Calisto

CAVALLI *8 performances*
(arr Raymond Leppard)

La Natura   Marjorie Biggar (*Canadian*)
L'Eternità   Enid Hartle (*English*)
Il Destino   Teresa Cahill (*English*)
Giove   Ugo Trama (*Italian*)
Mercurio   Peter Gottlieb (*French*)
Calisto   Ileana Cotrubas (*Rumanian*)
Endimione   James Bowman (*English*)
Diana   Janet Baker (*English*)
Linfea   Hugues Cuenod (*Swiss*)
Satirino   Janet Hughes (*English*)
Pane   Federico Davià (*Italian*)
Silvano   Owen Brannigan (*English*)
Giunone   Teresa Kubiak (*Polish*)
Echo   Isla Brodie (*Scottish*)

Conductor   RAYMOND LEPPARD
Producer   PETER HALL
Associate producer   PATRICK LIBBY
Design and Lighting   JOHN BURY

Ariadne auf Naxos

RICHARD STRAUSS *16 performances*

Major Domo   Richard Van Allan (*English*)
Music Master   Thomas Hemsley (*English*)
The Composer   Anne Howells (*English*)
  Delia Wallis (*English*)
Bacchus   Helge Brilioth (*Swedish*)
  Wilmer Neufeld (*Canadian*)
Officer   Terry Jenkins (*English*)
Dancing Master   Alexander Oliver (*Scottish*)
Wig Maker   William Elvin (*Scottish*)
Lackey   Thomas Lawlor (*Irish*)
Zerbinetta   Sylvia Geszty (*Hungarian*)
Ariadne   Helen Vanni (*American*)
Harlekin   John Gibbs (*English*)
Scaramuccio   Maurice Arthur (*English*)
Truffaldino   Dennis Wicks (*English*)
Brighella   John Fryatt (*English*)
Najade   Teresa Cahill (*English*)
Dryade   Enid Hartle (*English*)
Echo   Yvonne Fuller (*English*)

Conductor   ALDO CECCATO
Producer   JOHN COX
Designer   MICHAEL ANNALS

Così fan tutte

MOZART *12 performances*

Ferrando   Jerry Jennings (*American*)
Guglielmo   Knut Skram (*Norwegian*)
Don Alfonso   Paolo Montarsolo (*Italian*)
Fiordiligi   Margaret Price (*Welsh*)
  Elizabeth Harwood (*English*)
Dorabella   Edith Thallaug (*Norwegian*)
Despina   Jane Berbié (*French*)

Conductor   JOHN PRITCHARD
Original production by   FRANCO ENRIQUEZ
Revival produced by   PAOLO MONTARSOLO
Associate Producer   ROGER BRUNYATE
Designer   EMANUELE LUZZATI
Sponsored by the Peter Stuyvesant Foundation

---

248   *Così fan tutte* in rehearsal and
  performance, 1971

1972

Glyndebourne 21 May– 1 August: 65 performances

Ariadne auf Naxos

RICHARD STRAUSS *17 performances*

Major Domo   Richard Van Allan (*English*)
   James Atkins (*English*)
Music Master   Thomas Hemsley (*English*)
The Composer   Irmgard Stadler (*German*)
   Delia Wallis (*English*)
Bacchus   Maurice Maievsky (*French*)
   Wilmer Neufeld (*Canadian*)
Officer   James Anderson (*Scottish*)
Dancing Master   Alexander Oliver (*Scottish*)
Wig Maker   William Elvin (*Scottish*)
Lackey   Thomas Lawlor (*Irish*)
Zerbinetta   Sylvia Geszty (*Hungarian*)
   Patricia Wise (*American*)
Ariadne   Gloria Lane (*American*)
   Helen Vanni (*American*)
Harlekin   John Gibbs (*English*)
Scaramuccio   Terry Jenkins (*English*)
Truffaldino   Dennis Wicks (*English*)
Brighella   John Fryatt (*English*)
Najade   Janet Price (*Welsh*)
Dryade   Enid Hartle (*English*)
Echo   Yvonne Fuller (*English*)
   ★Lynn Channing (*1 perf*)

Conductors   MYER FREDMAN, ALDO CECCATO
Producer   JOHN COX
Designer   MICHAEL ANNALS

Die Entführung aus dem Serail

MOZART *18 performances*

Belmonte   Horst Laubenthal (*German*)
   Ryland Davies (*Welsh*)
   ★Anthony Roden (*1 perf*)
Osmin   Marius Rintzler (*Rumanian*)
   Noel Mangin (*New Zealand*)
   Richard Van Allan (*English*)
Pedrillo   Kimmo Lappalainen (*Finnish*)
Pasha Selim   Richard Van Allan (*English*)
   James Atkins (*English*)
Constanze   Sylvia Geszty (*Hungarian*)
   Margaret Price (*Welsh*)
Blonde   Danièle Perriers (*French*)

Conductors   BERNARD HAITINK, JOHN
   PRITCHARD
Producer   JOHN COX
Designer   EMANUELE LUZZATI

★role performed as understudy

Il ritorno d'Ulisse in patria

MONTEVERDI *14 performances*
(arr Raymond Leppard)

L'Humana fragiltà   Annabel Hunt (*English*)
Tempo   Ugo Trama (*Italian*)
Fortuna   Patricia Greig (*Scottish*)
Amore   Laureen Livingstone (*Scottish*)
Penelope   Janet Baker (*English*)
Ericlea   Virginia Popova (*Bulgarian*)
Melanto   Janet Hughes (*English*)
   ★Myrna Moreno (*1 perf*)
Eurimaco   John Wakefield (*English*)
Nettuno   Clifford Grant (*Australian*)
   Robert Lloyd (*English*)
Giove   David Hughes (*Welsh*)
   Brian Burrows (*English*)
Ulisse   Benjamin Luxon (*English*)
Minerva   Anne Howells (*English*)
Eumete   Richard Lewis (*English*)
Iro   Alexander Oliver (*Scottish*)
Telemaco   Ian Caley (*English*)
Antinöo   Ugo Trama (*Italian*)
Anfimono   Bernard Dickerson (*English*)
Pisandro   John Fryatt (*English*)
Giunone   Vivien Townley (*English*)

Conductor   RAYMOND LEPPARD
Producer   PETER HALL
Designer   JOHN BURY

Macbeth

VERDI *15 performances*

Macbeth   Kostas Paskalis (*Greek*)
   Delme Bryn-Jones (*Welsh*)
Banquo   James Morris (*American*)
Lady Macbeth   Joyce Barker (*South African*)
   Gloria Lane (*American*)
Gentlewoman   Rae Woodland (*English*)
   ★Patricia Greig (*1 perf*)
Macduff   Keith Erwen (*Welsh*)
Malcolm   Ian Caley (*English*)
Doctor   Brian Donlan (*English*)
Servant   Ian Caddy (*English*)
Murderer   John Tomlinson (*English*)

Conductors   JOHN PRITCHARD, MYER FREDMAN
Producer   MICHAEL HADJIMISCHEV
Designer   EMANUELE LUZZATI
Choreographer   PAULINE GRANT

★role performed as understudy

Flanders Festival 28–31 August: Brussels and Ghent

La Calisto

CAVALLI *2 performances*

La Natura   Marjorie Biggar (*English*)
L'Eternità   Annabel Hunt (*English*)
Il Destino   Penelope MacKay (*English*)
   Shelagh Squires (*English*)
Giove   Ugo Trama (*Italian*)
Mercurio   Alan Charles (*Welsh*)
Calisto   Jill Gomez (*Trinidadian*)
Endimione   James Bowman (*English*)
Diana   Delia Wallis (*English*)
Linfea   Hugues Cuenod (*Swiss*)
Satirino   Janet Hughes (*English*)
Pane   Simon Estes (*American*)
Silvano   Owen Brannigan (*English*)
   Gavin Walton (*English*)
Giunone   Irmgard Stadler (*Austrian*)
Echo   Isla Brodie (*Scottish*)

Conductor   RAYMOND LEPPARD
Producer   PETER HALL
Designer   JOHN BURY
Lighting   ROBERT BRYAN

BRT KAMERORKEST

249   Janet Baker and Benjamin Luxon as
   Penelope and Ulysses

1973

Glyndebourne 30 May–
14 August: 64 performances

Die Zauberflöte

MOZART *18 performances*

Tamino George Shirley (*American*)
 Anthony Roden (*Australian*)
Three Ladies Linda Esther Gray (*Scottish*)
 Doreen Cryer (*English*)
 Enid Hartle (*English*)
 Gwenyth Annear (*Australian*)
 Patricia Greig (*Scottish*)
 ★Lorna Brindley (*1 perf*)
 Angela Vernon Bates (*English*)
Papageno Thomas Allen (*English*)
 Peter-Christoph Runge (*German*)
Queen of the Night Edita Gruberova
 (*Czech*)
Three Boys Joy Roberts (*English*)
 ★Eiko Nakamura (*1 perf*)
 Annabel Hunt (*English*)
 Susan Lees (*English*)
Monostatos Brian Burrows (*English*)
 Alexander Oliver (*Scottish*)
Pamina Sheila Armstrong (*English*)
 Elisabeth Speiser (*Swiss*)
The Speaker Michael Rippon (*English*)
 Thomas Hemsley (*English*)
Sarastro Robert Lloyd (*English*)
 Manfred Schenk (*German*)
Priests and Men in Armour Anthony Roden
 (*Australian*), Athole Still (*Scottish*), John
 Tomlinson (*English*)
Papagena Elizabeth Gale (*English*)

Conductors BERNARD HAITINK, MYER FREDMAN
Associate Producers JOHN COX, ADRIAN SLACK
Designer EMANUELE LUZZATI

★role performed as understudy

---

250 *La Calisto*, 1970: Hugues Cuenod and
 Janet Hughes

The Visit of the Old Lady

GOTTFRIED VON EINEM *8 performances*
First performance in England

Claire Zachanassian Kerstin Meyer (*Swedish*)
Her Butler Edgar Evans (*Welsh*)
Koby Duncan Robertson (*Scottish*)
Loby Ian Caley (*English*)
Alfred Ill Donald Bell (*Canadian*)
His Wife Rae Woodland (*English*)
His Daughter Sara de Javelin (*Canadian*)
His Son Roderic Keating (*English*)
The Mayor Alan Crofoot (*Canadian*)
The Pastor Don Garrard (*Canadian*)
The Schoolmaster Derek Hammon-Stroud
 (*English*)
The Doctor Brian Donlan (*English*)
Police Chief Michael Rippon (*English*)
First Woman Isla Brodie (*Scottish*)
Second Woman Lorna Brindley (*Scottish*)
Hofbauer Anthony Bremner (*Australian*)
Helmesberger Edward Sadler (*English*)
Station Master Keith Brookes (*English*)
Ticket Inspector John Carr (*English*)
Guard Thomas Lawlor (*Irish*)
Cameraman John Tomlinson (*English*)

Conductors JOHN PRITCHARD, MYER FREDMAN
Producer JOHN COX
Designer MICHAEL ANNALS

Le nozze di Figaro

MOZART *17 performances*

Figaro Knut Skram (*Norwegian*)
Susanna Ileana Cotrubas (*Rumanian*)
 Britta Möllerström (*Swedish*)
Bartolo Marius Rintzler (*Rumanian*)
 Michael Rippon (*English*)
Marcellina Nucci Condò (*Italian*)
Cherubino Frederica von Stade (*American*)
Count Almaviva Benjamin Luxon (*English*)
Don Basilio John Fryatt (*English*)
The Countess Elizabeth Harwood (*English*)
 Kiri Te Kanawa (*New Zealand*)
Antonio Thomas Lawlor (*Irish*)
Barbarina Elizabeth Gale (*English*)
Don Curzio Bernard Dickerson (*English*)

Conductors JOHN PRITCHARD, MYER FREDMAN
Producer PETER HALL
Designer JOHN BURY
Choreographer PAULINE GRANT

Sponsored by the Peter Stuyvesant Foundation

Il ritorno d'Ulisse in patria

MONTEVERDI *11 performances*
(*arr Raymond Leppard*)

L'Humana fragiltà Annabel Hunt (*English*)
Tempo Ugo Trama (*Italian*)
Fortuna Patricia Greig (*Scottish*)
Amore Laureen Livingstone (*Scottish*)
Penelope Janet Baker (*English*)
Ericlea Virginia Popova (*Bulgarian*)
Melanto Janet Hughes (*English*)
Eurimaco John Wakefield (*English*)
Nettuno Robert Lloyd (*English*)
Giove Brian Burrows (*English*)
Ulisse Benjamin Luxon (*English*)
 Richard Stilwell (*American*)
Minerva Anne Howells (*English*)
Eumete Richard Lewis (*English*)
Iro Alexander Oliver (*Scottish*)
Telemaco Ian Caley (*English*)
Antinöo Ugo Trama (*Italian*)
Anfimono Bernard Dickerson (*English*)
Pisandro John Fryatt (*English*)
Giunone Rae Woodland (*English*)

Conductors RAYMOND LEPPARD, HENRY WARD
Producer PETER HALL
Associate Producer PATRICK LIBBY
Designer JOHN BURY

Capriccio

RICHARD STRAUSS *10 performances*

Flamand Leo Goeke (*American*)
Olivier Richard Stilwell (*American*)
La Roche Marius Rintzler (*Rumanian*)
The Countess Elisabeth Söderström (*Swedish*)
The Count Håkan Hagegård (*Swedish*)
Clairon Kerstin Meyer (*Swedish*)
Italian Tenor Ricardo Cassinelli
 (*Argentinian*)
Italian Soprano Eugenia Ratti (*Italian*)
Major Domo Thomas Lawlor (*Irish*)
Monsieur Taupe Hugues Cuenod (*Swiss*)

Conductors JOHN PRITCHARD, ANDREW DAVIS
Producer JOHN COX
Scenery DENNIS LENNON
Costumes MARTIN BATTERSBY
Choreographer PAULINE GRANT

1974
Glyndebourne 23 May– 5 August: 65 performances

La Calisto

CAVALLI *12 performances*
(arr Raymond Leppard)

La Natura   Cynthia Buchan (*Scottish*)
L'Eternità   Linda Esther Gray (*Scottish*)
   Jillian Crowe (*English*)
Il Destino   Patricia Greig (*Scottish*)
   Miriam Bowen (*Welsh*)
Giove   Ugo Trama (*Italian*)
Mercurio   John Fryatt (*English*)
Calisto   Barbara Hendricks (*American*)
Endimione   James Bowman (*English*)
Diana   Anne Howells (*English*)
Linfea   Hugues Cuenod (*Swiss*)
Satirino   Janet Hughes (*English*)
Pane   Ugo Trama (*Italian*)
Silvano   John Tomlinson (*English*)
Giunone   Janet Jacques (*English*)
Echo   Isla Brodie (*Scottish*)

Conductors RAYMOND LEPPARD, KENNETH
   MONTGOMERY
Original production by PETER HALL
Staged by PATRICK LIBBY
Designer JOHN BURY

Idomeneo

MOZART *17 performances*

Ilia   Glenys Fowles (*Australian*)
   Bozena Betley (*Polish*)
Idamante   Kimmo Lappalainen (*Finnish*)
   Leo Goeke (*American*)
Arbace   Alexander Oliver (*Scottish*)
   James Anderson (*Scottish*)
Electra   Krysztina Kujawinska (*Polish*)
   Linda Esther Gray (*Scottish*)
   Josephine Barstow (*English*)
Idomeneo   George Shirley (*American*)
   Richard Lewis (*English*)
High Priest   John Fryatt (*English*)
Voice of Neptune   Dennis Wicks (*English*)

Conductor JOHN PRITCHARD
Producer JOHN COX
Designer ROGER BUTLIN
Sponsored by the Peter Stuyvesant Foundation

Intermezzo

RICHARD STRAUSS *12 performances (in English)*

Christine   Elisabeth Söderström (*Swedish*)
Robert Storch   Marco Bakker (*Dutch*)
Anna   Elizabeth Gale (*English*)
Franzl   Richard Allfrey (*English*)
Therese   Angela Whittingham (*English*)
Fanny   Barbara Dix (*English*)
Marie   Susan Varley (*English*)
Baron Lummer   Alexander Oliver (*Scottish*)
The Lawyer's Wife   Rae Woodland
   (*English*)
Resi   Cynthia Buchan (*Scottish*)
The Commercial Counsellor   Donald Bell
   (*Canadian*)
The Opera Singer   Dennis Wicks (*English*)
Stroh, the Conductor   Anthony Rolfe
   Johnson (*English*)
The Legal Counsellor   Brian Donlan
   (*English*)
The Lawyer   Thomas Lawlor (*Irish*)

Conductor JOHN PRITCHARD
Producer JOHN COX
Designer MARTIN BATTERSBY
Choreographer PAULINE GRANT
Sponsored by the Fred Kobler Trust

Le nozze di Figaro

MOZART *18 performances*

Figaro   Knut Skram (*Norwegian*)
   Thomas Allen (*English*)
Susanna   Evelyn Mandac (*Filipino*)
   Elizabeth Gale (*English*)
Bartolo   Ugo Trama (*Italian*)
Marcellina   Nucci Condò (*Italian*)
Cherubino   Helena Jungwirth-Ahnsjö
   (*Swedish*)
   ★Joy Roberts (*1 perf*)
Count Almaviva   Michael Devlin (*American*)
   Håkan Hagegård (*Swedish*)
Don Basilio   John Fryatt (*English*)
The Countess   Kiri Te Kanawa (*New
   Zealand*)
   Helena Döse (*Swedish*)
Antonio   Thomas Lawlor (*Irish*)
Barbarina   Elizabeth Gale (*English*)
   Susanna Ross (*English*)
Don Curzio   Bernard Dickerson (*English*)

Conductors JOHN PRITCHARD, KENNETH
   MONTGOMERY, PETER GELLHORN
Producer PETER HALL
Associate Producer ADRIAN SLACK
Designer JOHN BURY
Choreographer PAULINE GRANT
Sponsored by the Peter Stuyvesant Foundation

★*role performed as understudy*

The Visit of the Old Lady

GOTTFRIED VON EINEM *6 performances*

Claire Zachanassian   Kerstin Meyer (*Swedish*)
Her Butler   Edgar Evans (*Welsh*)
Koby   Duncan Robertson (*Scottish*)
Loby   Ian Caley (*English*)
Alfred Ill   Donald Bell (*Canadian*)
His Wife   Rae Woodland (*English*)
His Daughter   Cynthia Buchan (*Scottish*)
His Son   Philip Griffiths (*Welsh*)
The Mayor   Alan Crofoot (*Canadian*)
The Pastor   Dennis Wicks (*English*)
The Schoolmaster   Derek Hammond-Stroud
   (*English*)
The Doctor   Brian Donlan (*English*)
Police Chief   Thomas Lawlor (*Irish*)
First Woman   Isla Brodie (*Scottish*)
Second Woman   Lorna Brindley (*Scottish*)
Hofbauer   Anthony Bremner (*Australian*)
Helmesberger   Alan Watt (*Scottish*)
Station Master   Keith Brookes (*English*)
Cameraman   Powell Harrison (*English*)

Conductor MYER FREDMAN
Producer JOHN COX
Designer MICHAEL ANNALS

---

251   Michael Devlin and Kiri Te Kanawa as
   Count and Countess Almaviva

1975

Glyndebourne 22 May– 6 August: 68 performances

The Cunning Little Vixen

JANÁČEK *13 performances (in English)*

The Forester   Benjamin Luxon (*English*)
The Vixen   Norma Burrowes (*Irish*)
The Forester's Wife   Enid Hartle (*English*)
The Dog   Alan Watt (*Scottish*)
The Cock   Hugues Cuenod (*Swiss*)
The Hen   Isla Brodie (*Scottish*)
The Badger   Richard Robson (*English*)
The Parson   Brian Donlan (*English*)
The Schoolmaster   Bernard Dickerson
   (*English*)
The Innkeeper   John Michael Flanagan
   (*English*)
The Fox   Robert Hoyem (*American*)
The Owl/Woodpecker   Enid Hartle (*English*)
The Poacher   Thomas Lawlor (*Irish*)
The Innkeeper's Wife   Barbara Dix (*English*)

Conductor   RAYMOND LEPPARD
Producer   JONATHAN MILLER
Scenery   PATRICK ROBERTSON
Costumes   ROSEMARY VERCOE
Movement   MARK FURNEAUX

Intermezzo

RICHARD STRAUSS *10 performances (in English)*

Christine   Elisabeth Söderström (*Swedish*)
Robert Storch   Marco Bakker (*Dutch*)
Anna   Elizabeth Gale (*English*)
Franzl   James Baker (*English*)
Therese   Catherine McCord (*Scottish*)
Fanny   Jean Williams (*New Zealand*)
Marie   Susan Varley (*English*)
Baron Lummer   Alexander Oliver (*Scottish*)
The Lawyer's Wife   Isla Brodie (*Scottish*)
Resi   Cynthia Buchan (*Scottish*)
The Commercial Counsellor   Alan Watt
   (*Scottish*), Donald Bell (*Canadian*)
The Opera Singer   Dennis Wicks (*English*)
Stroh, the Conductor   Anthony Rolfe
   Johnson (*English*)
The Legal Counsellor   Brian Donlan
   (*English*)
The Lawyer   Thomas Lawlor (*Irish*)

Conductor   JOHN PRITCHARD
Producer   JOHN COX
Designer   MARTIN BATTERSBY
Choreographer   PAULINE GRANT
Sponsored by the Fred Kobler Trust

Eugene Onegin

TCHAIKOVSKY *16 performances*

Larina   Pamela Bowden (*English*)
Tatyana   Galia Yoncheva (*Bulgarian*)
   Elizabeth Tippet (*Australian*)
Olga   Reni Penkova (*Bulgarian*)
   Cynthia Buchan (*Scottish*)
Filippyevna   Virginia Popova (*Bulgarian*)
Lensky   Ryland Davies (*Welsh*)
   Anthony Rolfe Johnson (*English*)
Onegin   Richard Stilwell (*American*)
Prince Gremin   Don Garrard (*Canadian*)
Petrovich   Alan Watt (*Scottish*)
Zaretsky   Thomas Lawlor (*Irish*)
Monsieur Triquet   Hugues Cuenod (*Swiss*)

Conductor   ANDREW DAVIS
Producer   MICHAEL HADJIMISCHEV
Designer   PIER LUIGI PIZZI
Choreographer   PAULINE GRANT

Così fan tutte

MOZART *16 performances*

Ferrando   Robert Johnson (*American*)
   Anson Austin (*Australian*)
Guglielmo   Knut Skram (*Norwegian*)
   Thomas Allen (*English*)
Don Alfonso   Michael Devlin (*American*)
   Frantz Petri (*French*)
Fiordiligi   Bozena Betley (*Polish*)
   Helena Döse (*Swedish*)
Dorabella   Reni Penkova (*Bulgarian*)
   Sylvia Lindenstrand (*Swedish*)
Despina   Evelyn Mandac (*Filipino*)
   Danièle Perriers (*French*)

Conductors   JOHN PRITCHARD, KENNETH
   MONTGOMERY
Producer   ADRIAN SLACK
Designer   EMANUELE LUZZATI
Sponsored by the Peter Stuyvesant Foundation

The Rake's Progress

STRAVINSKY *13 performances*

Anne   Jill Gomez (*Trinidadian*)
Tom Rakewell   Leo Goeke (*American*)
Trulove   Don Garrard (*Canadian*)
Nick Shadow   Donald Gramm (*American*)
Mother Goose   Thetis Blacker (*English*)
Baba the Turk   Rosalind Elias (*American*)
Sellem   John Fryatt (*English*)
Keeper of the Madhouse   Malcolm King
   (*English*)

Conductor   BERNARD HAITINK
Producer   JOHN COX
Designer   DAVID HOCKNEY

252   Raymond Leppard, Jonathan Miller
   and Steuart Bedford in a production
   rehearsal of *The Cunning Little Vixen*

1976

Glyndebourne 1 June–8 August:
62 performances

Falstaff

VERDI *15 performances*

Falstaff   Donald Gramm (*American*)
   Richard Cross (*American*)
Dr Caius   John Fryatt (*English*)
Bardolph   Bernard Dickerson (*English*)
Pistol   Ugo Trama (*Italian*)
Meg Page   Reni Penkova (*Bulgarian*)
Alice Ford   Kay Griffel (*American*)
Mistress Quickly   Nucci Condò (*Italian*)
Nannetta   Elizabeth Gale (*English*)
Fenton   Max-René Cosotti (*Italian*)
   Anthony Rolfe Johnson (*English*)
Ford   Richard Stilwell (*American*)
   Benjamin Luxon (*English*)

Conductors   JOHN PRITCHARD, KENNETH
   MONTGOMERY
Producer and Designer   JEAN-PIERRE PONNELLE
Sponsored by the Fred Kobler Trust and the
   Corbett Foundation of Cincinnati, Ohio

Le nozze di Figaro

MOZART *19 performances*

Figaro   Knut Skram (*Norwegian*)
   Samuel Ramey (*American*)
Susanna   Adrienne Csengery (*Hungarian*)
   Lillian Watson (*English*)
Bartolo   Ugo Trama (*Italian*)
Marcellina   Nucci Condò (*Italian*)
   Joyce McCrindle (*Scottish*)
Cherubino   Cynthia Buchan (*Scottish*)
   Delia Wallis (*English*)
Count Almaviva   Hans Helm (*German*)
   Michael Devlin (*American*)
Don Basilio   John Fryatt (*English*)
The Countess   Bozena Betley (*Polish*)
   Helena Döse (*Swedish*)
Antonio   Thomas Lawlor (*Irish*)
Barbarina   Susanna Ross (*English*)
Don Curzio   Bernard Dickerson (*English*)

Conductors   JOHN PRITCHARD, CALVIN
   SIMMONS
Producer   PETER HALL
Associate Producer   ADRIAN SLACK
Designer   JOHN BURY
Choreographer   PAULINE GRANT
Sponsored by the Peter Stuyvesant Foundation

Capriccio

RICHARD STRAUSS *9 performances*

Flamand   Ryland Davies (*Welsh*)
Olivier   Dale Duesing (*American*)
La Roche   Marius Rintzler (*Rumanian*)
The Countess   Elisabeth Söderström (*Swedish*)
The Count   Håkan Hagegård (*Swedish*)
Clairon   Kerstin Meyer (*Swedish*)
Italian Tenor   Ricardo Cassinelli
   (*Argentinian*)
Italian Soprano   Eugenia Ratti (*Italian*)
Major Domo   Thomas Lawlor (*Irish*)
Monsieur Taupe   Hugues Cuenod (*Swiss*)

Conductor   ANDREW DAVIS
Producer   JOHN COX
Scenery   DENNIS LENNON
Costumes and Furniture   MARTIN BATTERSBY
Choreographer   PAULINE GRANT

Così fan tutte

MOZART *10 performances*

Ferrando   David Kuebler (*American*)
   David Rendall (*English*)
Guglielmo   Knut Skram (*Norwegian*)
Don Alfonso   Frantz Petri (*French*)
Fiordiligi   Bozena Betley (*Polish*)

Dorabella   Trudeliese Schmidt (*German*)
Despina   Lillian Watson (*English*)
   Danièle Perriers (*French*)

Conductor   KENNETH MONTGOMERY
Producer   ADRIAN SLACK
Designer   EMANUELE LUZZATI
Sponsored by the Peter Stuyvesant Foundation

Pelléas et Mélisande

DEBUSSY *9 performances*

Pelléas   André Jobin (*French*)
Mélisande   Anne-Marie Blanzat (*French*)
Golaud   Michael Devlin (*American*)
Geneviève   Jocelyne Taillon (*French*)
Arkel   Don Garrard (*Canadian*)
Yniold   Elisabeth Conquet (*French*)
Doctor   Malcolm King (*English*)

Conductor   BERNARD HAITINK
Producer   RENÉ TERRASSON
Scenery   PATRICK ROBERTSON
Costumes   ROSEMARY VERCOE
Sponsored by the Lily and Henry Davis
   Charitable Trust

253   *Capriccio* (choreographer Pauline
   Grant): Håkan Hagegård, Marius Rintzler
   and Kerstin Meyer

1977

Glyndebourne 31 May– 7 August: 71 performances

Don Giovanni

MOZART *18 performances*

Leporello Stafford Dean (*English*)
 Richard Van Allan (*English*)
Donna Anna Joan Carden (*Australian*)
 Horiana Branisteanu (*Rumanian*)
Don Giovanni Benjamin Luxon (*English*)
 Thomas Allen (*English*)
The Commendatore Pierre Thau (*French*)
Don Ottavio Leo Goeke (*American*)
 Philip Langridge (*English*)
Donna Elvira Rosario Andrade (*Mexican*)
 Rachel Yakar (*French*)
Zerlina Elizabeth Gale (*English*)
 Adrienne Csengery (*Hungarian*)
Masetto John Rawnsley (*English*)

Conductors JOHN PRITCHARD
 BERNARD HAITINK, CALVIN SIMMONS
Producer PETER HALL
Designer JOHN BURY
Choreographer PAULINE GRANT
Sponsored by Imperial Tobacco Ltd

Falstaff

VERDI *17 performances*

Falstaff Renato Capecchi (*Italian*)
 Richard Cross (*American*)
Dr Caius John Fryatt (*English*)
Bardolph Bernard Dickerson (*English*)
Pistol Ugo Trama (*Italian*)
Meg Page Reni Penkova (*Bulgarian*)
Alice Ford Teresa Cahill (*English*)
 Kay Griffel (*American*)
Mistress Quickly Nucci Condò (*Italian*)
Nannetta Elizabeth Gale (*English*)
Fenton Max-René Cosotti (*Italian*)
Ford Brent Ellis (*American*)
 Benjamin Luxon (*English*)

Conductors JOHN PRITCHARD, CALVIN
 SIMMONS
Produced and designed by JEAN-PIERRE
 PONNELLE
Rehearsed by JULIAN HOPE
*Sponsored by the Fred Kobler Trust and the
 Corbett Foundation of Cincinnati, Ohio*

Die schweigsame Frau

RICHARD STRAUSS *10 performances*

Morosus Richard Cross (*American*)
Theodosia Johanna Peters (*English*)
Schneidebart Peter Gottlieb (*French*)
Henry Jerome Pruett (*American*)
Aminta Janet Perry (*American*)
Isotta Nan Christie (*Scottish*)
Carlotta Enid Hartle (*English*)
Morbio Alan Watt (*Scottish*)
Vanuzzi Federico Davià (*Italian*)
Farfallo Ugo Trama (*Italian*)

Conductor ANDREW DAVIS
Producer JOHN COX
Designer MICHAEL ANNALS

DOUBLE BILL: *9 performances*

La Voix humaine

POULENC

Elle Graziella Sciutti (*Italian*)

Conductor CALVIN SIMMONS
Producer GRAZIELLA SCIUTTI
Designer MARTIN BATTERSBY

The Cunning Little Vixen

JANÁČEK (*in English*)

The Forester Thomas Allen (*English*)
The Vixen Norma Burrowes (*Irish*)
 Eilene Hannan (*Australian*)
The Forester's Wife Enid Hartle (*English*)
The Dog Alan Watt (*Scottish*)
The Cock Hugues Cuenod (*Swiss*)
The Hen Isla Brodie (*Scottish*)
The Badger Michael Lewis (*English*)
The Parson Brian Donlan (*English*)
The Schoolmaster Bernard Dickerson (*English*)
The Innkeeper John Michael Flanagan
 (*English*)
The Fox Robert Hoyem (*American*)
The Owl/Woodpecker Enid Hartle (*English*)
The Poacher Thomas Lawlor (*Irish*)
The Innkeeper's Wife Phyllis Cannan
 (*Scottish*)

Conductor SIMON RATTLE
Producer JONATHAN MILLER
Scenery PATRICK ROBERTSON
Costumes ROSEMARY VERCOE
Movement STUART COX

The Rake's Progress

STRAVINSKY *8 performances*

Anne Felicity Lott (*English*)
Tom Rakewell Leo Goeke (*American*)
Trulove Richard Van Allan (*English*)
Nick Shadow Samuel Ramey (*American*)
Mother Goose Nuala Willis (*Irish*)
Baba the Turk Rosalind Elias (*American*)
Sellem John Fryatt (*English*)
Keeper of the Madhouse Thomas Lawlor
 (*Irish*)

Conductor BERNARD HAITINK
Producer JOHN COX
Designer DAVID HOCKNEY

254 *Die schweigsame Frau*, 1979: Kate
Flowers and Marius Rintzler

1978

Glyndebourne 28 May–
7 August: 64 performances

Die Zauberflöte

MOZART *16 performances*

Tamino Leo Goeke (*American*)
Three Ladies Mani Mekler (*Israeli*)
  Patricia Parker (*English*)
  Nucci Condò (*Italian*)
Papageno Benjamin Luxon (*English*)
Queen of the Night May Sandoz (*American*)
  Sylvia Greenberg (*Israeli*)
Three Boys Kate Flowers (*English*)
  Lindsay John (*English*)
  Elizabeth Stokes (*English*)
Monostatos John Fryatt (*English*)
Pamina Isobel Buchanan (*Scottish*)
  Felicity Lott (*English*)
The Speaker Willard White (*Jamaican*)
  ★Henry Herford (*2 perfs*)
Sarastro Thomas Thomaschke (*German*)
  Kolos Kovats (*Hungarian*)
Priest Richard Berkeley Steel (*English*)
Men in Armour Neil McKinnon (*Scottish*)
  John Rath (*English*)
Papagena Elisabeth Conquet (*French*)

Conductors ANDREW DAVIS, BERNARD HAITINK
Producer JOHN COX
Associate Producer GUUS MOSTART
Designer DAVID HOCKNEY
Sponsored by Imperial Tobacco Ltd

Don Giovanni

MOZART *9 performances*

Leporello Stafford Dean (*English*)
  Malcolm King (*English*)
Donna Anna Norma Sharp (*American*)
Don Giovanni Brent Ellis (*American*)
The Commendatore Leonard Mroż (*Polish*)
Don Ottavio Philip Langridge (*English*)
  Keith Lewis (*New Zealand*)
Donna Elvira Rosario Andrade (*Mexican*)
Zerlina Elizabeth Gale (*English*)
Masetto John Rawnsley (*English*)

Conductors KENNETH MONTGOMERY
  NICHOLAS BRAITHWAITE
Original production by PETER HALL
Staged by STEWART TROTTER
Designer JOHN BURY
Choreographer PAULINE GRANT
Sponsored by Imperial Tobacco Ltd

★role performed as understudy

La Bohème

PUCCINI *16 performances*

Marcello Brent Ellis (*American*)
  John Rawnsley (*English*)
Rodolfo Alberto Cupido (*Italian*)
Colline Willard White (*Jamaican*)
Schaunard Alan Charles (*Welsh*)
Benoît Thomas Lawlor (*Irish*)
Mimì Linda Zoghby (*American*)
Musetta Ashley Putnam (*American*)
Alcindoro Federico Davià (*Italian*)
Parpignol Neil McKinnon (*Scottish*)
Sergeant Brian Donlan (*English*)
Customs Officer Paul Nemeer (*English*)

Conductors NICOLA RESCIGNO, NICHOLAS
  BRAITHWAITE
Producer JOHN COX
Associate Producer JULIAN HOPE
Scenery HENRY BARDON
Costumes DAVID WALKER
Sponsored by the Peter Stuyvesant Foundation

---

255 *Die Zauberflöte*, 1978: Patricia Parker,
  Benjamin Luxon, Mani Mekler

Così fan tutte

MOZART *15 performances*

Ferrando Max-René Cosotti (*Italian*)
Guglielmo Håkan Hagegård (*Swedish*)
Don Alfonso Stafford Dean (*English*)
Fiordiligi Bozena Betley (*Polish*)
  ★Helen Walker (*2 perfs*)
Dorabella Maria Ewing (*American*)
  Patricia Parker (*English*)
Despina Nan Christie (*Scottish*)

Conductors BERNARD HAITINK, ED SPANJAARD
Producer PETER HALL
Designer JOHN BURY
Sponsored by National Westminster Bank

The Rake's Progress

STRAVINSKY *6 performances*

Anne Felicity Lott (*English*)
Tom Rakewell Leo Goeke (*American*)
Trulove John Michael Flanagan (*English*)
Nick Shadow Samuel Ramey (*American*)
Mother Goose Nuala Willis (*Irish*)
Baba the Turk Katherine Pring (*English*)
Sellem John Fryatt (*English*)
Keeper of the Madhouse Brian Donlan
  (*English*)

Conductor BERNARD HAITINK
Producer JOHN COX
Associate Producer JULIAN HOPE
Designer DAVID HOCKNEY

★role performed as understudy

1979

Glyndebourne 27 May– 7 August: 62 performances

Il ritorno d'Ulisse in patria

MONTEVERDI 10 performances
(arr Raymond Leppard)

L'Humana fragiltà Diana Montague (*English*)
Tempo Ugo Trama (*Italian*)
Fortuna Lynda Russell (*English*)
Amore Kate Flowers (*English*)
Penelope Frederica von Stade (*American*)
Ericlea Nucci Condò (*Italian*)
Melanto Patricia Parker (*English*)
Eurimaco Max-René Cosotti (*Italian*)
Nettuno Roger Bryson (*English*)
Giove Keith Lewis (*New Zealand*)
  ★Kevin John (*1 perf*)
Ulisse Richard Stilwell (*American*)
Minerva Ann Murray (*Irish*)
Eumete Richard Lewis (*English*)
Iro Alexander Oliver (*Scottish*)
Telemaco Patrick Power (*New Zealand*)
Antinöo Ugo Trama (*Italian*)
Anfimono Bernard Dickerson (*English*)
Pisandro John Fryatt (*English*)
Giunone Claire Powell (*English*)

Conductor RAYMOND LEPPARD
Original production PETER HALL
Revived by PATRICK LIBBY
Associate DAVE HEATHER
Designer JOHN BURY

La fedeltà premiata

HAYDN 12 performances

Nerina Kathleen Battle (*American*)
Lindoro James Atherton (*American*)
Melibeo Richard Van Allan (*English*)
Amaranta Sylvia Lindenstrand (*Swedish*)
Perrucchetto Thomas Allen (*English*)
Fileno Max-René Cosotti (*Italian*)
Celia Julia Hamari (*Hungarian*)
Diana Eiddwen Harrhy (*Welsh*)

Conductors BERNARD HAITINK, NICHOLAS
  BRAITHWAITE
Producer JOHN COX
Designer HUGH CASSON
Sponsored by the Fred Kobler Trust

Die schweigsame Frau

RICHARD STRAUSS 11 performances

Morosus Marius Rintzler (*Rumanian*)
Theodosia Johanna Peters (*English*)
Schneidebart Peter Gottlieb (*French*)
Henry Jerome Pruett (*American*)
Aminta Krisztina Laki (*Hungarian*)
Isotta Kate Flowers (*English*)
Carlotta Enid Hartle (*English*)
Morbio Alan Watt (*Scottish*)
Vanuzzi Joseph Rouleau (*Canadian*)
Farfallo Ugo Trama (*Italian*)

Conductors ANDREW DAVIS, STEPHEN BARLOW
Producer JOHN COX
Designer MICHAEL ANNALS
Sponsored by the Peter Stuyvesant Foundation

Così fan tutte

MOZART 17 performances

Ferrando John Aler (*American*)
Guglielmo Alan Titus (*American*)
  ★Richard Jackson (*1 perf*)
Don Alfonso Stafford Dean (*English*)
  ★Brian Donlan (*1 perf*)
Fiordiligi Bozena Betley (*Polish*)
Dorabella Patricia Parker (*English*)
Despina Nan Christie (*Scottish*)

Conductors BERNARD HAITINK, NICHOLAS
  BRAITHWAITE
Original production by PETER HALL
Staged by GUUS MOSTART
Designer JOHN BURY
Sponsored by National Westminster Bank

★role performed as understudy

---

256 Far left, Frederica von Stade as
  Penelope and Richard Stilwell as Ulysses
257 Left, *La fedeltà premiata*

1980

Glyndebourne 27 May– 11 August: 64 performances

Die Entführung aus dem Serail

MOZART *12 performances*

Belmonte   Gösta Winbergh (*Swedish*)
Osmin   Willard White (*Jamaican*)
Pedrillo   James Hoback (*American*)
Pasha Selim   Thomas Thomaschke
   (*German*)
   Christopher Blades (*English*)
Constanze   Valerie Masterson (*English*)
Blonde   Lillian Watson (*English*)

Conductor   GUSTAV KUHN
Producer   PETER WOOD
Associate Producer   GUUS MOSTART
Designer   WILLIAM DUDLEY
*Sponsored by Dredsner Bank and Deutsche BP
   A.G.*

Falstaff

VERDI *14 performances*

Falstaff   Renato Capecchi (*Italian*)
Dr Caius   John Fryatt (*English*)
Bardolph   Bernard Dickerson (*English*)
   ★Adrian Scott (*1 perf*)
Pistol   Ugo Trama (*Italian*)
Meg Page   Claire Powell (*English*)
Alice Ford   Teresa Cahill (*English*)
Mistress Quickly   Nucci Condò (*Italian*)
Nannetta   Lucia Aliberti (*Italian*)
Fenton   Max-René Cosotti (*Italian*)
Ford   Alberto Rinaldi (*Italian*)

Conductor   ANDREW DAVIS
Original Production and Designs by JEAN-
   PIERRE PONNELLE
Staged by JULIAN HOPE
*Revival sponsored by the Peter Stuyvesant
   Foundation*

★role performed as understudy

La fedeltà premiata

HAYDN *8 performances*

Nerina   Kate Flowers (*English*)
Lindoro   James Atherton (*American*)
Melibeo   Ferruccio Furlanetto (*Italian*)
Amaranta   Linda Zoghby (*American*)
Perrucchetto   John Rawnsley (*English*)
Fileno   Max-René Cosotti (*Italian*)
Celia   Evelyn Petros (*American*)
Diana   Elizabeth Ritchie (*English*)

Conductor   SIMON RATTLE
Producer   JOHN COX
Designer   HUGH CASSON
Sponsored by the Fred Kobler Trust

Die Zauberflöte

MOZART *14 performances*

Tamino   Ryland Davies (*Welsh*)
Three Ladies   Catherine McCord (*Scottish*)
   Maria Moll (*English*)
   Fiona Kimm (*English*)
Papageno   Stephen Dickson (*American*)
   Benjamin Luxon (*English*)
Queen of the Night   Rita Shane (*American*)
Three Boys   Deborah Rees (*Welsh*)
   ★Delith Brook (*1 perf*)
   Yvonne Lea (*English*), Jane Findlay (*English*)
Monostatos   Francis Egerton (*Irish*)
Pamina   Norma Burrowes (*Irish*)
   Isobel Buchanan (*Scottish*)
The Speaker   Willard White (*Jamaican*)
Sarastro   Thomas Thomaschke (*German*)
Priest   Hugh Hetherington (*English*)
Men in Armour   David Johnston (*English*)
   Roger Bryson (*English*)
Papagena   Meryl Drower (*Welsh*)

Conductors   ANDREW DAVIS, BERNARD HAITINK
Original production by JOHN COX
Rehearsed by JOHN COX *and* GUUS MOSTART
Designer   DAVID HOCKNEY
Sponsored by Imperial Tobacco Ltd

★role performed as understudy

Der Rosenkavalier

RICHARD STRAUSS *16 performances*

Oktavian   Felicity Lott (*English*)
Feldmarschallin   Rachel Yakar (*French*)
   Elizabeth Harwood (*English*)
Ochs   Donald Gramm (*American*)
   Artur Korn (*Austrian*)
Valzacchi   John Fryatt (*English*)
Annina   Nucci Condò (*Italian*)
Faninal   Derek Hammond-Stroud (*English*)
Sophie   Krisztina Laki (*Hungarian*)
   ★Deborah Rees (*1 perf*)
Duenna   Rae Woodland (*English*)
Singer   Dennis O'Neill (*Welsh*)
Landlord   Bernard Dickerson (*English*)
Police Inspector   David Wilson-Johnson
   (*English*)
   ★Andrew Gallacher (*1 perf*)

Conductor   BERNARD HAITINK
Producer   JOHN COX
Designer   ERTÉ
Sponsored by Imperial Tobacco Ltd

★role performed as understudy

258   Above, Willard White and Gösta
   Winbergh as Osmin and Belmonte

Fidelio

BEETHOVEN *12 performances*

Jaquino   Ian Caley (*English*)
Marzelline   Elizabeth Gale (*English*)
   ★Lynda Russell (*2 perfs*)
Rocco   Curt Applegren (*Swedish*)
Leonore   Elisabeth Söderström (*Swedish*)
Pizarro   Robert Allman (*Australian*)
Florestan   Anton de Ridder (*Dutch*)
Don Fernando   Michael Langdon (*English*)
   ★Phillip Bromley (*1 perf*)

Conductor   BERNARD HAITINK
Producer   PETER HALL
Associate Producer   GUUS MOSTART
Design and Lighting   JOHN BURY
Sponsored by Imperial Tobacco Ltd.

★role performed as understudy

1981

Paris 12–17 November: 4 performances

The Rake's Progress

As 1978 cast except

Trulove   Don Garrard (*Canadian*)
Baba the Turk   Rosalind Elias (*American*)
Nick Shadow   John Pringle (*Australian*)

259   Costume design by Michael Annals for
Ariadne auf Naxos

Glyndebourne Festival Opera 1971
Ariadne auf Naxos

Arlecchino. — Mr. John Gibbs.   Michael Annals 71.

Glyndebourne 27 May– 11 August: 64 performances

Il barbiere di Siviglia

ROSSINI   *16 performances*

Fiorello   Robert Dean (*English*)
Count Almaviva   Max-René Cosotti
   (*Italian*)
Figaro   John Rawnsley (*English*)
Rosina   Maria Ewing (*American*)
   Zehava Gal (*Israeli*)
   ★Yvonne Lea (*2 perfs*)
Bartolo   Claudio Desderi (*Italian*)
Berta   Catherine McCord (*Scottish*)
Basilio   Ferruccio Furlanetto (*Italian*)
Officer   Hugh Davies (*English*)

Conductors   SYLVAIN CAMBRELING, ELGAR
   HOWARTH
Producer   JOHN COX
Associate Producer   MICHAEL BEAUCHAMP
Designer   WILLIAM DUDLEY
Lighting Designer   ROBERT BRYAN
Sponsored by Imperial Tobacco Limited

A Midsummer Night's Dream

BRITTEN   *10 performances*

Cobweb   Martin Warr (*English*)
Mustardseed   Jonathan Whiting (*English*)
Peaseblossom   Stephen Jones (*English*)
Moth   Stuart King (*English*)
Puck   Damien Nash (*English*)
Tytania   Ileana Cotrubas (*Rumanian*)
   Lillian Watson (*English*)
Oberon   James Bowman (*English*)
Lysander   Ryland Davies (*Welsh*)
Demetrius   Dale Duesing (*American*)
Hermia   Cynthia Buchan (*Scottish*)
Helena   Felicity Lott (*English*)
Quince   Roger Bryson (*English*)
Snug   Andrew Gallacher (*English*)
Starveling   Donald Bell (*Canadian*)
Flute   Patrick Power (*New Zealand*)
Snout   Adrian Thompson (*English*)
Bottom   Curt Applegren (*Swedish*)
Theseus   Lieuwe Visser (*Dutch*)
Hippolyta   Claire Powell (*English*)

Conductor   BERNARD HAITINK
Producer   PETER HALL
Design and Lighting   JOHN BURY
*Sponsored by Commercial Union Assurance
   Company Limited*

★role performed as understudy

Le nozze di Figaro

MOZART   *16 performances*

Figaro   Alberto Rinaldi (*Italian*)
   Knut Skram (*Norwegian*)
Susanna   Norma Burrowes (*Irish*)
   Maria Fausta Gallamini (*Italian*)
Bartolo   Arthur Korn (*Austrian*)
   Roger Bryson (*English*)
Marcellina   Nucci Condò (*Italian*)
Cherubino   Faith Esham (*American*)
   Colette Alliot-Lugaz (*French*)
Don Basilio   John Fryatt (*English*)
Count Almaviva   Richard Stilwell
   (*American*)
   Alan Titus (*American*)
The Countess   Isobel Buchanan (*Scottish*)
   Felicity Lott (*English*)
Antonio   Brian Donlan (*English*)
Don Curzio   Bernard Dickerson (*English*)
Barbarina   Deborah Rees (*Welsh*)
   ★Delith Brook (*1 perf*)

Conductors   ELIAHU INBAL, GUSTAV KUHN,
   NICHOLAS KRAEMER
Producer   PETER HALL
Associate Producer   ROGER WILLIAMS
Choreographer   PAULINE GRANT
Design and Lighting   JOHN BURY
*Revival sponsored by Meridian International
   Credit Corporation Limited*

Fidelio

BEETHOVEN   *10 performances*

Jaquino   Patrick Power (*New Zealand*)
Marzelline   Elizabeth Gale (*English*)
Rocco   Curt Appelgren (*Swedish*)
Leonore   Josephine Barstow (*English*)
Don Pizarro   Malcolm Donnelly
   (*Australian*)
First Prisoner   David Johnston (*English*)
Second Prisoner   Roger Bryson (*English*)
Florestan   Anton de Ridder (*Dutch*)
Don Fernando   Roderick Kennedy (*English*)

Conductor   BERNARD HAITINK
Original production by   PETER HALL
Revival Producer   GUUS MOSTART
Design and Lighting   JOHN BURY
Sponsored by Imperial Tobacco Limited

★role performed as understudy

1982

Ariadne auf Naxos

RICHARD STRAUSS *12 performances*

Major Domo William Fox (*English*)
Music Master Donald Bell (*Canadian*)
The Composer Maria Ewing (*American*)
 ★Christine Botes (*1 perf*)
Bacchus Dennis Bailey (*American*)
Officer Hugh Hetherington (*English*)
Dancing Master Alexander Oliver (*Scottish*)
Wig Maker Omar Ebrahim (*English*)
Lackey John Hall (*English*)
Zerbinetta Gianna Rolandi (*American*)
Ariadne Helena Döse (*Swedish*)
Harlekin Dale Duesing (*American*)
Scaramuccio Alexander Oliver (*Scottish*)
Truffaldino Willard White (*Jamaican*)
Brighella John Fryatt (*English*)
Najade Deborah Rees (*Welsh*)
Dryade Fiona Kimm (*English*)
Echo Elizabeth Ritchie (*English*)

Conductors SIMON RATTLE, NICHOLAS
 KRAEMER, GUSTAV KUHN
Producer JOHN COX
Designer MICHAEL ANNALS
Lighting Designer ROBERT BRYAN
*Revival sponsored by the Peter Stuyvesant
 Foundation*

Il barbiere di Siviglia

ROSSINI *16 performances*

Fiorello Stephen Rhys-Williams (*English*)
Count Almaviva Robert Gambill
 (*American*)
 Ugo Benelli (*Italian*)
Figaro John Rawnsley (*English*)
Rosina Zehava Gal (*Israeli*)
 Maria Ewing (*American*)
 ★Yvonne Lea (*1 perf*)
Bartolo Andrew Foldi (*American*)
 Claudio Desderi (*Italian*)
Berta Catherine McCord (*Scottish*)
Basilio Curt Appelgren (*Swedish*)

Conductors SYLVAIN CAMBRELING, JANE
 GLOVER
Producer JOHN COX
Associate Producer STEFAN JANSKI
Designer WILLIAM DUDLEY
Lighting Designer ROBERT BRYAN
Sponsored by John Player & Sons

*role performed as understudy

Orfeo ed Euridice

GLUCK *10 performances*

Orfeo Janet Baker (*English*)
Amore Elizabeth Gale (*English*)
Euridice Elisabeth Speiser (*Swiss*)

Conductor RAYMOND LEPPARD
Producer PETER HALL
Associate Producer GUUS MOSTART
Design and Lighting JOHN BURY
Movement STUART HOPPS
Sponsored by John Player & Sons

---

260 *Ariadne auf Naxos*: Helena Döse and
 Dennis Bailey

Over page:
261 Above left, *Fidelio*: Curt Appelgren,
 Elisabeth Söderström and Elizabeth Gale
262 Below left, *Il barbiere di Siviglia*: John
 Rawnsley, Maria Ewing and Ugo Benelli
263 Right, Dame Janet Baker takes her
 final bow on stage after the last
 performance of *Orfeo*, 17 July 1982

L'Amour des Trois Oranges

PROKOFIEV *10 performances*

Herald   Roger Bryson (*English*)
The King   Willard White (*Jamaican*)
Pantalon   Peter-Christoph Runge (*German*)
Trouffaldino   Ugo Benelli (*Italian*)
Léandre   John Pringle (*Australian*)
Tchélio   Richard Van Allan (*English*)
Fata Morgana   Nelly Morporgo (*Dutch*)
Princess Clarice   Nucci Condò (*Italian*)
Sméraldine   Fiona Kimm (*English*)
The Prince   Ryland Davies (*Welsh*)
Farfarello   Derek Hammond-Stroud (*English*)
Cook   Roger Bryson (*English*)
Linette   Yvonne Lea (*English*)
Nicolette   Susan Moore (*Australian*)
Ninette   Colette Alliot-Lugaz (*French*)
Master of Ceremonies   Hugh Hetherington
   (*English*)

Conductor   BERNARD HAITINK
Producer   FRANK CORSARO
Associate Producer   ROBERT CARSEN
Designer   MAURICE SENDAK
Choreographer   PAULINE GRANT
Lighting   ROBERT BRYAN
Sponsored by Cointreau SA

Der Rosenkavalier

RICHARD STRAUSS *14 performances*

Oktavian   Felicity Lott (*English*)
Marschallin   Elizabeth Harwood (*English*)
   Rachel Yakar (*French*)
Baron Ochs   Artur Korn (*Austrian*)
   Donald Gramm (*American*)
Valzacchi   John Fryatt (*English*)
Annina   Nucci Condò (*Italian*)
Italian Singer   Pietro Ballo (*Italian*)
Faninal   Derek Hammond-Stroud (*English*)
Duenna   Rae Woodland (*English*)
Sophie   Lillian Watson (*English*)
   Deborah Rees (*Welsh*)

Conductor   SIMON RATTLE
Original production by   JOHN COX
Staged by   ROBERT CARSEN
Designer   ERTÉ
Lighting Designer   KEITH BENSON
Sponsored by John Player & Sons

264   *Der Rosenkavalier*: Krisztina Laki and
   Felicity Lott

Don Giovanni

MOZART *14 performances*

Don Giovanni   Thomas Allen (*English*)
Leporello   Richard Van Allan (*English*)
Donna Elvira   Elizabeth Pruett (*American*)
Donna Anna   Carol Vaness (*American*)
Don Ottavio   Keith Lewis (*New Zealand*)
   ★Glen Winslade (*1 perf*)
Zerlina   Elizabeth Gale (*English*)
Masetto   Gordon Sandison (*Scottish*)
The Commendatore   Dimitri Kavrakos (*Greek*)

Conductors   BERNARD HAITINK, JANE GLOVER
Producer   PETER HALL
Designer   JOHN BURY
Choreographer   PAULINE GRANT
Lighting designer   ROBERT BRYAN
Sponsored by John Player & Sons

★role performed as understudy

1983

Glyndebourne 26 May–
10 August: 64 performances

Idomeneo

MOZART *15 performances*

Ilia Margaret Marshall (*Scottish*)
  Yvonne Kenny (*Australian*)
Idamante Jerry Hadley (*American*)
Electra Carol Vaness (*American*)
Arbace Thomas Hemsley (*English*)
Idomeneo Philip Langridge (*English*)
High Priest Anthony Roden (*Australian*)
Voice of Neptune Roderick Kennedy (*English*)

Conductor BERNARD HAITINK
Director TREVOR NUNN
Associate Director ROBERT CARSEN
Designer JOHN NAPIER
Lighting Designer DAVID HERSEY
Movement MALCOLM GODDARD
Sponsored by Autobar

265 Design by Allen Charles Klein for *La Cenerentola*

La Cenerentola

ROSSINI *16 performances*

Clorinda Marta Taddei (*Italian*)
Tisbe Laura Zannini (*Italian*)
Angelina Kathleen Kuhlmann (*American*)
  ★Jenny Miller (*3 perfs*)
Alidoro Roderick Kennedy (*English*)
Don Magnifico Claudio Desderi (*Italian*)
Ramiro Laurence Dale (*English*)
Dandini Alberto Rinaldi (*Italian*)

Conductors DONATO RENZETTI, STEPHEN
  BARLOW
Director JOHN COX
Associate Director ANDY HINDS
Designer ALLEN CHARLES KLEIN
Lighting Designer ROBERT BRYAN
Sponsored by National Westminster Bank

★role performed as understudy

Die Entführung aus dem Serail

MOZART *11 performances*

Belmonte Ryland Davies (*Welsh*)
Osmin Willard White (*Jamaican*)
Pedrillo Petros Evangelides (*Cypriot*)
Bassa Selim Robert Atzorn (*German*)
Constanze Elizabeth Pruett (*American*)
Blonde Lillian Watson (*English*)
  ★Linda Kitchen (*1 perf*)

Conductors GUSTAV KUHN, JANE GLOVER
Director PETER WOOD
Associate Director STEFAN JANSKI
Designer WILIAM DUDLEY
Lighting Designer ROBERT BRYAN
Sponsored by Dresdner Bank AG and Deutsche
  BP AG

★role performed as understudy

L'Amour des Trois Oranges

PROKOFIEV *10 performances*

Herald Roger Bryson (*English*)
The King Willard White (*Jamaican*)
Pantalon Peter-Christoph Runge (*German*)
Trouffaldino Ugo Benelli (*Italian*)
Léandre John Pringle (*Australian*)
Tchélio Federico Davià (*Italian*)
Fata Morgana Nelly Morpurgo (*Dutch*)
Princess Clarice Nucci Condò (*Italian*)
Sméraldine Sally Burgess (*English*)
The Prince Ryland Davies (*Welsh*)
Farfarello Stephen Rhys-Williams (*English*)
Cook Roger Bryson (*English*)
Linette Anne Mason (*English*)
Nicolette Susan Moore (*Australian*)
Ninette Colette Alliot-Lugaz (*French*)
Master of Ceremonies Hugh Hetherington
  (*English*)

Conductor SIMON RATTLE
Director FRANK CORSARO
Associate Director ROBERT CARSEN
Designer MAURICE SENDAK
Lighting Designer KEITH BENSON
Choreographer PAULINE GRANT
Sponsored by Cointreau SA

Intermezzo

RICHARD STRAUSS *12 performances (in English)*

Christine Felicity Lott (*English*)
Robert Storch John Pringle (*Australian*)
Anna Elizabeth Gale (*English*)
  ★Catherine Benson (*1 perf*)
Franzl Rupert Ashford (*English*)
Therese Maria Jagusz (*English*)
Fanny Yvonne Howard (*English*)
Marie Delith Brook (*English*)
Baron Lummer Ian Caley (*English*)
The Lawyer's Wife Rae Woodland
  (*English*)
Resi Catherine Pierard (*New Zealand*)
The Commercial Counsellor Ian Caddy
  (*English*)
The Opera Singer Andrew Gallacher (*English*)
Stroh, the Conductor Glenn Winslade
  (*Australian*)
The Legal Counsellor Brian Donlan
  (*English*)
The Lawyer Roger Bryson (*English*)

Conductor GUSTAV KUHN
Director JOHN COX
Designer MARTIN BATTERSBY
Lighting Designer ROBERT BRYAN
Assistant Director/Choreographer MONIQUE
  WAGEMAKERS
Sponsored by the Fred Kobler Trust

★role performed as understudy

1984

General Administrator BRIAN DICKIE (1962)
Musical Director BERNARD HAITINK KBE (1972)
Artistic Director SIR PETER HALL CBE (1970)

Conductors BERNARD HAITINK, GUSTAV KUHN (1980), RAYMOND LEPPARD (1952), STEPHEN BARLOW (1977), JANE GLOVER (1979)
Head of Music Staff MARTIN ISEPP (1957)
Senior Coaches JONATHAN HINDEN (1966), JEAN MALLANDAINE (1966)
Chorus Director JANE GLOVER
Repetiteurs IVOR BOLTON (1982), ROBIN BOWMAN (1976), JOYCE FIELDSEND (1983), CHRISTOPHER FIFIELD (1971), HUGH KEELAN (1983), IAIN LEDINGHAM (1981), ANIKO PETER-SZABO (1976), JANE ROBINSON (1982), CRAIG RUTENBERG (1979), CHRISTOPHER WILLIS (1978)
Italian Coaches ROSETTA ELY (1976), GABRIELLA EZRA (1978)
German Coach GERALDINE FRANK (1980)
Librarian JONATHAN BURTON (1975)
Associate CHARMIAN HUGHES (1973)
Directors JOHN COX (1959), PETER HALL
Deputy to the Artistic Director GUUS MOSTART (1977)
Revival Directors MICHAEL MCCAFFERY (1981), ROGER WILLIAMS (1981)
Associate Directors STEPHEN LAWLESS (1976), MONIQUE WAGEMAKERS (1983), RENNIE WRIGHT (1984)
Staff Directors CHRISTOPHER NEWELL (1983), AIDAN LANG (1984), KATE BROWN (1984), LUCY BAILEY (1979)
Choreographers PAULINE GRANT (1950), MONIQUE WAGEMAKERS (1983)
Designers JOHN BURY (1970), JULIA TREVELYAN OMAN (1984)
Lighting Designers ROBERT BRYAN (Lighting Consultant) (1972), JOHN BURY
Production Manager TOM REDMAN (1968)
Personal Assistant to Production Manager SHEILA PURBROOK (1977)
Stage Manager VICTORIA WAKLEY (1982)
Deputy Stage Managers JULIE CROCKER (1978), DAVID LOCKER (1981), NICHOLAS MURRAY (1977)
Assistant Stage Managers CRISPIN AVON (1984), LAURA DEARDS (1984), IAN GLEDHILL (1983), VERONICA PEACE (1983)
Technical Manager ALBERT PULLEN (1951)
Stage Foreman IVOR GREEN (1959)
Staff Carpenters REX CARTER (1954), FRANK EADE (1949), MARTIN SHERIFF (1982)
Head Flyman ALLEN BYFORD (1973)
Deputy Flyman TIMOTHY PULLEN (1970)
Stage Staff GRAHAM ALBOROUGH, BERTIE ARNOLD, PETER SAUNDERS, ROB STEFANELLI, BRIAN THAIN, MARK VAUGHAN, ANDREW VIVIAN, GARY WELLS, CHRISTOPHER WOOD, JULIAN COURT, ADRIAN QUINN, ALAN ZEAL
Lighting Manager KEITH BENSON (1973)
Assistant PAUL PYANT (1974)

Production Electricians HUGH CHINNICK, GREG HAMLIN, PAUL HASTIE, MARK JONATHAN
Chief Electrical Technician PAUL HANRAHAN (1978)
Assistant GARY HANRAHAN (1982)
Wardrode Manager TONY LEDELL (1964)
Chief Cutters ANNIE HADLEY (Wardrobe) (1981), SYLVAN FORDE (Tailoring) (1984)
Junior Cutters HEATHER DICKENS, ANNE MARIE SHAW
Wardrobe Assistants JOANNA COE, TINA CORBETT, JANET GOODERHAM, SUSAN HUDSON, TRACEY MILLARD
Tailoring Assistants AUDREY BERNARD, JOAN COLLOM, GLENN HILLS, MAGGIE POWER, SANDRA VENTRIS
Wardrobe Mistress RUTH FEATHERSTONE (1970)
Assistants KATE HILTON (1982), CATHERINE POWELL (1984)
Chief Dresser KAY CHANDLER (1960)
Wig Manager BARBARA BURROWS (1969)
First Assistant GINA CYGANIK (1979)
Assistants SHAENA GAMBLE, MARIAN STREET, YVONNE SOUTH, CAROLE THOMPSON, TRACEY WINDEBANK, CAMILLA NOLAN
Make-up Manager JEANNIE OGDEN (1983)
Property Manager ANNABELLE HAWTREY (1965)
Assistants MICHAEL READ, TERRI ANDERSON, GRAHAM CONSTABLE, KATE LYONS, VIGEE HARDING, NEIL HARVEY, SALLY V. SMITH, ANTHONY BARNETT
Opera Manager ANTHONY WHITWORTH-JONES (1981)
Planning Co-ordinator CATHERINE LEE (1982)
Assistant to the Opera Manager ROSEMARY WHEELER (1981)
Personal Assistant to the General Administrator SUSAN BINNEY (1981)
Secretary to the General Administrator LUCY DE CASTRO (1983)
Secretary to the Chairman STEPHANIE WARD (1979)
Treasurer JOHN BARDEN (1962)
Assistant Treasurer ADRIAN WINES (1982)
Assistants LESLEY STANSFIELD (1978), KEN WATKINS (1981)
Editor, Festival Programme Book MORAN CAPLAT CBE (1945)
Accommodation Manager JANET MOORES (1934)
Secretary to the House and Accommodation Managers SALLY HART (1980)
House Manager GEOFFREY GILBERTSON (1957)
Chief Telephonists BRENDA HERMITAGE (1969), JOAN PULLEN (1965)
Transport Officer ROSEMARY MARTIN (1975)
Associate DESMOND WORSFOLD (1966)
Press and Public Relations HELEN O'NEILL (1957)
Appointed Photographer GUY GRAVETT (1951)

Information Secretary PAT WALKER (1981)
Gallery Manager JUNE DANDRIDGE (1951)
Assistant JOYCE AKINS (1968)
Head Gardener TERENCE PARKER (1980)
Publicity VIVIENNE MOORE (1983)
Assistant ANDREA EBERT (1983)
Press Secretary JOANNA TOWNSEND (1979)
Box Office Manager SHIRLEY HONER (1979)
Assistant Manager JANET BOYES (1979)
Catering by LETHEBY & CHRISTOPHER LTD

LONDON PHILHARMONIC ORCHESTRA

(Dates in parenthesis indicate year of first Glyndebourne engagement)

266   *Wild Things* rehearsal

Glyndebourne at the National Theatre 9–14 January 1984: 17 performances

Where the Wild Things Are

KNUSSEN *17 performances (World première)*

Max   Karen Beardsley
   Rosemary Hardy
Mama & Tzippy   Mary King
Moishe & Goat   Hugh Hetherington
Bruno   Jeremy Munro
Emile   Stephen Rhys-Williams
Bernard   Andrew Gallacher

Conductors OLIVER KNUSSEN, JANE GLOVER
Director FRANK CORSARO
Associate Director ROBERT CARSEN
Designer MAURICE SENDAK
Movement JONATHAN WOLKEN
Lighting ROBERT BRYAN

Glyndebourne 28 May– 17 August: 66 performances

Così fan tutte

MOZART *13 performances*

Ferrando   Ryland Davies (*Welsh*)
   *Glenn Winslade (*1 perf.*)
Guglielmo   J. Patrick Raftery (*American*)
Don Alfonso   Claudio Desderi (*Italian*)
Fiordiligi   Carol Vaness (*American*)
Dorabella   Delores Ziegler (*American*)
Despina   Jane Berbié (*French*)

Conductor GUSTAV KUHN
Director PETER HALL
Associate Director STEPHEN LAWLESS
Design and Lighting JOHN BURY
Sponsored by National Westminster Bank

*role performed as understudy

A Midsummer Night's Dream

BRITTEN *9 performances*

Cobweb   James Cook (*English*)
Mustardseed   Michael Brierley (*English*)
Peaseblossom   Christopher Hollands
   (*English*)
Moth   Richard Peachey (*English*)
Puck   Jamie Gates (*English*)
Tytania   Elizabeth Gale (*English*)
Oberon   James Bowman (*English*)
Lysander   Ryland Davies (*Welsh*)
Demetrius   Dale Duesing (*American*)
Hermia   Cynthia Buchan (*Scottish*)
Helena   Jill Gomez (*Trinidadian*)
Quince   Roger Bryson (*English*)
Snug   Andrew Gallacher (*English*)
Starveling   Geoffrey Moses (*Welsh*)
Flute   Patrick Power (*New Zealand*)
Snout   Adrian Thompson (*English*)
Bottom   Curt Applegren (*Swedish*)
Theseus   Roderick Kennedy (*English*)
Hippolyta   Jean Rigby (*English*)

Conductors BERNARD HAITINK, JANE GLOVER
Original Director PETER HALL
Revival Director MICHAEL MCCAFFERY
Design and Lighting JOHN BURY
Choreographer PAULINE GRANT
*Sponsored by Commercial Union Assurance
   Company plc*

Le nozze di Figaro

MOZART *16 performances*

Figaro   Claudio Desderi (*Italian*)
   Alberto Rinaldi (*Italian*)
Susanna   Gianna Rolandi (*American*)
   Faith Esham (*American*)
Bartolo   Artur Korn (*Austrian*)
Marcellina   Mimi Lerner (*American*)
Cherubino   Faith Esham (*American*)
   Carolyn Watkinson (*English*)
Don Basilio   Ugo Benelli (*Italian*)
Count Almaviva   Richard Stilwell
   (*American*)
   William Shimell (*English*)
The Countess   Isobel Buchanan (*Scottish*)
   Gabriele Fontana (*Austrian*)
Antonio   Federico Davià (*Italian*)
   Brian Donlan (*English*)
Barbarina   Anne Dawson (*English*)
Don Curzio   Hugues Cuenod (*Swiss*)
   David Johnston (*English*)

Conductors BERNARD HAITINK, GUSTAV KUHN
Original production by PETER HALL
Revival Director ROGER WILLIAMS
Design and Lighting JOHN BURY
Choreographer PAULINE GRANT
*Revival sponsored by the Michael & Ilse Katz
   Charitable Trust*

267 Above, *La Cenerentola*, 1983, Laurence Dale, Kathleen Kuhlmann, Alberto Rinaldi

268 Below, *Così fan tutte*, 1984, Jane Berbié, J. Patrick Raftery, Delores Ziegler, Carol Vaness and Ryland Davies

269 Above, *Le nozze di Figaro*, 1984: Artur Korn, Mimi Lerner, Claudio Desderi, Gianna Rolandi

270 *Arabella*, 1984: Below left, John Bröcheler, Keith Lewis, Gianna Rolandi. Below right, Ashley Putnam as Arabella

271 *Le nozze di Figaro*, 1984: Above, Faith Esham, Richard Stilwell, Gianna Rolandi. Below, Faith Esham, Gianna Rolandi, Isobel Buchanan

272 *Così fan tutte*, 1984: Above, J. Patrick Raftery, Delores Ziegler, Jane Berbie, Claudio Desderi, Carol Vaness, Ryland Davies. Below left, Delores Ziegler, Claudio Desderi, Carol Vaness. Below right, Delores Ziegler, J. Patrick Raftery

L'incoronazione di Poppea

MONTEVERDI *14 performances*

Fortuna Patricia Kern (*English*)
Virtù Helen Walker (*English*)
Amor Linda Kitchen (*English*)
Ottone Dale Duesing (*American*)
First Soldier Keith Lewis (*New Zealand*)
Second Soldier Donald Stephenson (*English*)
Poppea Maria Ewing (*American*)
  ★Helen Walker (*1 perf*)
Nerone Dennis Bailey (*American*)
Arnalta Anne-Marie Owens (*English*)
Ottavia Cynthia Clarey (*American*)
Drusilla Elizabeth Gale (*English*)
  ★Susan Bullock (*1 perf*)
Seneca Robert Lloyd (*English*)
  Roderick Kennedy (*English*)
Liberto Roderick Kennedy (*English*)
  Jeremy Munro (*English*)
Pallade Jenny Miller (*American*)
Damigella Lesley Garrett (*English*)
Valetto Petros Evangelides (*Cypriot*)
Lucano Keith Lewis (*New Zealand*)
Lictor Roger Bryson (*English*)
  ★Alan Fairs (*2 perfs*) Jeremy Munro (*Scottish*)

Conductor RAYMOND LEPPARD
Director PETER HALL
Associate Director RENNIE WRIGHT
Design and Lighting JOHN BURY
Sponsored by IBM United Kingdom Limited

Arabella

STRAUSS *14 performances*

Fortune-teller Enid Hartle (*English*)
Adelaide Regina Sarfaty (*American*)
Graf Waldner Artur Korn (*Austrian*)
Zdenka Gianna Rolandi (*American*)
  ★Louisa Kennedy (*1 perf.*)
Arabella Ashley Putnam (*American*)
Matteo Keith Lewis (*New Zealand*)
Mandryka John Bröcheler (*Dutch*)
Graf Elemer Glenn Winslade (*Australian*)
Graf Dominik Jeremy Munro (*Scottish*)
Graf Lamoral Geoffrey Moses (*Welsh*)
Fiakermilli Eileen Hulse (*English*)
  Gwendolyn Bradley (*American*)
Djura Timothy Evans-Jones (*Welsh*)
Jankel Peter Coleman-Wright (*English*)
Welko John Hall (*English*)
Waiter John Oakman (*English*)

Conductors BERNARD HAITINK, STEPHEN BARLOW
Director JOHN COX
Associate Director and Choreogapher MONIQUE
  WAGEMAKERS
Designer JULIA TREVELYAN OMAN
Lighting Designer ROBERT BRYAN
Sponsored by John Player Special

★role performed as understudy

273   Dennis Bailey and Maria Ewing as Nero and Poppea

OPERAS PERFORMED BY GLYNDEBOURNE TOURING OPERA, 1968–1984

1968

5 March–13 April:
41 performances Newcastle,
Liverpool, Manchester,
Oxford, Sheffield

L'Ormindo

CAVALLI *6 performances*

Ormindo   John Wakefield
Amida   Neil Howlett
Nerillo   Janet Hughes
Sicle   Elizabeth Tippett
Melide   Jean Allister
Erice   Minoo Golvala
Erisbe   April Cantelo
Mirinda   Mararet Lensky
King Ariadeno   Anthony Williams
Osmano   Richard Van Allan

Conductor RAYMOND LEPPARD
Original production by GÜNTHER RENNERT
Produced for the Tour by CHARLES HAMILTON
Designer ERICH KONDRAK

Don Giovanni

MOZART *11 performances*

Leporello   Richard Van Allan
Donna Anna   Maria Landis
Don Giovanni   Geoffrey Chard
The Commendatore   Anthony Williams
Don Ottavio   Alexander Oliver
Donna Elvira   Margaret Kingsley
Zerlina   Beverley Bergen
Masetto   Brian Donlan

Conductor MYER FREDMAN
Producer FRANCO ENRIQUEZ
Designer EMANUELE LUZZATI

Die Zauberflöte

MOZART *12 performances*

Tamino   John Serge
First Lady   Clare Walmsley
Second Lady   Elizabeth Tippett
Third Lady   Joy Domzalski
Papageno   John Gibbs
Queen of the Night   Jessica Cash
First Boy   Wendy Eathorne
Second Boy   Janet Hughes
Third Boy   Gillian Hull
Monostatos   Alexander Oliver
Pamina   Annon Lee Silver
The Speaker   James Christiansen
Sarastro   Noel Noble
Priests/Armed Men   John Perrin
  Ian Comboy
Papagena   Gillian Humphreys

Conductor MYER FREDMAN
Producer FRANCO ENRIQUEZ
Designer EMANUELE LUZZATI

L'elisir d'amore

DONIZETTI *12 performances*

Adina   Jill Gomez
Nemorino   Ryland Davies
Belcore   Terence Sharpe
Dulcamara   Ian Wallace
Giannetta   Beverely Bergen

Conductor KENNETH MONTGOMERY
Original production by FRANCO ZEFFIRELLI
Produced for the Tour by DENNIS MAUNDER
Designer FRANCO ZEFFIRELLI

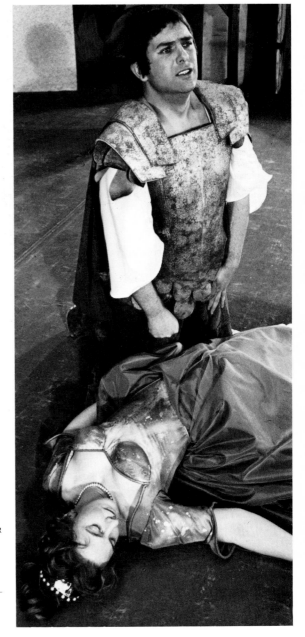

274   April Cantelo and John
Wakefield in *L'Ormindo*

275 Norma Burrowes and Richard Van Allan in *Il turco in Italia*

1969

17 March–19 April:
32 performances Manchester,
Leeds, Liverpool, Newcastle,
Nottingham

Eugene Onegin

TCHAIKOVSKY *10 performances*

Larina   Pamela Bowden
Tatyana   Elizabeth Tippett
Olga   Rosanne Creffield
Filippyevne   Enid Hartle
Onegin   Tom McDonnell
Lensky   Maurice Arthur
Prince Gremin   Anthony Williams
Petrovich   Erich Vietheer
Zaretsky   Richard Van Allan
Monsieur Triquet   Terry Jenkins

Conductor MYER FREDMAN
Producer MICHAEL HADJIMISCHEV
Designer PIER LUIGI PIZZI
Choreographer PAULINE GRANT

Macbeth

VERDI *10 performances*

Macbeth   Terence Sharpe
   Neil Howlett
Banquo   Anthony Williams
Lady Macbeth   Milla Andrew
   Maragret Kingsley
Gentlewoman   Joan Carden
Macduff   Ninian Walden
Malcolm   Terry Jenkins
Doctor   Brian Donlan
Servant   Neville Wilkie
Murderer   Erich Vietheer

Conductor MYER FREDMAN
Original production by FRANCO ENRIQUEZ
Produced for the Tour by GEOFFREY CONNOR
Designer EMANUELE LUZZATI

Die Entführung aus dem Serail

MOZART *12 performances*

Belmonte   Ryland Davies
   Kenneth Bowen
   ★Malcolm Williams
Osmin   Richard Van Allan
Pedrillo   Alexander Oliver
Pasha Selim   Otakar Kraus
Constanze   Mary O'Brian
Blonde   Annon Lee Silver

Conductor KENNETH MONTGOMERY
Original production by FRANCO ENRIQUEZ
Produced for the Tour by GEOFFREY CONNOR
Designer EMANUELE LUZZATI

★role performed as understudy

8–10 May: 2 performances
Glyndebourne

Die Entführung aus dem Serail

Same cast as UK tour

276   Richard Van Allan and Teresa Cahill as
Leporello and Donna Elvira

1970

16 March–18 April:
28 performances Manchester,
Oxford, Newcastle, Nottingham,
Southsea

Don Giovanni

MOZART *8 performances*

Leporello   Richard Van Allan
Donna Anna   Gwenyth Annear
Don Giovanni   Alan Charles
The Commendatore   Anthony Williams
Don Ottavio   Kenneth Bowen
Donna Elvira   Teresa Cahill
Zerlina   Norma Burrowes
Masetto   Brian Donlan

Conductor RAYMOND LEPPARD
Original production by FRANCO ENRIQUEZ
Produced for the Tour by PATRICK LIBBY
Designer EMANUELE LUZZATI

Così fan tutte

MOZART *11 performances*

Ferrando   Alexander Oliver
Guglielmo   Alan Opie
Don Alfonso   Richard Van Allan
Fiordiligi   Marie Hayward
Dorabella   Rosanne Creffield
Despina   Sandra Dugdale

Conductor MYER FREDMAN
Original production by FRANCO ENRIQUEZ
Produced for the Tour by ROGER BRUNYATE
Designer EMANUELE LUZZATI

Werther

MASSENET *9 performances*

The Bailiff   Brian Donlan
Johann   Gavin Walton
Schmidt   Terry Jenkins
Sophie   Wendy Eathorne
Werther   David Hughes
Charlotte   Yvonne Fuller
Albert   William Elvin

Conductor MYER FREDMAN
Original production by MICHAEL REDGRAVE
Assistant Producer GEOFFREY GILBERTSON
Designers HENRY BARDON (Scenery)
   DAVID WALKER (Costumes)

1971

30 March–17 April:
17 performances Liverpool,
Edinburgh, Southampton

Il turco in Italia

ROSSINI *6 performances*

Zaida   Penelope MacKay
Albazar   Malcolm Williams
The Poet   Alan Charles
Don Geronio   Wyndham Parfitt
Fiorilla   Norma Burrowes
Selim   Richard Van Allan
Narciso   Alexander Oliver

Conductor   MYER FREDMAN
Producer   JOHN COX
Designer   EMANUELE LUZZATI

Die Zauberflöte

MOZART *6 performances*

Tamino   Maurice Arthur
First Lady   Gwenyth Annear
Second Lady   Yvonne Fuller
Third Lady   Marjorie McMichael
Papageno   William Elvin
Queen of the Night   Jessica Cash
First Boy   Angela Whittingham
Second Boy   Alison MacGregor
Third Boy   Shelagh Squires
Monostatos   Anthony Bremner
Pamina   Teresa Cahill
The Speaker   Brian Donlan
Sarastro   Anthony Williams
Priests/Armed Men   Malcolm Williams
   John Tomlinson
Papagena   Sara de Javelin

Conductor   NICHOLAS BRAITHWAITE
Original production by   FRANCO ENRIQUEZ
Designer   EMANUELE LUZZATI

Eugene Onegin

TCHAIKOVSKY *5 performances*

Larina   Doreen Cryer
Tatyana   Elizabeth Tippett
Olga   Rosanne Creffield
Filippyevna   Enid Hartle
Onegin   Benjamin Luxon
Lensky   Anthony Roden
   Maurice Arthur
Prince Gremin   Anthony Williams
Petrovich   Brian Donlan
Zaretsky   Thomas Lawlor
Monsieur Triquet   Terry Jenkins

Conductor   MYER FREDMAN
Original production by   MICHAEL
   HADJIMISCHEV
Produced for the Tour by   CHARLES HAMILTON
Designer   PIER LUIGI PIZZI
Choreographer   PAULINE GRANT

6–25 September:
18 performances Leeds,
Norwich, Newcastle

Il turco in Italia

ROSSINI *6 performances*

Same as on Spring Tour, but conducted by
   LIONEL FRIEND

Ariadne auf Naxos

STRAUSS *6 performances*

Major Domo   Roderic Keating
Music Master   Brian Donlan
The Composer   Delia Wallis
Bacchus   Wilmer Neufeld
Officer   Malcolm Williams
Dancing Master   Anthony Bremner
Wig Maker   Edward Sadler
Lackey   Gavin Walton
Zerbinetta   Deborah Cook
Ariadne   Vivien Townley
Harlekin   Donald Rutherford
Scaramuccio   Terry Jenkins
Truffaldino   Wyndham Parfitt
Brighella   Ian Caley
Najade   Angela Whittingham
Dryade   Shelagh Squires
Echo   Angela Bostock

Conductor   MYER FREDMAN
Producer   JOHN COX
Designer   MICHAEL ANNALS

Così fan tutte

MOZART *6 performances*

Ferrando   John Brecknock
Guglielmo   William Elvin
Don Alfonso   Thomas Lawlor
Fiordiligi   Teresa Cahill
Dorabella   Rosanne Creffield
Despina   Sara de Javelin

Conductor   MYER FREDMAN
Original production by   FRANCO ENRIQUEZ
Produced for the Tour by   ROGER BRUNYATE
Designer   EMANUELE LUZZATI

277   Above, *Ariadne auf Naxos*: Delia
   Wallis and Deborah Cook
278   Below, *La Bohème*: Keith Erwen and
   Linda Esther Gray

1972

19 September–21 October:
25 performances Oxford,
Nottingham, Newcastle,
Liverpool, Manchester

La Bohème

PUCCINI *10 performances*

Marcello William Elvin
Rodolfo Keith Erwen
  Athole Still
Colline John Tomlinson
Schaunard Thomas Lawlor
Benoît Brian Donlan
Alcindoro Gavin Walton
Mimì Linda Esther Gray
Musetta Victoria Sumner
Parpignol James Anderson
Sergeant Paul Nemeer
Customs Officer Edward Sadler

Conductor MYER FREDMAN
Producer JOHN COX
Designers HENRY BARDON (Scenery)
  DAVID WALKER (Costumes)

La Calisto

CAVALLI *5 performances*

La Natura Marjorie Biggar
L'Eternità Annabel Hunt
Il Destino Penelope MacKay
Giove Robert Lloyd
Mercurio Alan Charles
Calisto Jill Gomez
  ★Lynn Channing
Endimione James Bowman
Diana Delia Wallis
Linfea John Fryatt
Satirino Janet Hughes
Pane Brian Donlan
Silvano Gavin Walton
Giunone Gwenyth Annear
Echo Isla Brodie

Conductors RAYMOND LEPPARD, HENRY WARD
Original production by PETER HALL
Produced for the Tour by PATRICK LIBBY
Designer JOHN BURY

★role performed as understudy

Die Entführung aus dem Serail

MOZART *10 performances*

Belmonte Anthony Roden
Osmin Thomas Lawlor
Pedrillo Ian Caley
Pasha Selim James Atkins
Constanze Valerie Masterson
Blonde Elizabeth Gale

Conductor LIONEL FRIEND
Producer JOHN COX
Designer EMANUELE LUZZATI

279 Left, Jill Gomez as Calisto
280 Right, *Die Entführung*, 1972: Elizabeth
  Gale and Thomas Lawlor

1973

25 September–27 October:
25 performances Norwich,
Bristol, Oxford, Southampton,
Manchester

Le nozze di Figaro

MOZART *7 performances*

Figaro   William Elvin
Susanna   Elizabeth Gale
Bartolo   Michael Rippon
Marcellina   Maureen Morelle
Cherubino   Joy Roberts
Count Almaviva   Peter Knapp
Don Basilio   Brian Burrows
The Countess   Linda Esther Gray
Antonio   Brian Donlan
Barbarina   Susanna Ross
Don Curzio   James Anderson

Conductor   MYER FREDMAN
Original production by PETER HALL
Produced for the Tour by ADRIAN SLACK
Designer   JOHN BURY
Choreographer   PAULINE GRANT

La Bohème

PUCCINI *10 performances*

Marcello   Alan Watt
Rodolfo   Carlo Millauro

Colline   John Tomlinson
Schaunard   Ian Caddy
Benoît   Brian Donlan
Alcindoro   Edward Sadler
Mimì   Patricia Greig
Musetta   Victoria Sumner
Parpignol   James Anderson
Sergeant   Powell Harrison
Customs Officer   Keith Brookes

Conductor   ROBIN STAPLETON
Producer   JOHN COX
Designers   HENRY BARDON (Scenery)
   DAVID WALKER (Costumes)

Macbeth

VERDI *8 performances*

Macbeth   Terence Sharpe
Banquo   John Tomlinson
Lady Macbeth   Janet Jacques
Gentlewoman   Eiddwen Harrhy
Macduff   Athole Still
Malcolm   Ian Caley
Doctor   Brian Donlan
Servant   Edward Sadler
Murderer   Keith Brookes

Conductor   MYER FREDMAN
Producer   MICHAEL HADJIMISCHEV
Designer   EMANUELE LUZZATI

1974

18 September–26 October:
28 performances Glyndebourne,
Southampton, Oxford,
Bristol, Manchester, Norwich

Eugene Onegin

TCHAIKOVSKY *11 performances*

Larina   Moreen Morelle
Tatyana   Linda Esther Gray
Olga   Cynthia Buchan
Filippyevna   Enid Hartle
Onegin   Marco Bakker
Lensky   Anthony Rolfe Johnson
Prince Gremin   Brian Holmes
Petrovich   Anthony Smith
Zaretsky   Thomas Lawlor
Monsieur Triquet   Dennis O'Neill

Conductor   MYER FREDMAN
Producer   MICHAEL HEDJIMISCHEV
Designer   PIER LUIGI PIZZI
Choreographer   PAULINE GRANT

281   *Eugene Onegin*: Marko Bakker and
Anthony Rolfe Johnson

Le nozze di Figaro
MOZART *11 performances*

Figaro   William Elvin
Susanna   Elizabeth Gale
Bartolo   Thomas Lawlor
Marcellina   Maureen Morelle
Cherubino   Joy Roberts
Count Almaviva   Peter Knapp
Don Basilio   Brian Burrows
The Countess   Patricia Greig
Antonio   Brian Donlan
Barbarina   Susanna Ross
Don Curzio   Dennis O'Neill

Conductor   KENNETH MONTGOMERY
Original production by   PETER HALL
Produced for the Tour by   ADRIAN SLACK
Designer   JOHN BURY
Choreographer   PAULINE GRANT

Intermezzo
STRAUSS *6 performances*
In the English translation made for
Glyndebourne by Andrew Porter

Christine   Janet Gail
Robert Storch   Donald Bell
Anna   Susan Varley
Franzl   Richard Allfrey
    Christopher Davis
Therese   Vida Schepens
Fanny   Jean Williams
Marie   Jennifer Heslop
Baron Lummer   Bernard Dickerson
The Lawyer's Wife   Isla Brodie
Resi   Julianna Bethlen
The Commercial Counsellor   Alan Watt
The Opera Singer   Charles Kerry
Stroh, the Conductor   David Cusick
The Legal Counsellor   Brian Donlan
The Lawyer   Powell Harrison

Conductor   MYER FREDMAN
Producer   JOHN COX
Designer   MARTIN BATTERSBY
Choreographer   PAULINE GRANT

1975
16 September–25 October:
30 performances Glyndebourne, Bristol, Oxford, Norwich, Manchester, Southampton

Der Freischütz
WEBER *12 performances*
In an English translation made for Glyndebourne by John Cox and David Parry

Killian   John Rawnsley
Max   Raymond Gibbs
    James Anderson
Cuno   Brian Donlan
Caspar   Malcolm King
Samiel   Brian Holmes
Agathe   Linda Esther Gray
Anna   Elizabeth Gale
Ottokar   Peter Knapp
The Hermit   Thomas Lawor

Conductor   KENNETH MONTGOMERY
Producer   JOHN COX
Designer   JOHN FRASER
Lighting   ROBERT BRYAN

Così fan tutte
MOZART *12 performances*

Ferrando   David Rendall
Guglielmo   Alan Watt
Don Alfonso   Thomas Lawlor
Fiordiligi   Patricia Greig
Dorabella   Cynthia Buchan
Despina   Lillian Watson

Conductor   CALVIN SIMMONS
Producer   ADRIAN SLACK
Designer   EMANUELE LUZZATI
Lighting   MATT L. ENGLISH

The Rake's Progress
STRAVINSKY *6 performances*

Anne   Susanna Ross
Tom Rakewell   Ian Caley
Trulove   John Michael Flanagan
Nick Shadow   Alan Charles
Mother Goose   Joyce McCrindle
Baba the Turk   Enid Hartle
Sellem   Graeme Matheson-Bruce
Keeper of the Madhouse   Keith Brookes

Conductor   SIMON RATTLE
Producer   JOHN COX
Designer   DAVID HOCKNEY
Lighting   ROBERT BRYAN

1976
14 September–23 October:
30 performances Glyndebourne, Norwich, Oxford, Manchester, Bristol, Southampton

Capriccio
STRAUSS *6 performances*
In the English translation by Maria Massey

Flamand   Richard Berkeley Steele
Olivier   Richard Jackson
La Roche   Malcolm King
The Countess   Felicity Lott
The Count   Ian Caddy
Clairon   Phyllis Cannan
Italian Tenor   Eduardo Velazco
Italian Soprano   Catherine McCord
Major Domo   John Rae
Monsieur Taupe   Adrian Scott

Conductor   KENNETH MONTGOMERY
Producer   JOHN COX
Designers   DENNIS LENNON (Scenery)
    MARTIN BATTERSY (Costumes and Furniture)

Le nozze di Figaro
MOZART *12 performances*

Figaro   Alan Watt
Susanna   Lillian Watson
Bartolo   Thomas Lawlor
Marcellina   Joyce McCrindle
Cherubino   Cynthia Buchan
Count Almaviva   Anthony Smith
Don Basilio   Brian Burrows
The Countess   Rosalind Plowright
Antonio   Richard Robson
Barbarina   Kate Flowers
Don Curzio   Philip Griffiths

Conductors   DIEGO MASSON, KENNETH MONTGOMERY
Original production by   PETER HALL
Produced for the Tour by   CHRISTOPHER RENSHAW
Designer   JOHN BURY
Choreographer   PAULINE GRANT
Lighting   ROBERT BRYAN

Falstaff

VERDI *12 performances*

Falstaff   Jonathan Summers
Dr Caius   John Fryatt
   Graeme Matheson-Bruce
Bardolph   Bonaventura Bottone
Pistol   John Rea
Meg Page   Joyce McCrindle
Alice Ford   Teresa Cahill
Mistress Quickly   Enid Hartle
Nannetta   Elizabeth Gale
   Miriam Bowen
Fenton   Anthony Rolfe Johnson
Ford   John Rawnsley

Conductors   KENNETH MONTGOMERY, DAVID
   PARRY
Original production by   JEAN-PIERRE PONNELLE
Produced for the Tour by   JULIAN HOPE
Designer   JEAN-PIERRE PONNELLE
Lighting   ROBERT BRYAN

---

282   Jonathan Summers as Falstaff

1977

4–10 February: 4 performances Angers (France)

The Rake's Progress

STRAVINSKY

Anne   Susanna Ross
Tom Rakewell   Ian Caley
Trulove   John Michael Flanagan
Nick Shadow   Alan Charles
Mother Goose   Joyce McCrindle
Baba the Turk   Enid Hartle
Sellem   Graeme Matheson-Bruce
Keeper of the Madhouse   Keith Brookes

Conductor   SIMON RATTLE
Producer   JOHN COX
Designer   DAVID HOCKNEY
Lighting   ROBERT BRYAN

13 September–22 October: 30 performances Glyndebourne, Norwich, Bristol, Oxford, Southampton, Manchester

DOUBLE BILL: *6 performances*
La Voix humaine

POULENC

Elle   Felicity Lott

Conductor   NICHOLAS BRAITHWAITE
Producer   GRAZIELLA SCIUTTI
Designer   MARTIN BATTERSBY
Lighting   ROBERT BRYAN

The Cunning Little Vixen

JANÁČEK
In an English translation by Norman Tucker

The Forester   Henry Herford
The Vixen   Kate Flowers
The Forester's Wife   Phyllis Cannan
The Dog   Michael Carlyle
The Cock   Graeme Matheson-Bruce
The Hen   Beryl Korman
The Badger   David Todd
The Parson   John Michael Flanagan
The Schoolmaster   Nigel Robson
The Innkeeper   Michael Carlyle
The Poacher   Paul Nemeer
The Innkeeper's Wife   Nuala Willis
The Fox   Neil McKinnon
The Gnat   Adrian Scott

Conductor   SIMON RATTLE
Original production by   JONATHAN MILLER
Produced for the Tour by   GRAHAM VICK
Designers   PATRICK ROBERTSON (Scenery)
   ROSEMARY VERCOE (Costumes)
Movement   STUART COX
Lighting   ROBERT BRYAN

Falstaff

VERDI *12 performances*

Falstaff   Jonathan Summers
Dr Caius   Graeme Matheson-Bruce
Bardolph   Adrian Scott
Pistol   John Rea
Meg Page   Joyce McCrindle
Alice Ford   Catherine McCord
Mistress Quickly   Enid Hartle
Nannetta   Miriam Bowen
Fenton   Richard Berkeley Steele
Ford   John Rawnsley

Conductor   NICHOLAS BRAITHWAITE
Original production by   JEAN-PIERRE PONNELLE
Produced for the Tour by   JULIAN HOPE
Designer   JEAN-PIERRE PONNELLE
Lighting   ROBERT BRYAN

Don Giovanni

MOZART *12 performances*

Leporello   Malcolm King
Donna Anna   Eiddwen Harrhy
Don Giovanni   Thomas Allen
The Commendatore   John Tranter
Don Ottavio   Keith Lewis
   *Peter Richfield
Donna Elvira   Rosalind Plowright
Zerlina   Patricia Price
   Diana Montague
Masetto   John Rath

Conductors   CALVIN SIMMONS, NICHOLAS
   BRAITHWAITE
Original production by   PETER HALL
Produced for the Tour by   STEWART TROTTER
Designer   JOHN BURY
Choreographer   PAULINE GRANT
Lighting   ROBERT BRYAN

*role performed as understudy

1978

19 September–28 October:
30 performances Glyndebourne,
Norwich, Nottingham, Oxford,
Southampton, Birmingham

Così fan tutte

MOZART *12 performances*

Ferrando   Keith Lewis
Guglielmo   John Rath
Don Alfonso   Michael Lewis
Fiordiligi   Felicity Lott
Dorabella   Patricia Parker
Despina   Kate Flowers

Conductor SIMON RATTLE
Original production by PETER HALL
Produced for the Tour by STEWART TROTTER
Designer JOHN BURY
Lighting ROBERT BRYAN

---

283   Rosalind Plowright and Thomas Allen
in *Don Giovanni*

Die Zauberflöte

MOZART *12 performances*

Tamino   Richard Berkeley Steele
   Adrian Martin
First Lady   Patricia Richards
   Catherine McCord
Second Lady   Elizabeth Stokes
   Claire Powell
Third Lady   Fiona Kimm
   Nuala Willis
Papageno   Richard Jackson
   Paul Nemeer
Queen of the Night   Sunny Joy Langton
   Lynda Russell
First Boy   Roslyn Riley
Second Boy   Lindsay John
Third Boy   Jane Findlay
Monostatos   Armistead Wilkinson
   Adrian Scott
Pamina   Helen Walker
   Miriam Bowen
The Speaker   Henry Herford
   Phillip Bromley
Sarastro   Willard White
Priest   Adrian Thompson
Men in Armour   Neil McKinnon, Roger
   Bryson
Papagena   Fiona Dobie

Conductor NICHOLAS BRAITHWAITE
Original production by JOHN COX
Produced for the Tour by GUUS MOSTART
Designer DAVID HOCKNEY
Lighting ROBERT BRYAN

The Rake's Progress

STRAVINSKY *6 performances*

Anne   Susanna Ross
Tom Rakewell   Ian Caley
Trulove   John Michael Flanagan
Nick Shadow   John Rawnsley
Mother Goose   Nuala Willis
Baba the Turk   Enid Hartle
Sellem   Nigel Robson
Keeper of the Madhouse   Phillip Bromley

Conductor STEPHEN BARLOW
Original production by JOHN COX
Produced for the Tour by JULIAN HOPE
Designer DAVID HOCKNEY
Lighting ROBERT BRYAN

1979

18 September–3 November:
36 performances Glyndebourne,
Norwich, Southampton, Oxford,
Nottingham, Liverpool

Fidelio

BEETHOVEN *15 performances*

Jaquino   William Pool
Marzelline   Lynda Russell
Rocco   Roger Bryson
Leonore   Maria Moll
Pizarro   Malcolm Donnelly
Florestan   Philip Langridge
   ★David Johnston
Don Fernando   Phillip Bromley

Conductors NICHOLAS BRAITHWAITE,
   NICHOLAS CLEOBURY
Original production by PETER HALL
Produced for the Tour by GUUS MOSTART
Designer JOHN BURY
Lighting ROBERT BRYAN

Così fan tutte

MOZART *15 performances*

Ferrando   Alexander Oliver
   Adrian Thompson
Guglielmo   Richard Jackson
Don Alfonso   Brian Donlan
Fiordiligi   Helen Walker
Dorabella   Jane Findlay
   ★Christine Botes
Despina   Catherine McCord

Conductors NICHOLAS BRAITHWAITE, STEPHEN
   BARLOW
Original production by PETER HALL
Produced for the Tour by STEPHEN LAWLESS
Designer JOHN BURY
Lighting ROBERT BRYAN

★*role performed as understudy*

1980

La fedeltà premiata

HAYDN *6 performances*

Nerina Kate Flowers
Lindoro Adrian Thompson
Melibeo John Rath
Amaranta Claire Powell
Perrucchetto Jacek Strauch
  ★Omar Ebrahim
Fileno Ian Caley
Celia Fiona Kimm
Diana Elizabeth Ritchie

Conductors SIMON RATTLE, NICHOLAS
  BRAITHWAITE
Original production by JOHN COX
Produced for the Tour by JEREMY JAMES
  TAYLOR
Designer HUGH CASSON
Lighting ROBERT BRYAN

★role performed as understudy

7–11 November: 3 performances Nancy (France)

La fedeltà premiata

As UK Tour

---

284 *La fedeltà premiata*: Fiona Kimm as
  Celia

23 September–1 November: 30 performances Glyndebourne, Norwich, Coventry, Oxford, Nottingham, Southampton

Die Entführung aus dem Serail

MOZART *12 performances*

Belmonte Keith Lewis
Osmin Roger Bryson
Pedrillo Adrian Thompson
Pasha Selim Christopher Blades
Constanze Yvonne Kenny
Blonde Deborah Rees

Conductors NICHOLAS KRAEMER, JANE GLOVER
Original production by PETER WOOD
Produced for the Tour by GUUS MOSTART
Designer WILLIAM DUDLEY
Lighting ROBERT BRYAN

La Bohème

PUCCINI *12 performances*

Marcello Christopher Blades
Rodolfo Pietro Ballo
Colline Andrew Gallacher
Schaunard Omar Ebrahin
Benoît Michael Carlyle
Alcindoro Charles Kerry
Mimì Helen Field
  ★Rosamund Illing
Musetta Maria Moll
  Catherine McCord
Parpignol Mark Curtis
Sergeant Neil Jansen
Customs Officer Paul Hodges

Conductor NICHOLAS BRAITHWAITE
Original production by JOHN COX
Produced for the Tour by MICHAEL BEAUCHAMP
Designers HENRY BARDON (Scenery)
  DAVID WALKER (Costumes)
Lighting KEITH BENSON

★role performed as understudy

The Rake's Progress

STRAVINSKY *6 performances*

Anne Helen Walker
Tom Rakewell Peter Jeffes
Trulove Roger Bryson
Nick Shadow John Pringle
Mother Goose Christine Batty
Baba the Turk Mary King
Sellem John Fryatt
Keeper of the Madhouse Brendan Wheatley

Conductor STEPHEN BARLOW
Original production by JOHN COX
Produced for the Tour by JULIAN HOPE
Designer DAVID HOCKNEY
Lighting ROBERT BRYAN

21–27 November: 4 performances Nancy (France)

The Rake's Progress

As UK Tour but Tom Rakewell sung at 1
  performance by
Grant Shelley

1981

22 September–31 October:
31 performances Glyndebourne,
Oxford, Nottingham,
Southampton, Manchester

Le nozze di Figaro

MOZART *12 performances*

Figaro   Christopher Blades
Susanna   Deborah Rees
   ★Delith Brook
Bartolo   Roger Bryson
Marcellina   Mary King
Cherubino   Beverley Mills
Count Almaviva   Robert Dean
Don Basilio   David Johnston
   ★Alan Duffield
The Countess   Elizabeth Ritchie
Antonio   Andrew Gallacher
Barbarina   Delith Brook
   ★Alison Higham-Bell
Don Curzio   Alan Duffield
   ★David McCord

Conductor   NICHOLAS KRAEMER
Original production by   PETER HALL
Produced for the Tour by   ROGER WILLIAMS
Designer   JOHN BURY
Choreographer   PAULINE GRANT
Lighting   KEITH BENSON

Falstaff

VERDI *12 performances*

Falstaff   Renato Capecchi
   Thomas Hemsley
   ★Brian Donlan
Dr Caius   Hugh Hetherington
Bardolph   Adrian Scott
Pistol   Charles Kerry
Meg Page   Christine Botes
Alice Ford   Elizabeth Byrne
Mistress Quickly   Anne-Marie Owens
Nannetta   Rosamund Illing
Fenton   Mark Curtis
Ford   Neil Jansen

Conductor   ELGAR HOWARTH
Original production by   JEAN-PIERRE PONNELLE
Produced for the Tour by   JULIAN HOPE
Designer   JEAN-PIERRE PONNELLE
Lighting   KEITH BENSON

★role performed as understudy

A Midsummer Night's Dream

BRITTEN *7 performances*

Cobweb   Martin Warr
Mustardseed   Jonathan Whiting
Peaseblossom   Stephen Jones
Moth   Stuart King
Puck   Dexter Fletcher
Tytania   Gillian Sullivan
Oberon   Robin Martin-Oliver
Lysander   Peter Jeffes
Demetrius   Henry Herford
Hermia   Jane Findlay
Helena   Helen Walker
Quince   Roger Bryson
Snug   Christopher Ross
Starveling   Michael Carlyle
Flute   Adrian Thompson
Snout   Grant Shelley
Bottom   John Michael Flanagan
Theseus   Hugh Davies
Hippolyta   Yvonne Lea

Conductor   JANE GLOVER
Original production by   PETER HALL
Produced for the Tour by   GUUS MOSTART
Designer   JOHN BURY
Lighting   PAUL PYANT

1982

28 September–6 November:
30 performances Glyndebourne,
Manchester, Plymouth, Oxford,
Southampton, Norwich

Don Giovanni

MOZART *12 performances*

Leporello   Michael Rippon
Donna Anna   Marie Slorach
Don Giovanni   Robert Dean
The Commendatore   Geoffrey Moses
Don Ottavio   Glenn Winslade
Donna Elvira   Elizabeth Byrne
Zerlina   Catherine Benson
Masetto   John Hall

Conductors   NICHOLAS KRAEMER, JANE GLOVER
Original production by   PETER HALL
Produced for the Tour by   STEPHEN LAWLESS
Designer   JOHN BURY
Choreographer   PAULINE GRANT
Lighting   KEITH BENSON

285   Robert Dean in *Don Giovanni*

Il barbiere di Siviglia

ROSSINI *12 performances*

Count Almaviva   Patrick Power
Figaro   Gordon Sandison
Rosina   Yvonne Lea
Bartolo   Stephen Rhys-Williams
Basilio   Geoffrey Moses
Fiorello   Omar Ebrahim
   ★Alan Duffield
Berta   Catherine McCord
Ambrogio   Martyn Harrison
Officer   Jeremy Munro
Notary   Anthony Buckeridge

Conductor JANE GLOVER
Original production by JOHN COX
Produced for the Tour by STEFAN JANSKI
Designer WILLIAM DUDLEY
Lighting KEITH BENSON

★role performed as understudy

Orfeo ed Euridice

GLUCK *6 performances*

Orfeo   Carolyn Watkinson
Amore   Delith Brook
Euridice   Anne Dawson

Conductor STEPHEN BARLOW
Original production by PETER HALL
Produced for the Tour by GUUS MOSTART
Designer JOHN BURY
Movement STUART HOPPS
Lighting PAUL PYANT

1983

*3 October–19 November:
37 performances Glyndebourne,
Plymouth, Oxford, Norwich,
Southampton, Nottingham*

La Cenerentola

ROSSINI *14 performances*

Clorinda   Catherine Benson
Tisbe   Louise Winter
Cenerentola   Carolyn Watkinson
Alidoro   Jeremy Munro
Don Magnifico   Philip O'Reilly
Ramiro   Gary Bennett
Dandini   William Shimell

Conductor JAMES JUDD
Original production by JOHN COX
Produced for the Tour by ANDY HINDS
Designer ALLAN CHARLES KLEIN
Lighting KEITH BENSON

Fidelio

BEETHOVEN *14 performances*

Jaquino   Mark Curtis
Marzelline   Faith Elliot
Rocco   Roderick Kennedy
Leonore   Elizabeth Vaughan
Pizarro   Michael Rippon
Florestan   Rowland Sidwell
Don Fernando   Matthew Best

Conductor JANE GLOVER
Original production by PETER HALL
Produced for the Tour by STEFAN JANSKI
Designer JOHN BURY
Lighting KEITH BENSON

The Love for Three Oranges

PROKOFIEV *9 performances*
*In an English translation made for Glyndebourne
by Tom Stoppard*

The King   Roger Bryson
   Matthew Best
Pantaloon   John Hancorn
Truffaldino   Hugh Hetherington
Leander   John Hall
Tchelio   Charles Kerry
Fata Morgana   Elizabeth Byrne
Princess Clarissa   Linda McLeod
Smeraldina   Colette McGahon
The Prince   Glenn Winslade
Farfarello   Stephen Rhys-Williams
The Cook   Michael Carlyle
Linetta   Catriona Bell
Nicoletta   Catherine Pierard
Ninetta   Helen Walker
Master of Ceremonies   David McCord
The Herald   Christopher Ross

Conductor STEPHEN BARLOW
Original production by FRANK CORSARO
Produced for the Tour by ROBERT CARSEN
Designer MAURICE SENDAK
Choreographer PAULINE GRANT
Lighting PAUL PYANT

---

286   Left, *Orfeo* rehearsal: Guus Mostart
   and Carolyn Watkinson
287   Below, A scene from *L'Amour des
   Trois Oranges*: Elizabeth Byrne as Fata
   Morgana

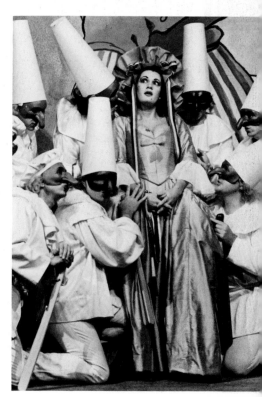

1984

9 October–17 November:
33 performances Glyndebourne,
Oxford, Southampton, Norwich,
Plymouth, Manchester

Così fan tutte

MOZART *12 performances*

Ferrando   Glenn Winslade
Guglielmo   Peter Coleman-Wright
Don Alfonso   Roger Bryson
Fiordiligi   Eiddwen Harrhy
Dorabella   Louise Winter
Despina   Lesley Garrett

Conductor   JANE GLOVER
Original production by   PETER HALL
Produced for the Tour by   LUCY BAILEY
Designer   JOHN BURY
Lighting   MARK JONATHAN

Le nozze di Figaro

MOZART *12 performances*

Figaro   John Hall
Susanna   Anne Dawson
Bartolo   Geoffrey Moses
Marcellina   Yvonne Howard
Cherubino   Jenny Miller
Count Almaviva   Jeremy Munro
Don Basilio   Adrian Thompson
The Countess   Rita Cullis
Antonio   Alan Fairs
Barbarina   Linda Kitchen
Don Curzio   Martyn Harrison

Conductors   LOTHAR ZAGROSEK, MARTIN ISEPP
Original production by   PETER HALL
Produced for the Tour by   ROGER WILLIAMS
Designer   JOHN BURY
Choreographer   PAULINE GRANT
Lighting   KEITH BENSON

DOUBLE BILL: *9 performances*

Where the Wild Things Are

KNUSSEN

Max   Rosemary Hardy
    Eileen Hulse
Mama/Tzippy   Linda Hirst
Moishe/Goat   Hugh Hetherington
Bruno   Stephen Richardson
Emile   Stephen Rhys-Williams
Bernard   Andrew Gallacher

289   *Where the Wild Things Are*, drawn by
    Maurice Sendak ©

Higglety Pigglety Pop!

KNUSSEN

Baby/Mother Goose/Flower   Deborah Rees
Rhoda   Rosemary Hardy
    Eileen Hulse
Jennie   Cynthia Buchan
Cat   Hugh Hetherington
Pig   Andrew Gallacher
Lion   Stephen Richardson
Narrator   Bamber Gascoigne

Conductors   OLIVER KNUSSEN, STEPHEN
    BARLOW
Director   FRANK CORSARO
Associate Director   ROBERT CARSEN
Designer   MAURICE SENDAK
Lighting   ROBERT BRYAN

288   Cynthia Buchan in *Higglety Pigglety Pop!*

GLYNDEBOURNE FESTIVAL OPERA

Operas performed 1934–1984

(Dates of new productions set in bold)

Beethoven *Fidelio*: **1959**, 61, 63, **79**, 81
Bellini *I Puritani*: **1960**
Britten *The Rape of Lucretia*: **1946** (world première), 1947; *Albert Herring*: **1947** (world première); *A Midsummer Night's Dream*: **1981**, 84
Busoni *Arlecchino*: **1954**, 60
Cavalli *L'Ormindo*: **1967**, 68, 69; *La Calisto*: **1970**, 71, 72, 73, 74
Cimarosa *Il matrimonio segreto*: **1965**, 67
Debussy *Pelléas et Mélisande*: **1962**, 63, 69, 70, **76**
Donizetti *Don Pasquale*: **1938**, 39; *L'elisir d'amore*: **1961**, 62, 67; *Anna Bolena*: **1965**, 68
Gay *The Beggar's Opera*: **1940**
Gluck *Orfeo ed Euridice*: **1947**, **1982**; *Alceste*: **1953**, 54, 58
Handel *Jephtha*: **1966**
Haydn *La fedeltà premiata*: **1979**, 80
Henze *Elegy for Young Lovers*: **1961**
Janáček *The Cunning Little Vixen*: **1975**, 77
Knussen *Where the Wild Things Are*: **1984** (world première)
Massenet *Werther*: **1966**, 69
Maw *The Rising of the Moon*: **1970** (world première), 71
Monteverdi *L'incoronazione de Poppea*: **1962**, 63, 64, **84**; *Il ritorno d'Ulisse in patria*: **1972**, 73, 79
Mozart *Le nozze di Figaro*: **1934**, 35, 36, 37, 38, 39, 47, **50**, **51**, **55**, 56, 58, 59, 62, 63, 65, **73**, 74, 76, 81, 84; *Così fan tutte*: **1934**, 35, 36, 37, 38, 39, **48**, 49, 50, 51, 52, 53, 54, 56, 59, 62, **69**, 71, 75, 76, **78**, 79, 84; *Die Zauberflöte*: **1935**, 36, 37, **56**, 57, 60, **63**, 64, 66, 70, 73, **78**, 80; *Die Entführung aus dem Serail*: **1935**, 36, 37, **50**, 53, **56**, 57, 61, **68**, **72**, 73, **80**, 83; *Don Giovanni*: **1936**, 37, 38, 39, 48, **51**, 54, 55, 56, **60**, 61, **67**, 69, **77**, 78,

82; *Idomeneo*: **1951**, 52, 53, 56, 59, 64, **74**, **83**; *Der Schauspieldirektor*: **1957**
Poulenc *La Voix humaine*: **1960**, 77
Prokofiev *L'Amour des Trois Oranges*: **1982**, 83
Puccini *La Bohème*: **1967**, 78
Purcell *Dido and Aeneas*: **1966**
Ravel *L'Heure espagnole*: **1966**
Rossini *La Cenerentola*: **1952**, 53, 54, 56, 59, 60, **83**; *Il barbiere di Siviglia*: **1954**, 55, 61, **81**, 82; *Le comte Ory*: **1954**, 55, 57, 58; *L'italiana in Algeri*: **1957**; *La pietra del paragone*: **1964**, 65; *Il turco in Italia*: **1970**
R. Strauss *Ariadne auf Naxos*: **1950**, **53**, 54, 57, 58, 62, **71**, 72, 81; *Der Rosenkavalier*: **1959**, 60, 65, **80**, 82; *Capriccio*: **1963**, 64, **73**, 76; *Intermezzo*: **1974**, 75, 83; *Die schweigsame Frau*: **1977**, 79; *Arabella*: **1984**
Stravinsky *The Rake's Progress*: **1953**, 54, 55, 58, 63, **75**, 77, 78, 80
Tchaikovsky *Eugene Onegin*: **1968**, 70, 75; *The Queen of Spades*: **1971**
Verdi *Macbeth*: **1938**, 39, 47, 52, 64, 65, **72**; *Un ballo in maschera*: **1949**; *La forza del destino*: **1951**, 55; *Falstaff*: **1955**, 57, 58, 60, **76**, 77, 80
Von Einem *The Visit of the Old Lady*: **1973**, 74
Wolf-Ferrari *Il segreto di Susanna*: **1958**, 60

Artists in principal roles 1934–1984

(Dates in italics indicate role performed as understudy)

Abercrombie, Elisabeth 1938
Adani, Mariella 1960
Alan, Hervey 1949, *1952–7*, 59, 60
Alarie, Pierrette 1951

Alberti, Walter 1962–5
Aler, John 1979
Alexander, Carlos 1961
Allfrey, Richard 1974
Alberti, Lucia 1980
Allen, Paschal 1965
Allen, Thomas 1973–5, 77, 79, 82
Allin, Norman 1934
Alliot-Lugaz, Colette 1981–3
Allister, Jean 1962, 63, 66, 68
Allman, Robert 1979
Alnar, Ayhan 1947
Alsen, Herbert 1937
Alva, Luigi 1961, 62
Amara, Lucine 1954, 55, 57, 58
Anders, Peter 1950
Anderson, James 1972, 74
Andrade, Rosario 1977, 78
Andrésen, Ivar 1935
Andrew, Jon 1965
Andrew, Milla 1968
Annear, Gwenyth 1965, 70, 73
Applegren, Curt 1979, 81, 82, 84
Armstrong, Sheila 1966, 67, 69, 70, 73
Arnaud, Claudine 1963, 64
Arthur, Maurice 1971
Ashford, Rupert 1983
Atherton, James 1979, 80
Atkins, James 1954–6, 72
Attwood, Audrey 1965
Atzorn, Robert 1983
Austin, Anson 1975
Autran, Victor 1966
Ayars, Ann 1947

Baccaloni, Salvatore 1936–9
Bacquier, Gabriel 1962
Badioli, Carlo 1961, 65, 67
Bailey, Dennis 1981, 84
Baillie, Peter 1968
Bainbridge, Elizabeth 1963, 64
Baker, James 1975
Baker, Janet 1966, 1970–3, 82
Bakker, Marco 1974, 75

Wixell, Ingvar   1962
Wolansky, Raymond   1963, 64
Woodland, Rae   *1960*, 64, 66, 1970–4, 80, 82, 83

Yakar, Rachel   1977, 80, 82
Yoncheva, Galia   1975
Young, Alexander   1950–3, 57

Zadek, Hilde   1950, 51
Zannini, Laura   1983
Zanolli, Silvana   1959, 60
Zareska, Eugenia   1948
Zeri, Maria   1962–4
Ziegler, Delores   1984
Ziegler, Edwin   1935
Zoghby, Linda   1978, 80
Zylis-Gara, Teresa   1965, 67

Conductors

Ansermet, Ernest   1946
Austin, Frederic   1940
Balkwill, Bryan   1954–8, 60, 63, 64
Barlow, Stephen   1979, 80, 83, 84
Beecham, Sir Thomas   1950
Bernard, Anthony   1940
Braithwaite, Nicholas   1978, 79
Busch, Fritz   1934–9, 1950, 51
Cambreling, Sylvain   1981, 82
Ceccato, Aldo   1971, 72
Cellini, Renato   1947
Cillario, Carlo Felice   1961, 62, 66, 67
Davis, Andrew   1973, 1975–80
Davis, Colin   1960
Erede, Alberto   1938, 39, 55
Fredman, Myer   1963–74
Fricsay, Ferencç   1950
Gardelli, Lamberto   1964, 65
Gavazzeni, Gianandrea   1965
Gelhorn, Peter   1956–61, 74
Gierster, Hans   1966
Giulini, Carlo Maria   1955
Glover, Jane   1982–4
Goldschmidt, Berthold   1947
Goodall, Reginald   1946
Gui, Vittorio   1948, 49, 1952–64
Haitink, Bernard   1972, 73, 1975–84
Henze, Hans Werner   1961
Howarth, Elgar   1981
Inbal, Eliahu   1981
Knussen, Oliver   1984
Kraemer, Nicholas   1981
Kubelik, Rafael   1948
Kuhn, Gustav   1980, 81, 83, 84
Leppard, Raymond   1964, 67, 68, 1970–5, 82, 84
Ludwig, Leopold   1959, 66
Maag, Peter   1959
Montgomery, Kenneth   1967, 68, 1974–6, 78
Mudie, Michael   1940

Oppenheim, Hans   1935, 36, 46, 49
Peters, Reinhard   1969, 70
Pritchard, John   1951–77
Rattle, Simon   1977, 1980–3
Renzetti, Donato   1983
Rescigno, Nicola   1978
Sacher, Paul   1954–8, 63
Schmidt-Issertedt, Hans   1958
Sillem, Maurits   1956
Simmons, Calvin   1976, 77
Solti, Georg   1954
Spanjaard, Ed   1978
Stiedry, Fritz   1947
Susskind, Walter   1947
Varviso, Silvio   1962, 63
Wallenstein, Alfred   1953
Ward, Henry   1973

Heads of music staff

Strasser, Jani   1934–72
Isepp, Martin   1978–

Producers

Besch, Anthony   1957
Cocteau, Jean   1960
Corsaro, Frank   1982–4
Cox, John   1970–84
Crozier, Eric   1946
Ebert, Carl   All operas up to and including 1939. Subsequently: 1947–63
Ebert, Peter   1954–8, 60, 61, 63
Enriquez, Franco   1960, 1963–71, 73
Gielgud, John   1940
Graham, Colin   1970, 71
Hadjimischev, Michael   1968, 70–2, 75
Hall, Peter   1970–4, 1976–9, 81, 82, 84
Hauser, Frank   1965, 67
Leveugle, Daniel   1965
Maunder, Dennis   1966, 67
Médecin, Pierre   1969
Miller, Jonathan   1975, 77
Montarsolo, Paolo   1971
Neugebauer, Hans   1965
Nunn, Trevor   1983
Ponnelle, Jean-Pierre   1976, 77, 80
Redgrave, Michael   1966, 67, 69
Rennert, Günther   1959–68
Sciutti, Graziella   1977
Slack, Adrian   1973, 75, 76
Terrasson, René   1976
Wood, Peter   1980, 83
Zeffirelli, Franco   1961, 62, 67

Designers

Annals, Michael   1971–4, 77, 79, 81
Bardon, Henry   1966, 67, 69, 78
Battersby, Martin   *1973–7, 83
Bury, John   1970–4, 1976–9, 81, 82, 84

Butlin, Roger   1974
Carl, Joseph   1947
Casson, Hugh   1953, 54, 58, 1962–4, 78, 80
Cocteau, Jean   1960
Dudley, William   1980–3
Erté   1980, 82
Evans, Conwy   *1962–4
Gérard, Rolf   1948–53, 56, 59, 62; *1951
Ghiglia, Lorenzo   1965, 66, 68
Green, Kenneth   *1938, 39
Heckroth, Hein   *1936–9, 48
Heeley, Desmond   1960, 65
Hockney, David   1975, 77, 78, 80
Hurry, Leslie   1951, 55
Klein, Allen Charles   1983
Lancaster, Osbert   1953–5, 57, 58, 60, 63, 64
Lennon, Dennis   1963, 64, 73, 76
Litherland, Ann   *1934–9, 47
Luzzati, Emanuele   1963–73, 76
Maximowna, Ita   1959–61, 63
Messel, Oliver   1950–65
Montresor, Beni   1962, 63
Motley   1940
Napier, John   1983
Neher, Caspar   1938, 39, 47, 49, 52
Nevill, Bernard   *1962
Nobili, Lila de   1961
Oman, Julia Trevelyan   1984
Piper, John   1946, 51, 54–6
Ponnelle, Jean-Pierre   1976, 77, 80
Powell, Anthony   1963, 64
Rice, Peter   1954, 57, 60
Robertson, Patrick   1975–7
Scott, Hutchinson   1951
Sendak, Maurice   1982–4
Toms, Carl   1958, 60
Vercoe, Rosemary   *1953, 54, 56, 58, 59, 1975–7
Walker, David   *1966, 67, 69, 78
Wilson, Hamish   1934–9, 47, 48
Zeffirelli, Franco   1961, 62, 67

*costumes only

Choreographers

Ellis, David   1956, 57
Furneaux, Mark   1975
Gilbert, Terry   1979, 80
Grant, Pauline   1950–6, 64–6, 68, 70–8, 81–4
Harrold, Robert   1959–65
Holmes, Michael   1962
Hopps, Stuart   1982
Talbot, Oenone   1967, 69
Wagemakers, Monique   1983, 84

General Managers/Administrators

Nightingale, Alfred   1934–5
Bing, Rudolph   1936–48
Caplat, Moran   1949–81
Dickie, Brian   1982–

GLYNDEBOURNE
TOURING OPERA

Administrator: 1968–80 Brian Dickie
1981– Anthony Whitworth-Jones
Musical Director: 1968–74 Myer Fredman
1975–6 Kenneth Montgomery
1977–80 Nicholas Braithwaite
1982– Jane Glover
Director of Production: 1974–9 John Cox
1980– Guus Mostart
Manager: 1968–78 Geoffrey Gilbertson
1979– Tom Redman
Orchestra: 1968–73 Northern Sinfonia
1974– Bournemouth Sinfonietta

Operas performed

1968 *Don Giovanni, Die Zauberflöte, L'elisir d'amore, L'Ormindo*
1969 *Die Entführung aus dem Serail, Eugene Onegin, Macbeth*
1970 *Don Giovanni, Così fan tutte, Werther*
1971 (spring) *Die Zauberflöte, Eugene Onegin, Il turco in Italia*; (autumn) *Così fan tutte, Il turco in Italia, Ariadne auf Naxos*
1972 *Die Entführung aus dem Serail, La Bohème, La Calisto*
1973 *Macbeth, La Bohème, Le nozze di Figaro*
1974 *Eugene Onegin, Le nozze di Figaro, Intermezzo*
1975 *Così fan tutte, Der Freischütz, The Rake's Progress*
1976 *Le nozze di Figaro, Falstaff, Capriccio*
1977 *Don Giovanni, Falstaff, La Voix humaine/The Cunning Little Vixen/The Rake's Progress*
1978 *Die Zauberflöte, Così fan tutte, The Rake's Progress*
1979 *Così fan tutte, Fidelio, La fedeltà premiata*
1980 *Die Entführung aus dem Serail, La Bohème, The Rake's Progress*
1981 *Le nozze di Figaro, Falstaff, A Midsummer Night's Dream*
1982 *Il barbiere di Siviglia, Orfeo ed Euridice, Don Giovanni*
1983 *The Love for Three Oranges, Fidelio, La Cenerentola*
1984 *Le nozze di Figaro, Così fan tutte, Where the Wild Things Are/Higglety, Pigglety Pop!*

Artists in principal roles

Allen, Thomas 1977
Allfrey, Richard 1974
Allister, Jean 1968
Anderson, James 1972, 73, 75
Andrew, Milla 1969
Annear, Gwenyth 1970–2
Arthur, Maurice 1969, 71
Atkins, James 1972

Bakker, Marco 1974
Ballo, Pietro 1980
Batty, Christine 1980
Bell, Donald 1974
Bell, Catriona 1983
Bennett, Gary 1983
Benson, Catherine 1982, 83
Bergen, Beverley 1968
Best, Matthew 1983
Bethlen, Julianna 1974
Biggar, Marjorie 1972
Blades, Christopher 1980, 81

Bostock, Angela 1971
Botes, Christine 1979, 81
Bottone, Bonaventura 1976
Bowden, Pamela 1969
Bowen, Kenneth 1969, 70
Bowen, Miriam 1976–8
Bowman, James 1972
Brecknock, John 1971
Bremner, Anthony 1971
Brodie, Isla 1972, 74
Bromley, Phillip 1978, 79
Brook, Delith 1981, 82
Brookes, Keith 1973, 75
Bryson, Roger 1978–81, 83, 84
Buchan, Cynthia 1974–6, 84
Buckeridge, Anthony 1982
Burrowes, Norma 1970, 71
Burrows, Brian 1973, 74, 76
Byrne, Elizabeth 1981–3

Caddy, Ian 1973, 76
Cahill, Teresa 1970, 71, 76
Caley, Ian 1971–3, 75, 78, 79
Cannan, Phyllis 1976, 77
Cantelo, April 1968
Capecchi, Renato 1981
Carden, Joan 1969
Carlyle, Michael 1977, 80, 81, 83
Carr, John 1974
Cash, Jessica 1968, 71
Channing, Lynn 1972
Chard, Geoffrey 1968
Charles, Alan 1970–2, 75
Christiansen, James 1968
Coleman-Wright, Peter 1984
Cook, Deborah 1971
Creffield, Rosanne 1969–71
Cryer, Doreen 1971
Cullis, Rita 1984
Curtis, Mark 1980, 81, 83
Cusick, David 1974

De Javelin, Sara 1971
Davies, Hugh 1981
Davies, Ryland 1968, 69

Wakefield, John   1968
Walden, Ninian   1969
Walker, Helen   1978–81, 83
Wallace, Ian   1968
Wallis, Delia   1971, 72
Walmesley, Clare   1968
Walton, Gavin   1970–2
Warr, Martin   1981
Watkinson, Carolyn   1982, 83
Watson, Lillian   1975, 76
Watt, Alan   1973–6
Wheatley, Brendan   1980
White, Willard   1978
Whiting, Jonathan   1981
Whittingham, Angela   1971
Wilkie, Neville   1969
Wilkinson, Armistead   1978
Williams, Anthony   1968–71
Williams, Jean   1974
Williams, Malcolm   *1969*, 71
Willis, Nuala   1977, 78
Winslade, Glenn   1982–4
Winter, Louise   1983, 84

Hinds, Andy   1983
Hope, Julian   1976, 1977–8, 80, 81
Janski, Stefan   1982, 83
Lawless, Stephen   1979, 82
Libby, Patrick   1970, 72
Maunder, Dennis   1968
Mostart, Guus   1978–82
Renshaw, Christopher   1976
Sciutti, Graziella   1977
Slack, Adrian   1973–5
Taylor, Jeremy James   1979
Trotter, Stewart   1977, 78
Vick, Graham   1977
Williams, Roger   1981, 84

Conductors

Barlow, Stephen   1978–80, 1982–4
Braithwaite, Nicholas   1971, 1977–80
Cleobury, Nicholas   1979
Fredman, Myer   1968–74
Friend, Lionel   1971, 72
Glover, Jane   1980–4
Howarth, Elgar   1981
Isepp, Martin   1984
Judd, James   1983
Knussen, Oliver   1984
Kraemer, Nicholas   1980–2
Leppard, Raymond   1968, 70, 72
Masson, Diego   1976
Montgomery, Kenneth   1968, 69, 1974–6
Parry, David   1976
Rattle, Simon   1975, 1977–9
Simmons, Calvin   1975, 77
Stapleton, Robin   1973
Ward, Henry   1972
Zagrosek, Lothar   1984

Producers

Bailey, Lucy   1984
Beauchamp, Michael   1980
Brunyate, Roger   1970, 71
Carsen, Robert   1983, 84
Connor, Geoffrey   1969
Corsaro, Frank   1984
Cox, John   1970–6
Hadjimischev, Michael   1969, 73
Hamilton, Charles   1968, 71

Designers

All productions as at Glyndebourne Festival, except:
Fraser, John   1975 *Der Freischütz*

Television transmissions and recordings

*Recording available on Video

1951   *Così fan tutte*   BBC
1952   *Macbeth*   BBC
1953   *Die Entführung aus dem Serail*   BBC
1954   *Don Giovanni*   BBC
1955   *Il barbiere di Siviglia*   BBC
1956   Scenes from all five Mozart operas: *Die Entführung*, *Don Giovanni*, *Figaro*, *Così* and *Die Zauberflöte*   BBC
1957   *Le Comte Ory*   BBC
1958   *The Rake's Progress*   BBC
1959   *La Cenerentola*   BBC (also on Eurovision to Italy, France, Belgium, Denmark, Switzerland, Holland)
1960   *Falstaff*   BBC (also on Eurovision to Italy, Denmark, Switzerland, Belgium)
1961   *Il barbiere di Siviglia*   BBC (also on Eurovision to Belgium, Austria, Switzerland, Italy, Denmark, Sweden)
1962   *L'elisir d'amore*   BBC (also on Eurovision to Belgium, Denmark, Sweden, Norway, Holland, Switzerland, Portugal)
1963   *Le nozze di Figaro*   BBC (also to Eire and West Germany)
1964   *Die Zauberflöte*   BBC (also to Denmark, Holland, Switzerland, Belgium, Eire)
1965   *La pietra del paragone*; *Dido & Aeneas*; *Arlecchino*; *L'Heure espagnole*   BBC
1970   *La Calisto*   BBC
1972   ★*Macbeth*; *Die Entführung aus dem Serail*   SOUTHERN
1973   ★*Le nozze di Figaro*; *Il ritorno d'Ulisse in patria*   SOUTHERN
1974   *Idomeneo*   SOUTHERN
1975   *Così fan tutte*   SOUTHERN
1976   ★*Falstaff*   SOUTHERN
        Capriccio   BBC
1977   *Don Giovanni*; *The Rake's Progress*   SOUTHERN
1978   ★*Die Zauberflöte*; *Così fan tutte*   SOUTHERN
1979   *Fidelio*   SOUTHERN
1980   ★*Die Entführung aus dem Serail*   SOUTHERN
1981   *Il barbiere di Siviglia*; *A Midsummer Night's Dream*   TVS
1982   *Orfeo ed Euridice*; *L'Amour des Trois Oranges*   TVS
1983   ★*La Cenerentola*; ★*Intermezzo*; ★*Idomeneo*   BBC
1984   ★*Arabella*; ★*L'incoronazione di Poppea*   BBC

All transmissions up to 1962 were broadcast live. All Southern Television/TVS recordings were transmitted on the full IBA network.

Gramophone recordings

Le nozze di Figaro   1934, 1955
Così fan tutte   1935, 1950 (excerpts)
Don Giovanni   1936, 1982
Orfeo ed Euridice   1947 (abridged), 1982
Idomeneo   1951 (excerpts), 1956
La Cenerentola   1953
Arlecchino   1954
Le Comte Ory   1955
Il barbiere di Siviglia   1962 (with Victoria de los Angeles, Luigi Alva, Sesto Bruscantini, Carlo Cava, Ian Wallace)
L'incoronazione di Poppea   1963 (abridged)
L'Ormindo   1968
La Calisto   1971
Die Entführung aus dem Serail   1972 (excerpts)
Il ritorno d'Ulisse in patria   1979
Where the Wild Things Are   1984

Dates denote year of production, not necessarily of recording.

Chronological lists compiled by Helen O'Neill.

Picture Credits and Acknowledgments

The author, Glyndebourne Festival Opera and the publishers would like to thank everyone who so kindly loaned material, whether it has been used in the book or not, and in particular the following owners of designs used:
Aldeburgh Festival, nos 52, 66–8; Mr John Armstrong, no. 218; Mr Paul Cannon, no. 176; Mr Moran Caplat, CBE, nos 48, 68, 73, 90, 237; Sir Hugh Casson, nos 94, 95, 97; Sir George Christie, no. 21; Dr Jerome Cotter, nos 174, 265; Mr John Cox, no. 151; Mrs Kenneth Dibben, no. 146; Mr Leslie Esterman, nos 72, 103; Hon. Mrs Julian Fane, no. 110; Mr Richard Gayner, no. 104; Mr Geoffrey Gilbertson, no. 148; Mr Dave Heather, no. 108; Mr Peter Herbert, no. 145; Mr Martin Isepp, no. 112; Mr Steve Jetton, no. 109; Mrs Rosemary Jones, no. 91; Mr Richard Lewis, CBE, nos 57, 74, 96; Miss Helen O'Neill, nos 31, 171; Mr G. Richardson, no. 177; Mr Jeremy Rowe, no. 77; Mr van den Bergh, no. 101; the V & A Theatre Museum, nos 57, 60–3; Mr T. R. Watts, CBE, nos 76, 111, 259; Mrs Wimbush, no. 102; and Mrs Wollaston, no. 144.

They also acknowledge with thanks the following copyright owners:
Aldeburgh Archive and John Piper, nos 52, 66–8; Michael Annals, nos 146 and 259; Henry Bardon, nos 103–4; Bassano Studios, nos 30, 40; Martin Battersby, nos 145, 149, 151; BBC Hulton Picture Library, nos 3, 8, 20, 26–7, 50, 53–4, 167, 205–7, 217, 222; Ilse Bing, nos 16, 28, 42–4, 201; Jane Bown and the Observer, no. 191; Bill Brandt, no. 25; Elizabeth Bury, nos 174, 177; John Bury, nos 187–8; Henri Cartier-Bresson, no. 2; Sir Hugh Casson, nos 94–7; Donald Cooper, no. 172; Anthony Crickmay, nos 126, 130–2; the Daily Herald, nos 21, 24, 28; J. W. Debenham, nos 203–4; Patrick Dickie, no. 194; Zoë Dominic, nos 113, 241, 250, 263, 280; Malcolm Dunbar, no. 208; Erté (© Sevenarts Limited London), no. 171; Lorenzo Ghiglia, no. 237; Glyndebourne Festival Opera, nos 141–2, 140, 160 (photographer Christopher Cormack), nos 65, 70–1, 84, 86–7, 98, 100, 105–6, 114–18, 120, 122–4, 134–9, 143, 147–8, 154, 156, 163–5, 168, 196, 198, 220–1, 226–7, 229, 232, 236, 238–9, 242–5, 247–8 (two photographs), 249, 251–8, 260–2, 264, 266–70 (two photographs), 271 (two photographs), 272–3, 275, 277–9, 281, 283–7, 289 (photographer Guy Gravett), nos 161–2, 185, 282 (photographer Philip Ingram); Graphic Photos, no. 6; Guy Gravett, nos 79, 81–2, 85, 88–9, 92, 99, 107, 119, 121, 125, 150, 152–3, 170, 175, 178–81, 183 (two photographs), 184 (two photographs), 189–90, 195, 200, 211, 216 (above), 223–5, 230, 233–5; Kenneth Green, no. 12; Desmond Heeley, no. 91; HMV, no. 37; David Hockney, nos 155, 157, 159–60; Hubman, Munich, no. 59; Leslie Hurry, no. 218; Allen Charles Klein, no. 265; Osbert Lancaster, the cartoon on p. 4 and nos 31, 72–7, 90; London News Agency, nos 19, 22, 36, 38; L. S. Lowry, the illustration on p. 3, Emanuele Luzzati, nos 108–12; Angus McBean, nos 49, 56, 58, 64, 80, 209 (two photographs), 210, 212, 213–15; Eammon McCabe, no. 182; Beni Montresor, no. 231 (above); John Napier, no. 193; Caspar Neher, no. 48; Lila de Nobili, the illustration on p. 18; Reeves of Lewes, no. 15; John St Clair, no. 128; the Scotsman, nos 69, 78; Maurice Sendak, no. 288; Lord Snowdon, nos 57, 60–3 (Oliver Messel illustrations), nos 83, 93, 216 (below), 219; SPADEM, Paris, no. 231 (below) (Jean Cocteau); Sport & General, no. 23; Sussex Express, no. 47; Homer Sykes and the Sunday Telegraph, nos 169, 199; The Times, nos 14, 35, 39; Rosemary Vercoe, no. 144; Vivienne, no. 41; David Walker, nos 102, 240; Hamish Wilson, no. 33; Reg Wilson nos 133, 158, 173, 176, 186, 192, 246; Roger Wood, no. 55; Franco Zeffirelli, no. 101; other photographs by unknown hands belong to the Christie family (nos 9–11, 13) or are in the Glyndebourne archives (nos 1, 4, 5, 7, 29, 32, 34, 51, 127, 129, 202).

Picture research by Victoria Dickie and Helen O'Neill.